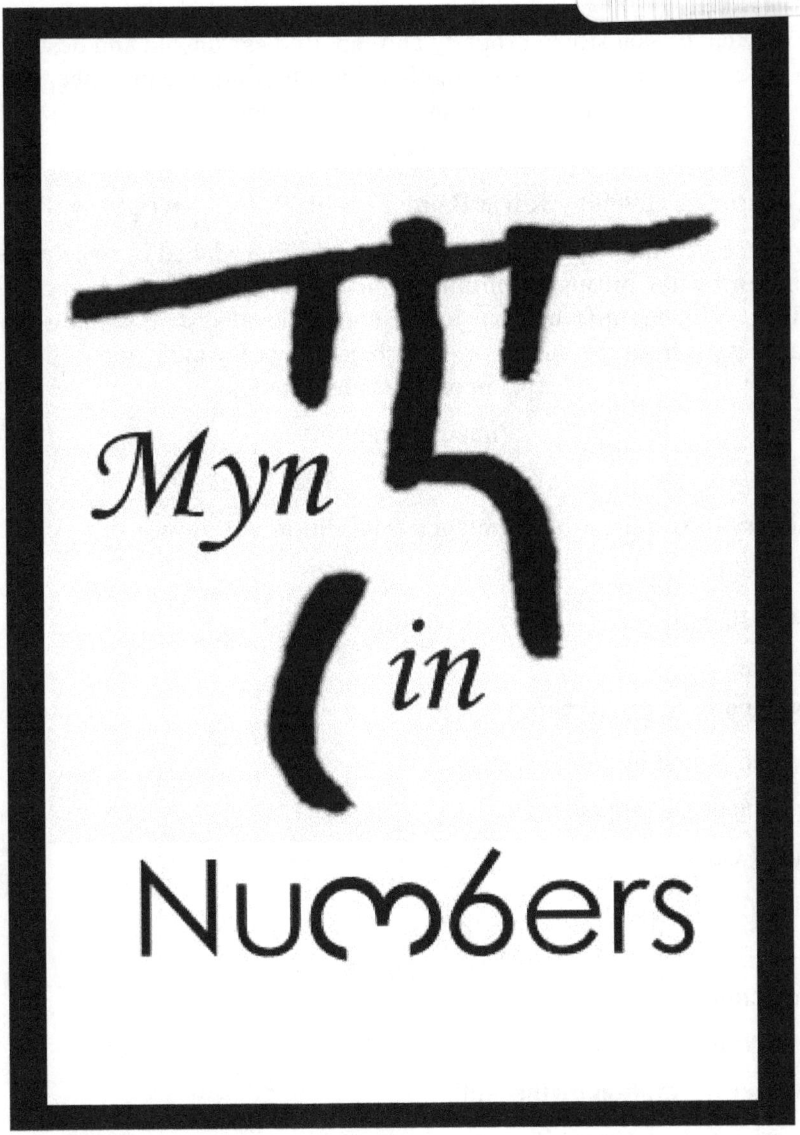

Myn (in Numbers

Kevin J. Baird

www.templeofgaia.com

If you purchased this book without a cover you should be aware that this book may have been stolen property and reported as "unsold and destroyed" to the publisher. In such case neither the author nor the publisher has received any payment for this "stripped book."

***

Copyright © 2009 by Kevin Baird (Alt-0169) for copyright symbol

All rights reserved. No part of this book may be reproduced or transmitted in any form or by any means, electronic or mechanical, including photocopying, recording, or by any information storage and retrieval system without written permission from the author or publisher, except for inclusion of brief excerpts in reviews and articles.

First edition 2009

10 9 8 7 6 5 4 3 2 1

The Library of Congress has cataloged this edition as follows:

Baird, Kevin

    Myn In Numbers

    P. cm.

    ISBN 978-0-578-01740-2

Printed and bound in the U. S. A.

Please contact the publisher at:

Temple of Gaia

www.templeofgaia.com

e-mail: Kevin@templeofgaia.com

Myn In Numbers

By Kevin Baird

Front Cover Illustration by the Author

Foreword and Back Cover Photography by ©Abigail Knutson 2009

Book Design & Typesetting by the Author

Edited by L. Grant

---

www.templeofgaia.com

Kevin J. Baird

Foreword

Imagine having a question on your mind and receiving the answer just by paying attention to clues around you. Reverend Kevin Baird, a gifted psychic medium his entire lifetime and ordained minister, shows us just how to do this in his new book, Myn in Numbers. By learning about the spirit angelic language of Myn in numbers, we will receive messages to guide us on our life path.

During the time I've known Rev. Kevin, and the many conversations we've had, the energy of Myn has caused a profound shift in my life. As I read Myn in Numbers, and put my red pen to it, I heard Rev. Kevin's voice in each page. His wisdom and knowledge of spirit is evident in how he shares with us how to use the messages given to us through the repeating of numbers that we are shown every day.

As you use this guide to look up the recurring numbers you are seeing, have fun with it, consider the interpretations, and know that Myn is the energy that drives manifestation and 386 = Myn Building Joy!

Lois Gant
Joyful Lightworker

Photo ©by Abigail Knutson

www.templeofgaia.com

Myn in Numbers

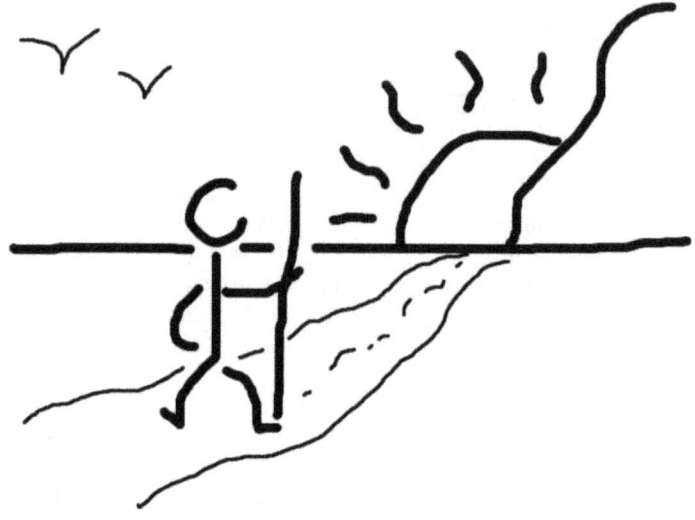

A Number of Myn is an angelic language code that serves the manifestation of guiding messages.

The origin of the language is older than the spoken word. The code goes back to the first intellects that realized a repeat in patterns and that specific events followed the patterns.

Reverend Kevin Baird is a renowned psychic medium and ordained minister in the greater Washington D.C. area. As a psychic he has a better grasp of understanding the elements of life in motion, i.e., knowing about some things before they happen, and as a medium he is a conduit for the people without flesh who exist in this world with us.

Here Kevin presents himself as a partner to the universe's plan to help others along their path by decoding daily clues for answers and new directions.

As a child, Kevin's grandmother taught him to monitor the repeat of patterns, but he felt she had scholastic intentions instead of developing his ability to work with the trust. As he grew up he continued to study the patterns. This study lead him to a career in computer science where his ability to observe patterns became more refined. Through that study he developed a knack, really a metaphysical knack, for realizing coming events based on present patterns.

His metaphysical knack has gone much further than how it was back in the day. Today he receives mental images that serve as information patterns about coming attractions as he goes about his day.

One of the best examples of Kevin's mediumship is a story about a young lady and her mother who are from Thailand. The young lady sat for a session with Kevin one morning and later that afternoon she returned with her mother. The story goes on that the two sat with Kevin and he shared that the mother had a sister that was present in spirit and was pressed to share something. A moment later Kevin was inspired to write on his tablet and after making some notes he went on with the session.

www.templeofgaia.com

Kevin J. Baird

  Later on in the session he was inspired to write again. Then the tone in the air released Kevin from writing and pressed him to share what he had written with the mother. The woman read the notes, but they made no sense; a bunch of words that were not English, but were written in the English alphabet. Kevin asked the lady to read the phonetic words out loud. As she spoke the words she realized that the language was Thai. As she continued, she began stumbling as she read.

The daughter put her hand on her mother's arm and said something in Thai that had a tone of concern. The mother responded in Thai and for a minute they exchanged a conversation with a tone that they were trying to understand the situation. The mother then spoke in English saying, "Kevin, my sister said to me before she passed away in April of 2008, that I was not to be sad because she was going to a better place. What you have written here is my name, Noy, and the words, *Why are you still sad?*"

The lady went on to explain how she did not believe her sister and had been very depressed for the last three months, but now she had closure and could start living her life again. For the record, Kevin only speaks English and a little Spanish, but through the work of mediumship, has received phonetic written languages of Farsi, Thai, Mandarin Chinese, Korean and Hindi. Kevin says he attributes this to his attending many Pentecostal church services as a child where speaking in tongues was a normal occurrence.

Kevin works with his spirit guides to receive psychic and mediumship information. His guides have shared with him that Myn in numbers is a code that all spirit guides understand and use to work with their charges on the physical plane. You can find out more about Kevin and his life by reading his first book, Myn and Angels, text that assists entry level psychics and mediums with learning the language of their angels and spirit guides.

Over the last several years, spirit angelic language has become very evident through the occurrence in the pattern of recurring number groups.

As you thumb through the pages and look at the numbers connected with the phrases, you will activate the energy of creation, Myn. It is an energy that is easily accessed or tapped to bring hopes and wishes into solid form, manifestation. Keep this personal journey to yourself except when sharing with brothers and sisters on the same walk.

Animate and inanimate objects enter and pass out of our lives; the only constant is you. These objects come in for a time, a season or a reason. All in one way or another teach us *how to be* or *how not to be*. The positive from a bad relationship, now exited, taught us *how not to be*. The observation of a friend who has been on a health program with visible proof of success *is teaching us how to be.*

One realizes the drive of Myn through the birth of a notion or an understanding following an action. The energy that increments numbers is myn energy. An example is numbers that pop up in lottery and bingo drawings.

Myn in Numbers will help people develop a specific hope to their specific needs. When they follow the coding and develop their own language culled from the mass of confusion, they will find themselves ascending through manifestation driven by the energy that drives their specific hope. The mass of confusion is that of the

Myn in Numbers

information overload received during a normal day's conduct. Numb by the confusion, they bumble along in the hopes that some sense will come of this deluge. Working with the myn in numbers they will develop a mast and sail that will give them the control of their seas.

Here is an opportunity for you to begin communicating with the people in spirit who are trying to help us avoid problems ahead or to hear that a friend or relative who passed away some time ago is saying hello.

The summation of two elements has valid myn outcome realized through the bottom line, the total of the equation and the number of myn.

There are two categories of divine language. Global, where the whole world sees the numbers, as in the lottery. Personal, where only a few see the numbers, as in a receipt or on a license plate that is in front of you while you are driving.

Mother communicates with us through symbols that are cryptic, because like gifts received on special occasions, we have to work at unwrapping the mystery.

Issues with dragons help keep our blood pumping. Tame the dragon and you add to your resources. Slay the dragon now and you lose saved resources.

www.templeofgaia.com

Kevin J. Baird

Myn in Numbers
Sandcastle stompers

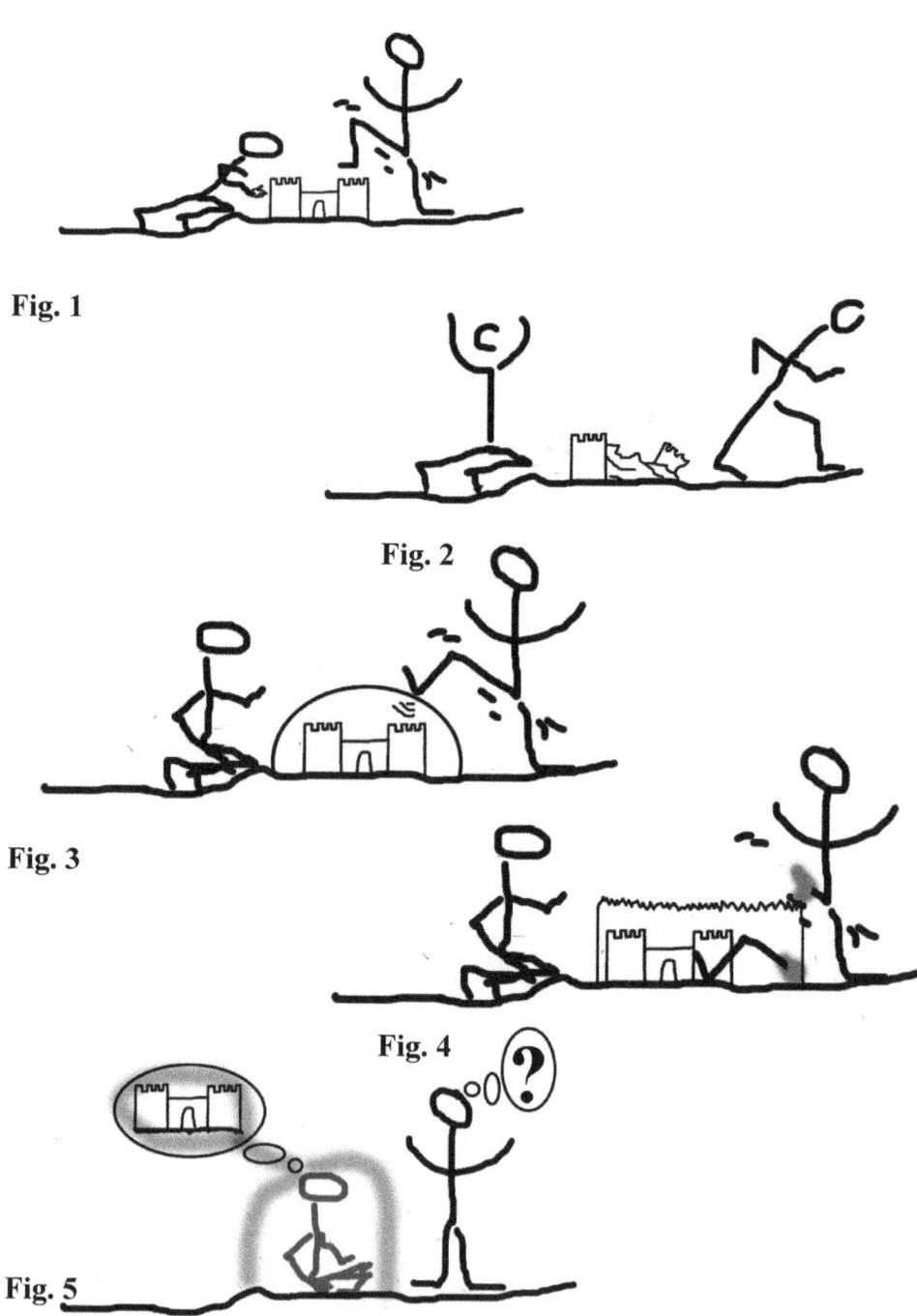

Fig. 1

Fig. 2

Fig. 3

Fig. 4

Fig. 5

Kevin J. Baird

Sandcastle stompers are the agents of evolution:

Nothing lasts forever. The only constant in life is change. Myn, the energy that drives manifestation, reminds us that things are always changing. The lesson is to never be certain of anything, and that which supports us now will eventually hold us back later. Also, the blame is not on the stomper but on the builder assuming an end-all be-all solution.

When you are visited by a stomper, they are telling you 111 (this is now) or 911 (action is now). 911, Action Is Now. Plan for a solid condition for the present and also plan that it will change later. Plan to cope.

Figure 1. An attempt to build a solution for protection.

Figure 2. Reaction to the failing of the protection.

Figure 3. Rebuilt, it is now an impenetrable protection. Now, no one can get in.

Figure 4. Modified, it now produces casualties to friend and foe.

Figure 5. Concern is now released. Protection now happens naturally by not being in threatening conditions. By learning to follow the signs and to go with the flow, coexistence is created.

Figures 1 through 4 are mental states that transmit expatiation vibrations that challenge and invite adversity. The mental states are the same, where rare objects are possessed by some and coveted by others.

Myn in Numbers

Myn

Myn tingles the sense of what just happened may be a sign or an omen.

Myn is the chemical experience that is the first attraction between lovers.

Myn is the spark that thrusts one into knowing from not knowing.

Myn is the glue that connects you to that which guides you.

Myn is the particles of sand in the hourglass of patience.

Myn is the air that gives angels the power of flight.

Myn holds some topics from conclusion.

Myn is the glue in the mosaic of dreams.

Myn is the mass of the etheric layer.

Myn revives obscure memories.

Myn is the zeal of passion.

You are myn.

Myn serves through:

Mynd (mend): To repair or heal.

Mynute (minute): A measure of time or substance.

Ad**myn**ister (administer): To apply.

Mynister (Minister): Spiritual counsel.

Mynimal (minimal): The smallest measure.

Myne (mine): Now possessed by you through external means.

Myner (Miner): A seeker of new things never before discovered.

Mynd (mind): The place where thoughts occur.

Myngle (mingle): To mix together.

Myn in Numbers

Personify sources:

When we are in thought, we process problems and hopes. When we process problems, we are working to solve them and plan so that we prevent them from happening again.

When we think of our children, their problems are our problems, their joys are our joys. As parents, we are at a place where we sometimes have to let the child overcome the problem themselves, because we know it helps develop their intellect. We represent a source that monitors their progress and lends a hand from time to time.

The same is true for adults where maturity grows as problems are overcome sometimes by ourselves and other times by some unseen force. There are many religions that have a defined personification of that source, be it God, Jesus, Allah, Loki, Devil or Buddha just to name a few.

However, sometimes the saving force does not have the feel of the sources we have been taught about. Kevin refers to them as spirit guides, fairy godmothers or godfathers. Kevin has a primary guide he works with and he says her name is Stacey. She looks and acts like a regular person you would meet on the street and is his external positive source.

For the sake of this discussion we will use the following image as a symbol for sources:

It has an expression with eyes and a nose line, but the gender and age are not known.

Kevin J. Baird

The following are personified mental conditions:

The doom/gloom manager (Dave):

Dave sends us mental information that makes us uncomfortable about problems and situations that we are unable to overcome at the present time. He also clouds our minds with doom-clutter to distract us from the present course.

The joy manager (Jimmy)

Jimmy sends us mental information that makes us happy as we are reminded about the joys and successes in our lives.

The planning manager (Pat)

Pat works with us so that we can process outcomes and defining steps for overcoming problems.

The boundary manager (Boris)

Boris blocks from our view things that we do not understand or because it is a low threat as we move along in our day, allows it to pass unnoticed.

The animal drive manager (Devin)

Devin drives us through chemical experiences, such as when we are hungry or by pheromones (pheromones: a chemical substance that is usually produced by an animal and serves especially as a stimulus to other individuals of the same species for one or more behavioral responses (Merriam-Webster Online Dictionary)).

The reasons manager (Denise)

Denise has the lens so we can focus on facts that brought about a state or condition.

Positive outside event sources (Abby)

Abby helps us find objects and positive things by accident. Or she sends someone to make our day through a positive act.

Myn in Numbers

Negative outside event sources (George)

George inventories our past and finds mistakes that affect our day and progress in life. Or he sends someone by happenstance that acts upon us as they project frustration that we were not due.

Places

There are physical places and there are mental places. At times physical places bring reactions from mental places.

You can be at a place, where there is a surprise heated discussion taking place, and in turn you may find that Boris joins you in the mental place where he closes the gate providing you with protection to the farthest possible extent.

You can be at a physical place where you overhear news about job cuts, and in turn you may find that Dave joins you in the mental place where he presents to you an inventory for all the reasons you should be a part of the job cuts as well.

You are the common denominator in every mental and physical place. You are the boss. When one manager has a primary voice there is imbalance. Mentally hand them a cookie as a token to hush for a minute. Now sort through your managers to see which one can serve you in the moment of imbalance.

Office space

Create a mental office space with a big table and chairs all around. Now, see doors around this space. These doors are the access points for your individual managers.

Let us return now to the discussion about job cuts and your doom manager, Dave, presenting you with his inventory of reasons you could be cut. Here Dave is a lone manager in the room with you.

A car honks behind you and you are brought back to the present reality that you are driving to work. You look at the clock on the dashboard of your car and see 7:14. You will have fifteen minutes to get a cup of coffee and a quick chat with colleagues before you sit down at your place of employment.

Up ahead, you see a flurry of brake lights as you make your way down the highway. This time when you look at the clock you see 7:17. Brake lights mean traffic issues and delays. Delays force adjustments to agendas. You can still get the cup of coffee, but will have to skip the chat time until break time later in the day or at lunch. Again you see brake lights and the thought enters your mind that you could be late for work.

You are distracted by a panicked driver as he makes his move for a last minute exit off the highway. A wave of agitation passes over as you make a quick adjustment to cope with this interruption. You glace down at his license plate to see LVI 7171.

Kevin J. Baird

The driver's hasty exit prompts you to consider making an exit too. While thinking about the driver you begin sorting the details of the last events. You are intrigued by the repeat of the number 717. First the number group showed itself when you looked at the time of the clock, now it has shown itself again on the license plate, LVI **7171**.

Distracted, you decide to take the same exit as the driver who just cut you off. You drive up the ramp and come to a stop at the cross road, route 717. You about have an out of body experience as you cope with yet another 717 event.

The number events began with seeing 7:14. The myn of this number is: Work is supported. This is the number that was presented to you while you were pondering whether your job would be cut. Work is supported, means things are just fine…for now.

Then 7:17 was next seen, meaning work is work or work is working. This translates to what you are doing in your work is serving a divine plan somewhere and you validate your connection through the process or outcome of the work that you do.

Then you were cut off abruptly by the driver with the license plate that had 7171. Work is working now. The divine entity helping you with the present situation is telling you to relax and cool off for a while. Everything is fine. It is going as planned.

Ending with you coming upon route 717, where the abrupt driver lead you to change the topic and direction you were going and taking you to the 717 (work is working) path.

The Myn message in numbers can happen to this extent and even to a point greater than this. The measure of the extent depends on how close you pay attention.

Myn in Numbers

Kevin J. Baird

The Angelic Coding

0 = Release, my, soul, self.
1 = Is, done, this, now.
2 = Join, compromise, partner, friend.
3 = Trust, myn, blessing, prosperity.
4 = Support, through, means, convey.
5 = Receive, accept, grant, present.
6 = Joy, laugh, serve, content.
7 = Work, ability, enable, capable.
8 = Build, form, store, structure.
9 = Action, feel, move, test.

Number messages show up everywhere:

Street signs

License plates

Phone calls that are wrong numbers (if you have caller I.D.)

Times of the day

The total of a receipt

The price of a single item

Lottery tickets

…and even in dreams.

For example, you wake up at 6:10 in the morning. Later in the day, you buy something that adds up to $6.10. A meeting at work is scheduled in Room 610. When you get in your car to go home from work, it is 6:10. Someone is trying to tell you something! Start paying attention to numbers and see what the universe is trying to tell you.

610 = Joy is releasing. What does that mean to you? How do you interpret it?

The message is for you if the number catches your attention and you see it repeatedly. You may notice the number and feel that is it meaningful, while someone else may not notice it at all.

Myn in Numbers

The journey of our life path is loaded with prosperity and misfortune and it is the Universe that puts these obstacles in front of us as a challenge to overcome or to go around. The element of the Myn in numbers is the force of the Universe as a teacher helping us along with hints about our present situation. We are not here to fail, but to learn, sometimes the hard way, but still to learn and to grow.

Let's use a computer video game as an example, and our soul, which is timeless, is playing this video game, the video game of life. So, a thousand lifetimes ago, earthly lifetimes, we began playing the game of life. The first couple of attempts at playing the game we opted out early in the game by turning off the machine and starting again from scratch, then starting anew with the hope that the process will be more successful this time around.

Examples of Myn in number groups:

Remember, Myn is the energy that drives manifestation.

10 Now release.

- The situation associated with '10' is related to where you are or what you are thinking. Dismiss the concerns relating to the condition or situation.

64 Content means.

- The situation associated with '64' states that it is okay to enjoy the element of the present situation. You are in a safe place and comfort is here. Rest easy.

42 Support compromise.

- The situation associated with '42' states that you should consider giving a little to the present situation.

57 Receive ability.

- The situation associated with '57' states that you will gain knowledge of how to do something in the present situation.

11 Is now.

- The situation associated with '11' states that you should go with what you have; wait no longer.

1064 Is my joy supported?

Kevin J. Baird

- The situation associated with '1064' asks if there is supporting value for you in the present situation. Ask yourself if your interests are considered in the element of the present situation?

1614 This joy is supported.

- You are in a place where you are thinking if this one thing would happen, you would be very happy, be it love, finances, or some other success.

425711 Through friend receiving ability is now.

- The situation associated with '425711' states that working with a partner you will gain understanding and capability in the now situation.

000 My soul self.

- When we are naked, we just have our flesh and blood to sustain us. We are at a place where we discover that all or a part of our world has changed and we stand, "naked" because we possess no prior experiences that we can call upon from our memories that can help make a part of the situation familiar.

111 This is now.

- No further thinking about the situation. You can choose to act or let the situation pass you by. If your hands are full and you can't add anything new to the present process, then by all means pass it up knowing that you will have another chance to choose again.

210 Join this self.

- We have many selves. One that exists in the workplace, as we drive, as we walk, as we shop, as children, as young adults, as parents, just to name a few. There is the self that we want to be, in a new job or new relationship, a future self for how we would like to be known by parents, employers, children, grandchildren, neighbors, and the person on the highway in the lane next to us while we are driving. There is also the self we don't want to see, such as the self realizing an unpleasant separation or receiving a penalty, such as getting fired or getting a ticket. When 210 becomes known to you, trust that your trust source for guidance is inviting you to consider participating in the "self condition" whether it is presented to you or a condition you are considering applying yourself.

www.templeofgaia.com

Myn in Numbers

222 Join partner compromise.

- Here is a place where two or more must agree that the situation is positive and supports all participants.

311 Trust this now.

Stop waiting for more information. Trust the information you have and make a decision.

313 Trust is trust.

- Trust is strengthened with caution. Trust, but don't be stupid. We are living so that we can learn how to be and how not to be. Most of the time we are learning how not to be. The outcome of easy lessons come and go quickly, but the hard lessons hang around for a while.

333 Trust trust trust.

- This is a place or situation where creative energy is at its strongest. On the clock, 3:33 a.m. is the window of spirit. It is the middle of the night and we have just awaken from the first batch of dreaming for the night. It is at this point we are on break and are digesting the wisdom received from the last dreaming. This is also the time where we press the Trust with our hopes that we may realize our future wishes and prayers for assistance to overcome fears. When 333 shows up in other places it is a heads up to be careful, because you may get what you asked for, but you have to trust.

354 Trust receiving support.

- The situation is that you are in a place that is new and you don't know how to trust a new person or organization to help you overcome a hurdle. Life is about taking risks, within reason, of course.

444 Supported through support.

- As you help others, so you will be helped in the same manner. While helping someone paint a room, consider how this process can work for you at a place specific to you.

555 Receive presenting acceptance.

Kevin J. Baird

- Understand that it takes time before something is accepted. Show acceptance (don't judge). Take your time at building relationships when working with a new group or person.

666 Content happy laugh.

- A place or feeling of happiness should be considered for the situation at hand. Take yourself to a place in your thoughts where you last laughed, followed by creating a new memory equal to that place.

777 Capable working ability.

- Work at improving that which you do best. Hone the skills you are known for. Take that class you were thinking about.

838 Store prosperity building.

- This can be related to working on a product for sales or doing work to grow a relationship. The angels are trying to get a message to you hoping you will see it. Myn energy helps this by making the numbers stand out from common details as we go about our day.

888 Form building structure.

- Create a framework that can house materials and thoughts that you can return to so that it can support you during your activities.

999 Test active feelings.

- Time to bring your ideas and notions out into the open and take action.

At the back of the book you will find a chart for you to use to track numbers and the date that they happen so that you can begin to monitor patterns. These patterns will be the beginning of your language with your angels, just like when we learn our first words as a child.

Define the language as you see fit, for now you have a chance to start truly defining how you now live your life. As you work with this new language you will find coincidences in what you are thinking and what is going on around you. For example, you see the number, 312. Trust this friend. As you word the numbers in your head trying to understand the message, you will hear someone use one of the three words, or see one or all of the words on the same sign. This is a message that

Myn in Numbers

your guides are working with you using their new language. It works - you just have to pay attention. You will find that you will be more connected to the things going on around you than ever before. I promise.

Kevin J. Baird

Angelic text presence

When a conversation is occurring, words and pauses occur. The same for written text. The same for music. When music is played, notes occur separately. The space between is the angelic presence in the situation.

The motion when drawing cards or tumbling dice is the angelic presence.

Here the poker hand says: "something is building." The tumbled dice say: "Trust joy accept friend support."

We can also see numbers in the sky.

Here three geese are telling us with their group of three, to trust that which is in preponderance.

10-sided dice

Here the 10-sided dice rolled one at a time end with the number: 1146.

The answer to your question: This is through joy.

Kevin J. Baird

If you asked a question about a relationship, be it partner, job or object, such as your car or house, the answer is to take steps to find the path to happiness.

When asking your spirit guide a question about a situation in your life, toss one dice cube at a time for a specific answer or toss all at once to get a message that shares a view from different angels

Variations of 1146:

Done this supports joy.

Now is supporting joy.

Is now supporting joy.

Is this supporting joy.

This is supporting joy.

Is done supporting joy.

This now supports joy.

This is through joy.

Now this means joy.

Now this serves joy

This is serving joy.

There are many ways to translate the 1146 quad. The words that stand out in the myn number code are the words to be used in the translation. The intent here is to understand the clue for solving the situation.

Myn in Numbers

FedEx Kinko's
9101 St...

3/19/2009   5:32:51 PM EST
Trans.: 0416
Register: 002
Team Member: Claudia M.
Customer: Kevin Baird

SALE

binding   8.47
                 1 @ 8.4700

Bind CoilMixed > 1"   5.49 T
0886   1.00 @ 5.4900

Cutting per Cut   2.98 T
0376   2.00 @ 1.4900

Sub-Total   8.47
Deposit   0.00
Tax   0.42
Total   8.89
  Cash   20.00
Total Tender   20.00
Change Due   (11.11)

Thank you for visiting
FedEx Kinko's
Make It. Print It. Pack It. Ship It.
www.fedexkinkos.com

Customer Copy

1111

A validation that this activity is supported by the angels and guides.

A deck of cards

The kings in the deck represent men in your life that are your age or order.

The aces represent gain, loss, love and hate.

The queens represent women your age or older.

The jacks represent men or women younger than you and they provide a service.

Follow the numbers on the cards along with the Myn in numbers.

The clubs represent tools that can help or hurt.

The diamonds represent money and assets.

The spades represent the use of yours and other people's words, either written or spoken.

The hearts represent emotions.

The spread below (king 8,8,8 and 8) talks about a male that is your age or older who will and can help you in many ways.

Myn in Numbers

When you are at a place where you need some answers to the mysteries in your life, in the middle of craziness and need some information, go to your local mini mart and request a random pick lottery ticket.

The first position represents information about you.

36 Trust Joy. You have to trust joy.

The second position represents your job.

55 Receiving acceptance.

The third position is information about your spouse or partner.

01 Release Now. Be open to who you are close to.

The fourth position is information about your family

11 Now done. This could be about closure to something you have been trying to get rid of.

The fifth position is information about strangers you will meet

24 Join support: You could find yourself in a place where you find a stranger in a position that needs your support. Call it a random act of kindness.

The sixth position is about your hopes and fears.

56 Receive joy. This could be a message about how you have been hesitant about taking some time out for yourself. Time to do so now.

We are here living our lives to learn soul development. This lottery ticket message shares clues to overcoming the situation at hand.

Myn in time

General times:

6:00 a.m. Rise to begin the day.
8:00 a.m. On the job.
10:15 a.m. Mid-morning break.
12:00 p.m. Lunch time.
2:30 p.m. Mid-afternoon break.
3:00 p.m. Kids let out from school.
3:33 a.m. First dream class break time
4:20 p.m. Snack time.
6:30 p.m. Dinner Time
8:00 p.m. Bed time for kids.
12:00 a.m. Bedtime for adults (generally)

When numbers show up in the day that match a number in our time schedules your guide is trying to help connect the dots. 12:10

Myn in Numbers

Digits

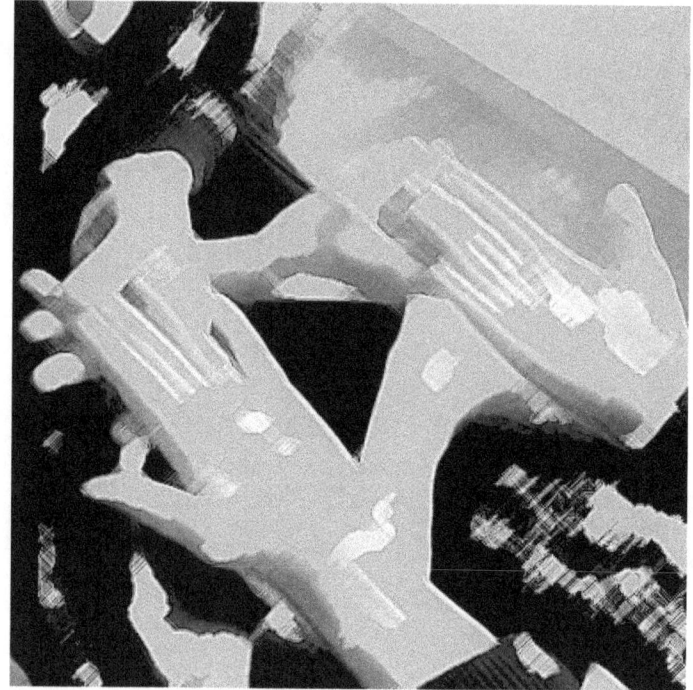

Kevin J. Baird
Your Hands and Feet

Pay attention to the digits on your hands and feet.

0 = the thumb on your dominant hand

1 = index finger

2 = middle finger

3 = ring finger

4 = small finger

Then moving on to your next hand.

5 = thumb

6 = index finger

7 = middle finger

8 = ring finger

9 = small finger

Your toes follow the same rules. If you're ambidextrous, you can interchange the hands. Your intuition will tell you which one to use.

Does your non-dominant hand's small finger hurt all the time? 9 = Action, move. Perhaps you need to be taking some action.

For nothing to exist, everything has to be absent. For something to exist, nothing has to be absent. For 0 to exist, everything has to be absent.

Self

<u>Zero</u> - The whole of one's self. The single cell. The origin of all things. We know what "my" is. It is the position that states a given ownership of that which can be contained. Property, positions and talents fall under the light of my. The circle is complete.

Kevin J. Baird

My

Of or relating to me or myself especially as possessor, agent, object of an action, or familiar person. (Merriam-Webster's online dictionary)

- My is about that which is personal to you such as feelings or possessions.

Release

To set free from restraint, confinement, or servitude. (Merriam-Webster's online dictionary)

- Release is about a pending outcome, positive/negative is now in motion. The positive is a wish granted. The negative is that which is restrictive is/will be removed.

Soul

An active or essential part; the moral and emotional nature. (Merriam-Webster's online dictionary)

- Soul is about the essence of conduct for everything that exists.

Self

An individual's typical character or behavior. (Merriam-Webster's online dictionary)

- Self is about the quality of conduct of a person, place or thing.

www.templeofgaia.com

Myn in Numbers

Now

<u>One</u> - To be one, is to be now - in the now. Is now done? What are you now doing? Are you now where you want to be? The sole source of energy.

www.templeofgaia.com

Done

Of or relating to fixed, permanent, or immovable things. (Merriam-Webster's online dictionary)

- Done is about an experience or relationship now finished, or a request is now in motion.

Is

An order of form. (Merriam-Webster's online dictionary)

- Is is about a static condition, person, place or thing that now exists.

This

The person, thing, or idea that is present or near in place, time, or thought or that has just been mentioned. (Merriam-Webster's online dictionary)

- This is about a condition, person, place or thing is at present the primary focus.

Now

At the present time or moment. (Merriam-Webster's online dictionary)

- Now is about a condition, a person, place or thing is poised for a pending action.

www.templeofgaia.com

Myn in Numbers

Join

<u>Two</u> - One and One are Two. The two are now in partnership, friendship. One works, one rests.

---

www.templeofgaia.com

Join

To put or bring into close association or relationship. (Merriam-Webster's online dictionary)

- Join is about moving from a single condition into a group condition, or a group or entity joins and eliminates the single condition.

Compromise

To adjust or settle by mutual concessions. (Merriam-Webster's online dictionary)

- Compromise is about relaxing pressed personal requirements so that they can have a common coexistence with a person(s), place or thing.

Partner

A person with whom one shares a close relationship. (Merriam-Webster's online dictionary)

- Partner is about building a relationship for a lengthy project such as spousehood where we join with a best friend who we sleep with at night (night spouse) or a best friend we will work with on an hourly basis during the day (day spouse).

Friend

Someone who is not hostile. (Merriam-Webster's online dictionary)

- Friend is about casual interactions between strangers and the people with whom we are acquainted.

Trust

Three – Above all else, trust! Followers of Faith, wait for it. As you study myn watch for phenomena of manifestation. To be born is a physical manifestation for the vehicle of your soul. Unique opportunities are divine blessings and do happen. The challenge is how do we make them more frequent? You have to trust.

Myn

The energy that drives manifestation. (Kevin Baird, 2005)

- Myn is about using deep contemplation for building hopes and forming dreams.

Trust

Assured reliance on the character, ability, strength, or truth of someone or something. (Merriam-Webster's online dictionary)

- Trust is about releasing control of that which is being pressed to form a specific outcome and letting it develop through Myn on its own.

Blessing

A thing conducive to happiness or welfare. (Merriam-Webster's online dictionary)

- Blessings are the product of dreams and hopes made solid, manifested through myn energy.

Prosperity

The condition of being successful or thriving. (Merriam-Webster's online dictionary)

- Prosperity is about the condition of continuous positive outcomes driven by cycling myn energy.

Myn in Numbers

Support

Four - Now support in groups of two. Now the group must decide, the One has the idea, do the three support? Agree? "Supported" means that the Universe agrees with the object related to the situation.

www.templeofgaia.com

Kevin J. Baird

Support

Something or someone to which one looks for support. (Merriam-Webster's online dictionary)

- Support is about receiving help from a person place or thing to achieve an outcome.

Through

Using the means or agency of. (Merriam-Webster's online dictionary)

- Through is about accessing an external system for achieving an outcome.

Means

Something used to achieve an end. (Merriam-Webster's online dictionary)

- Means is about a method or resource for achieving a desired outcome or the definition for a situation.

Convey

To support and take from one place to another. (Merriam-Webster's online dictionary)

- Convey is about a gentle transfer of substance or knowledge with the intent to coax a transformation of person, persons or condition.

www.templeofgaia.com

Myn in Numbers

Accept

Five - Now receive. The four support the one. The one now considers receiving instead of supporting. "Receive" that which is good or bad into our lives, teaching us how to be or how not to be. Is this granted?

Receive

To come into possession of. (Merriam-Webster's online dictionary)

- Receive is about physical body language or personal internal realization acknowledging a change in conditions that has the potential for changing a conduct.

Accept

To hold willingly. (Merriam-Webster's online dictionary)

- Accept is about now combining an object or notion and incorporating it with process or conduct.

Grant

To permit as a right. (Merriam-Webster's online dictionary)

- Grant is about now having permission to proceed or take possession of an object or situation.

Present

To give or bestow formally. (Merriam-Webster's online dictionary)

- Present is about the ceremony of gift giving or how we are formally received by others.

---

www.templeofgaia.com

Myn in Numbers

Joy

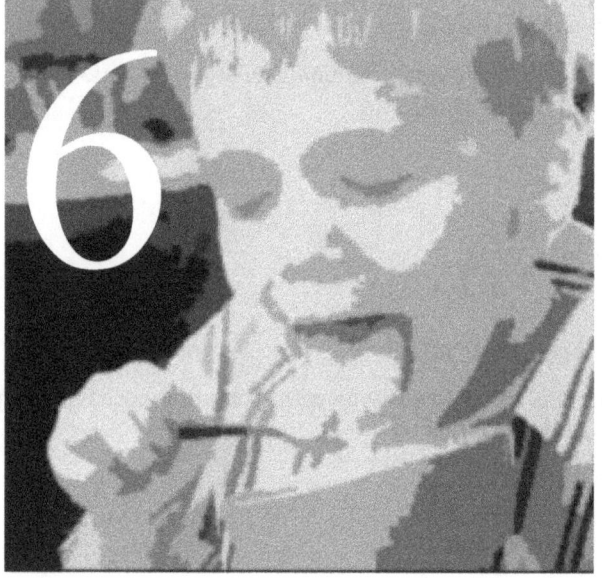

<u>Six</u> - Now joy and peace. Now some give and some receive, some work and some rest.

Serve

To answer the needs of a person or situation. (Merriam-Webster's online dictionary)

- Serve is about helping someone or a condition in need of specific skills.

Laugh

To find amusement or pleasure in something. (Merriam-Webster's online dictionary)

- Laugh is about releasing the physical expression of joy that can be witnessed by others.

Content

The feeling experienced when one's wishes are met. (Merriam-Webster's online dictionary)

- Content is about an unstable/unbalanced condition that is now stable or balanced.

Joy

The emotion evoked by well-being, success, or by the prospect of possessing what one desires. (Merriam-Webster's online dictionary)

- Joy is about a situation, person, place or thing that produces a quality or essence that brings about joy.

Myn in Numbers

Work

Seven - Now one stands able with a specific talent. Now three provide while four support. "Work" is a function that develops due to the reaction to a positive or negative object in motion in our arena of existence.

www.templeofgaia.com

Kevin J. Baird

Work

Activity in which one exerts strength or faculties to do or perform something. (Merriam-Webster's online dictionary)

- Work is about applying skills to form an outcome or bring about change in a condition.

Ability

Natural aptitude or acquired proficiency to form an outcome. (Merriam-Webster's online dictionary)

- Ability is about the quality of a specific skill and the condition it creates.

Enable

To make possible, practical, or easy. (Merriam-Webster's online dictionary)

- Enable is about removing bonds that restrict progress or movement.

Capable

Having or showing general efficiency and ability. (Merriam-Webster's online dictionary)

- Capable is about defining the quality of a skill to render an outcome or product with a single application of effort.

Myn in Numbers

Building

Eight – Now building. Now each one supports as a part of the four, and the other four now see that more will follow and that a preparation must begin and a growing follows. "Build," a task that develops a product which serves in both physical and material situations. Building a structure.

Build

To make an integral part of. (Merriam-Webster's online dictionary)

- Build is about the accumulation of matter or energy for the purpose of capturing and containing an external element.

Form

To give a particular shape to. (Merriam-Webster's online dictionary)

- Form is about defining how objects and ideas are received.

Store

To save provisions. (Merriam-Webster's online dictionary)

- Store is about considering what the necessary extras should be.

Structure

Something arranged in a definite pattern of organization. (Merriam-Webster's online dictionary)

- Structure is about bridges that reach upward and outward creating a network of support that has room to breath.

Action

<u>Nine</u> – Action. The birth of a group understanding and so follows a collective action, a growing and developing of more than what is here and now. Begin. Take the leap.

Feel

To be aware of by instinct or inference. (Merriam-Webster's online dictionary)

- Feel is about how the senses react to stimulation and then act or not act.

Move

To carry on one's life or activities in a specified environment. (Merriam-Webster's online dictionary)

- Move is about not being in the same place for very long.

Test

A process for measuring the skill, knowledge, intelligence, capacities, or aptitudes of an individual, group or an object(s). (Merriam-Webster's online dictionary)

- Test is about evaluating if a condition is secure or valid.

Action

An effort to produce an effect. (Merriam-Webster's online dictionary)

- Act is about reacting to given conditions or situations.

Myn in Numbers

Number Meanings

The following are guiding phrases. Use this compilation as a system to understand the messages intended to guide us. It will become a record of the messages you receive over a period of time. As time goes on, you will find meaningful messages may be repeating themselves, urging you to pay attention and take action. Make a notation of the dates you see the numbers. You may find a pattern in the dates as well.

As the numbers start to build, define them in your own way. Here 111 is represented as **This is Now**. However, each 1 can be something different from the 1 group of meanings depending on how you interpret it for yourself: **Is Now Done, Now Is Done or now-now-now**. Now, what does your intuition tell you about the message when you see the numbers?

0	My.	(Reason for living.)
1	Now.	(Here you are.)
2	Join.	(You are not alone.)
3	Trust.	(Live a little.)
4	Support.	(Help where you can.)
5	Accept.	(Consider new ideas.)
6	Joy.	(Consider the invitation.)
7	Work.	(It can be done.)
8	Build.	(Plan to see more.)
9	Action.	(Make it happen.)
10	Now releasing.	(You can take.)
11	Now is.	(No time like the present.)
12	Now join.	(Let others have a little.)
13	Now trust.	(Take a chance.)
14	Now supported.	(The angels are with you.)
15	Now accept.	(It is what it is.)
16	Now joy.	(Take time out for fun.)
17	Now working.	(Go with this idea.)
18	Now building.	(Be patient.)
19	Now action.	(No more waiting.)
20	Join release.	(Relax and let go.)
21	Join now.	(Look for help with this.)
22	Join friend.	(Agree with group agreement.)
23	Join trusting.	(Someone else has the lead on this.)

www.templeofgaia.com

24	Join supported.	(You have back up.)
25	Join acceptance.	(Show you care.)
26	Join joy.	(Help others have fun.)
27	Join working.	(Take the training.)
28	Join building.	(Team building.)
29	Join action.	(Team building.)
30	Trust self.	(You know you can do it.)
31	Trust now	(No guts, no glory.)
32	Trust joining.	(The plan is solid.)
33	Trust prosperity.	(It is true…trust it.)
34	Trust support.	(The others have the action.)
35	Trust acceptance.	(Ignore the body language.)
36	Trust joy.	(You are happy…go with it.)
37	Trusting works.	(You can do it.)
38	Trust builds	(Believe it or not.)
39	Trust action.	(Take the risk)
40	Supports release.	(Help someone feel better.)
41	Supports this.	(Give and you will receive.)
42	Support joining.	(A balance is necessary.)
43	Support trust.	(Teach how to trust.)
44	Support means.	(Help the efforts.)
45	Support receiving.	(Teach others to trust.)
46	Support joy.	(Help throw a party.)
47	Support works.	(Help others achieve.)
48	Support building.	(Help and be helped.)
49	Support action.	(Help and be helped.)
50	Accept self.	(Mistakes teach.)
51	Accept now.	(Go with it.)
52	Accept joining.	(Two heads are better than one.)
53	Accept trust.	(Earn you place.)
54	Accept support.	(You will have help with this.)
55	Accept acceptance.	(Your efforts are valid.)
56	Accept joy.	(Take a break.)
57	Accept work.	(Go on and do it.)

Myn in Numbers

58	Accept building.	(Mistakes teach.)
59	Accept action.	(You earned it.)
60	Joy releases.	(Find peace…NOW!)
61	Joy now.	(Take a break.)
62	Joy compromise.	(Go with the group idea.)
63	Joy trust.	(The outcome will leave you relieved.)
64	Joy support.	(Find your happy place.)
65	Joy accepted.	(This is good.)
66	Joy serves.	(Laughing sets the mood.)
67	Joy working.	(Make them laugh.)
68	Joy building.	(More laughter is needed.)
69	Joy action.	(Tell a joke.)
70	Work release.	(Take steps to improve yourself.)
71	Work now.	(Make this condition better.)
72	Work compromise.	(Teach others to compromise.)
73	Work trusting.	(Show you can be trusted.)
74	Work support.	(Be the example for helping others.)
75	Work accepted.	(You are good.)
76	Work joy.	(Work towards long term happiness.)
77	Work ability.	(Show others how good they are.)
78	Work building.	(The job grows.)
79	Work action.	(Practice getting busy.)
80	Build releasing.	(Grow dismissing expectations.)
81	Builds now.	(Waiting has paid off.)
82	Build joining.	(Teaming has benefits.)
83	Build trust.	(Show what you know.)
84	Build support.	(Don't spend it all in one place.)
85	Build acceptance.	(Show what you know.)
86	Build joy.	(Save for good times.)
87	Build work.	(Saving pays off.)
88	Build building.	(Save with others saving.)
89	Build feelings.	(Attachment grows roots.)
90	Act releasing.	(Your heart opens.)
91	Act now.	(Don't wait for more information.)

www.templeofgaia.com

92	Act joining.	(Can you trust?)
93	Act trusting.	(Take a chance.)
94	Act supporting.	(Will it/they be there?)
95	Act accepting.	(Fake it for now.)
96	Act joyful.	(Take some time for yourself.)
97	Active work.	(You CAN do it!)
98	Act building.	(Be prepared.)
99	Act feeling.	(How do you really feel?)

Myn in Numbers

Now

100

When "1" leads the pack your source is inviting you to be in the "Now" as you conduct yourself in the personal moment of the trailing numbers. Weigh the points and ponder the outcome.

****

100   Now my release.
101   Now releasing now.
102   Now my compromise.
103   Now my trust.
104   Now my support.
105   Now my acceptance.
106   Now my joy.
107   Now my ability.
108   Now my building.

www.templeofgaia.com

109   Now my action.
110   Now is releasing.
111   Now is done.
112   Now is friendship.
113   Now is trusted.
114   Now is supported.
115   Now is received.
116   Now is joy.
117   Now is ability.
118   Now is building.
119   Now is action.
120   Now join release.
121   Now join this.
122   Now join compromise.
123   Now join trust.
124   Now join support.
125   Now join acceptance.
126   Now join joy.
127   Now join ability.
128   Now join building.
129   Now join action.
130   Now trust self.
131   Now trust this.
132   Now trust joins.
133   Not trust blessing.
134   Now trust support.
135   Now trust accepted.
136   Now trust joy.
137   Now trust ability.
138   Now trust building.
139   Now trust action.
140   Now supports me.
141   Now supports this.
142   Now supports compromise.

Myn in Numbers

143	Now supports prosperity.
144	Now means support.
145	Now supports acceptance.
146	Now supports joy.
147	Now supports ability.
148	Now supports building.
149	Now supports action.
150	Now receive self.
151	Now receive this.
152	Now receive compromise.
153	Now receive trust.
154	Now receive support.
155	Now receive acceptance.
156	Now receive joy.
157	Now receive ability.
158	Now receive building.
159	Now receive action.
160	Now serves release.
161	Now serve this.
162	Now serve compromise.
163	Now serve blessing.
164	Now serve support.
165	Now serve accepting.
166	Now serve joy.
167	Now serve ability.
168	Now serve building.
169	Now serve action.
170	Now work release.
171	Now work this.
172	Now work compromise.
173	Now work trust.
174	Now work support.
175	Now work acceptance.
176	Now work joy.

177	Now work ability.
178	Now work building.
179	Now work feelings.
180	Now build release.
181	Now build this.
182	Now build friendship.
183	Now build trust.
184	Now build support.
185	Now build acceptance.
186	Now build joy.
187	Now build ability.
188	Now build structure.
189	Now build action.
190	Now action releases.
191	Now action is.
192	Now action joins.
193	Now action blessed.
194	Now action supported.
195	Now action received.
196	Now action serves.
197	Now action ability.
198	Now action building.
199	Now testing feelings.

Myn in Numbers

Join

200

When "2" leads the pack your source is inviting you to "Join-in" as you conduct yourself in the personal moment of the trailing numbers. Weigh the points and ponder the outcome.

***

200	Joins my self.
201	Joins my now.
202	Joins my friendship.
203	Joins my trust.
204	Joins my support.
205	Joins my acceptance.
206	Joins my joy.
207	Joins my ability.
208	Joins my building.
209	Joins my action.

www.templeofgaia.com

210 Joins this release.
211 Join this now.
212 Join this compromise.
213 Join this trust.
214 Join this support.
215 Join this acceptance.
216 Join this joy.
217 Join this ability.
218 Join this building.
219 Join this action.
220 Join partner release.
221 Join partner now.
222 Join partner compromise.
223 Join partner trust.
224 Join partner support.
225 Join partner acceptance.
226 Join partner serving.
227 Join partner ability.
228 Join partner building.
229 Join partner action.
230 Join trusting me.
231 Join trusting this.
232 Join trusting compromise.
233 Join trusting blessing.
234 Join trusting support.
235 Join trusting acceptance.
236 Join trusting joy.
237 Join trusting ability.
238 Join trusting structure.
239 Join trusting action.
240 Join supporting release.
241 Join supporting this.
242 Join supporting compromise.
243 Join supporting trust.

Myn in Numbers

244   Join supporting means.
245   Join supporting acceptance.
246   Join supporting joy.
247   Join supporting ability.
248   Join supporting building.
249   Join supporting action.
250   Join accepting self.
251   Join accepting this.
252   Join accepting compromise.
253   Join accepting blessing.
254   Join accepting support.
255   Join granting acceptance.
256   Join accepting joy.
257   Join accepting ability.
258   Join accepting building.
259   Join accepting action.
260   Joining serves self.
261   Joining serves now.
262   Joining serves friendship.
263   Joining serves trust.
264   Joining serves support.
265   Joining serves acceptance.
266   Joining serves joy.
267   Joining serves ability.
268   Joining serves building.
269   Joining serves feelings.
270   Join working release.
271   Join working now.
272   Join working compromise.
273   Join working trust.
274   Join working support.
275   Join working acceptance.
276   Join working joy.
277   Join working ability.

www.templeofgaia.com

278   Join working building.
279   Join working action.
280   Join building release.
281   Join building now.
282   Join building compromise.
283   Join building trust.
284   Join building support.
285   Join building acceptance.
286   Join building joy.
287   Join building ability.
288   Friendship builds structure.
289   Friendship builds action.
290   Joining tests release.
291   Joining tests now.
292   Joining tests compromise.
293   Joining tests trust.
294   Joining tests support.
295   Joining tests acceptance.
296   Joining tests joy.
297   Joining tests ability.
298   Joining tests building.
299   Joining tests feelings.

Trust

300

When "3" leads the pack your source is inviting you to "Look to the Source" as you conduct yourself in the personal moment of the trailing numbers. Weigh the points and ponder the outcome. In the end, trust that everything will work.

***

300	Trust my self.
301	Trust my now.
302	Trust my compromise.
303	Trust my blessing.
304	Trust my support.
305	Trust my acceptance.
306	Trust my joy.
307	Trust my ability.
308	Trust my building.

309 Trust my action.
310 Trust this release.
311 Trust this now.
312 Trust this compromise.
313 Trust this blessing.
314 Trust this supported.
315 Trust this acceptance.
316 Trust this joy.
317 Trust this ability.
318 Trust this building.
319 Trust this action.
320 Trust joining release.
321 Trust joining now.
322 Trust joining compromise.
323 Trust joining prosperity.
324 Trust joining support.
325 Trust joining acceptance.
326 Trust joining joy.
327 Trust joining ability.
328 Trust joining building.
329 Trust joining action.
330 Trust prosperity releasing.
331 Trust prosperity now.
332 Trust prosperity compromise.
333 Trust blesses prosperity.
334 Trust prosperity support.
335 Trust prosperity received.
336 Trust blessing joy.
337 Trust blessing ability.
338 Trust blessings building.
339 Trust prosperity action.
340 Trust supports release.
341 Trust support now.
342 Trust supports companionship.

Myn in Numbers

343	Trust supports blessings.
344	Trust supports support.
345	Trust supports acceptance.
346	Trust supports joy.
347	Trust supports ability.
348	Trust supports building.
349	Trust supports action.
350	Trust accepting self.
351	Trust acceptance now.
352	Trust accepting compromise.
353	Trust accepting blessing.
354	Trust accepting support.
355	Trust accepting acceptance.
356	Trust accepting joy.
357	Trust accepting ability.
358	Trust accepting builds.
359	Trust accepting action.
360	Trust serves self.
361	Trust joy now.
362	Trust joy compromise.
363	Trust joy blessings.
364	Trust joy supported.
365	Trust joy acceptance.
366	Trust joy serves.
367	Trust joy ability.
368	Trust joy building.
369	Trust joy action.
370	Trust works releasing.
371	Trust works this.
372	Trust works compromise.
373	Trust works prosperity.
374	Trust works supported.
375	Trust works acceptance.
376	Trust works joy.

www.templeofgaia.com

377   Trust works ability.
378   Trust works building.
379   Trust works testing.
380   Trust builds releasing.
381   Trust builds now.
382   Trust builds compromise.
383   Trust builds blessings.
384   Trust builds support.
385   Trust builds acceptance.
386   Trust builds joy.
387   Trust builds ability.
388   Trust builds building.
389   Trust builds action.
390   Trust active release.
391   Trust active now.
392   Trust active compromise.
393   Trust active blessing.
394   Trust active support.
395   Trust active acceptance.
396   Trust active joy.
397   Trust active ability.
398   Trust active structure.
399   Trust active feelings.

Myn in Numbers

Support

400

When "4" leads the pack your source is inviting you to "Support" as you conduct yourself in the personal moment of the trailing numbers. Weigh the points and ponder the outcome.

***

400	Supports my releasing.
401	Supports my now.
402	Supports my compromise.
403	Supports my trust.
404	Supports my means.
405	Supports my receiving.
406	Supports my joy.
407	Supports my ability.
408	Supports my building.
409	Supports my action.

www.templeofgaia.com

410   Supports this releasing.
411   Support is now.
412   Support is compromise.
413   Support is blessing.
414   Support is means.
415   Support is received.
416   Support is joy.
417   Support is ability.
418   Support is building.
419   Support is tested.
420   Support joins me.
421   Support joins now.
422   Support joins compromise.
423   Support joins trust.
424   Support joining means.
425   Support joins acceptance.
426   Support joins joy.
427   Support joins ability.
428   Support joins building.
429   Support joins action.
430   Support trusting release.
431   Support trusting now.
432   Support trusting compromise.
433   Support trusting blessing.
434   Support trusting means.
435   Support trusting acceptance.
436   Support trusting joy.
437   Support trusting ability.
438   Support trusting building.
439   Support trusting action.
440   Means supports release.
441   Means supports now.
442   Means supports compromise.
443   Means supports trust.

Myn in Numbers

444	Supported through means.
445	Means supports acceptance.
446	Means supports joy.
447	Means supports ability.
448	Means supports building.
449	Means supports action.
450	Support accepting release.
451	Support accepting now.
452	Support accepting compromise.
453	Support accepting trust.
454	Support accepting means.
455	Support receiving acceptance.
456	Support accepting joy.
457	Support accepting ability.
458	Support accepting building.
459	Support accepting action.
460	Support serves release.
461	Support serves now.
462	Support serves compromise.
463	Support serves trust.
464	Means serves support.
465	Support serves acceptance.
466	Support serves joy.
467	Support serves ability.
468	Support serves building.
469	Support serves action.
470	Support enables release.
471	Support works now.
472	Support works compromise.
473	Support works trust.
474	Support works means.
475	Support works acceptance.
476	Support works joy.
477	Support works ability.

478   Support works building.
479   Support works active.
480   Supports building release.
481   Support building this.
482   Support building compromise.
483   Support building trust.
484   Support building conveyance.
485   Support building acceptance.
486   Support building joy.
487   Through building ability.
488   Support building building.
489   Support building action.
490   Support active release.
491   Support active now.
492   Support active friendship.
493   Support active trust.
494   Support active means.
495   Support active acceptance.
496   Support active joy.
497   Support active ability.
498   Support active building.
499   Support active feelings.

Myn in Numbers

Accept

500

When "5" leads the pack your source is inviting you to "Be open" as you conduct yourself in the personal moment of the trailing numbers. Weigh the points and ponder the outcome.

***

500	Accepts my release.
501	Accepts my now.
502	Accepts my compromise.
503	Accepts my trust.
504	Accepts my support.
505	Accepts my presence.
506	Accepts my joy.
507	Accepts my ability.
508	Accepts my building.
509	Accepts my feelings.
510	Accept this release.
511	Accept this now.
512	Accept this compromise.
513	Accept this trusting.
514	Accept this support.

515   Accept this granted.
516   Accept this joy.
517   Accept this ability.
518   Accept this building.
519   Accept this action.
520   Accept friendship release.
521   Accept friendship now.
522   Accept friendship compromise.
523   Accept friendship trust.
524   Accept friendship support.
525   Accept friendship granted.
526   Accept friendship serves.
527   Accept friendship ability.
528   Accept friendship building.
529   Accept friendship action.
530   Accept trusting release.
531   Accept trusting now.
532   Accept trusting friendship.
533   Accept trusting blessing.
534   Accept trusting support.
535   Accept trusting presence.
536   Accept trusting joy.
537   Accept trusting ability.
538   Accept trust building.
539   Accept trusting action.
540   Acceptance through release.
541   Acceptance through now.
542   Acceptance through compromise.
543   Acceptance through trust.
544   Acceptance through support.
545   Acceptance through presence.
546   Acceptance through serving.
547   Acceptance through ability.
548   Acceptance through building.

Myn in Numbers

549	Acceptance through action.
550	Acceptance grants release.
551	Acceptance grants done.
552	Acceptance grants compromise.
553	Acceptance grants trust.
554	Acceptance grants means.
555	Acceptance grants presence.
556	Acceptance grants joy.
557	Acceptance grants ability.
558	Acceptance grants building.
559	Acceptance grants action.
560	Acceptance serves release.
561	Acceptance serves now.
562	Acceptance serves compromise.
563	Acceptance serves trust.
564	Acceptance serves means.
565	Acceptance serves receiving.
566	Acceptance serves laughing.
567	Acceptance serves ability.
568	Acceptance serves building.
569	Acceptance serves action.
570	Acceptance enables release.
571	Acceptance works this.
572	Acceptance works compromise.
573	Acceptance works trust.
574	Acceptance works support.
575	Acceptance works receiving.
576	Acceptance works joy.
577	Acceptance works ability.
578	Acceptance works building.
579	Acceptance works feelings.
580	Acceptance builds releasing.
581	Acceptance builds now.
582	Acceptance builds compromise.

www.templeofgaia.com

583	Acceptance builds trust.
584	Acceptance builds support.
585	Acceptance builds receiving.
586	Acceptance builds joy.
587	Acceptance builds ability.
588	Acceptance builds structure.
589	Acceptance builds action.
590	Acceptance acts releasing.
591	Acceptance acts now.
592	Acceptance acts joining.
593	Acceptance acts trusting.
594	Acceptance acts supportive.
595	Acceptance acts receiving.
596	Acceptance acts serving.
597	Acceptance acts able.
598	Acceptance acts building.
599	Acceptance acts feeling.

Joy

600

When "6" leads the pack your source is inviting you to "Smile" as you conduct yourself in the personal moment of the trailing numbers. Weigh the points and ponder the outcome.

***

600	Joy my release.
601	Joy my now.
602	Joy my compromise.
603	Joy my trust.
604	Joy my supportive.
605	Joy my acceptance.
606	Joy my serving.
607	Joy my ability.
608	Joy my building.
609	Joy my action.

610   Joy is releasing.
611   Joy now is.
612   Joy now compromise.
613   Joy now trust.
614   Joy now supported.
615   Joy now accepted.
616   Joy now joy.
617   Joy now working.
618   Joy now building.
619   Joy now action.
620   Joy joins releasing.
621   Joy joins now.
622   Joy joins compromise.
623   Joy joins trusting.
624   Joy joins supported.
625   Joy joins received.
626   Joy joins serving.
627   Joy joins ability.
628   Joy joins building.
629   Joy joins feelings.
630   Joy trusting release.
631   Joy trusting now.
632   Joy trusting compromise.
633   Joy trusting blessing.
634   Joy trusting support.
635   Joy trusting acceptance.
636   Joy trust serves.
637   Joy trusting ability.
638   Joy trusting building.
639   Joy trusting action.
640   Joy supports release.
641   Joy supports now.
642   Joy supports compromise.
643   Joy supports trust.

Myn in Numbers

644	Joy supports means.
645	Joy supports acceptance.
646	Joy supports joy.
647	Joy supports ability.
648	Joy supports building.
649	Joy supports action.
650	Joy accepting self.
651	Joy accepting this.
652	Joy accepting compromise.
653	Joy accepting trust.
654	Joy accepting support.
655	Joy accepting acceptance.
656	Joy accepting joy.
657	Joy accepting ability.
658	Joy acceptance building.
659	Joy accepting action.
660	Joy serves releasing.
661	Joy serves now.
662	Joy serves compromise.
663	Joy serves blessing.
664	Joy serves supportive.
665	Joy serves acceptance.
666	Joy serves laughing.
667	Joy serves ability.
668	Joy serves building.
669	Joy serves feelings.
670	Joy working release.
671	Joy working now.
672	Joy working compromise.
673	Joy working trust.
674	Joy working supported.
675	Joy working accepted.
676	Joy working joy.
677	Joy working ability.

678	Joy working building.
679	Joy working action.
680	Joy building release.
681	Joy building now.
682	Joy building compromise.
683	Joy building trust.
684	Joy building supported.
685	Joy building received.
686	Joy building joy.
687	Joy building ability.
688	Joy building structure.
689	Joy building action.
690	Joy action releasing.
691	Joy action now.
692	Joy action joining.
693	Joy action trusted.
694	Joy action supported.
695	Joy action granted.
696	Joy action serves.
697	Joy action enabled.
698	Joy action building.
699	Joy action felt.

Myn in Numbers

Work

700

When "7" leads the pack your source is inviting you to "Work it" as you conduct yourself in the personal moment of the trailing numbers. Weigh the points and ponder the outcome.

***

700	Works my release.
701	Works my now.
702	Works my compromise.
703	Works my trust.
704	Works my support.
705	Works my acceptance.
706	Works my joy.
707	Works my ability.
708	Works my building.
709	Works my feelings.
710	Work now releasing.

www.templeofgaia.com

711 Work now is.
712 Work now compromise.
713 Work now trusted.
714 Work now supported.
715 Work now accepted.
716 Work now serving.
717 Work now working.
718 Work now building.
719 Work now active.
720 Work joins self.
721 Work joins now.
722 Work joins compromise.
723 Work joins trusting.
724 Work joins supported.
725 Work joins accepted.
726 Work joins serving.
727 Work joins ability.
728 Work joins building.
729 Work joins action.
730 Work trusting self.
731 Work trusting this.
732 Work trusting compromise.
733 Work trusting prosperity.
734 Work trusting means.
735 Work trusting acceptance.
736 Work trusting joy.
737 Work trusting ability.
738 Work trusting building.
739 Work trusting feelings.
740 Work supporting self.
741 Work supporting now.
742 Work supporting compromise.
743 Work supporting trust.
744 Work supporting means.

Myn in Numbers

745   Work supporting acceptance.
746   Work supporting joy.
747   Work supporting ability.
748   Work supporting building.
749   Work supporting feelings.
750   Work accepting self.
751   Work accepting now.
752   Work accepting compromise.
753   Work accepting trust.
754   Work accepting support.
755   Work accepting granted.
756   Work accepting joy.
757   Work accepting ability.
758   Work accepting building.
759   Work accepting action.
760   Work joy release.
761   Work joy now.
762   Work joy compromise.
763   Work joy trust.
764   Work joy support.
765   Work joy acceptance.
766   Work joy serves.
767   Work joy ability.
768   Work joy building.
769   Work joy action.
770   Work capable release.
771   Work capable now.
772   Work capable compromise.
773   Work capable trust.
774   Work capable support.
775   Work capable acceptance.
776   Work capable joy.
777   Work capable ability.
778   Work capable building.

779   Work capable action.
780   Work building self.
781   Work building now.
782   Work building compromise.
783   Work building trust.
784   Work building support.
785   Work building acceptance.
786   Work building joy.
787   Work building ability.
788   Work building building.
789   Work building feelings.
790   Work action releasing.
791   Work action now.
792   Work action compromise.
793   Work action trusting.
794   Work action supporting.
795   Work action accepting.
796   Work action serves.
797   Work action ability.
798   Work action building.
799   Work action testing.

Myn in Numbers

Building

800

When "8" leads the pack your source is inviting you to "Build" as you conduct yourself in the personal moment of the trailing numbers. Weigh the points and ponder the outcome.

***

800	Build my release.
801	Build my now.
802	Build my compromise.
803	Build my blessing.
804	Build my support.
805	Build my acceptance.
806	Build my serving.
807	Build my ability.
808	Build my structure.

www.templeofgaia.com

809 Build my feelings.
810 Build this releasing.
811 Build this now.
812 Build this friendship.
813 Build now blessing.
814 Build now supported.
815 Build now received.
816 Build this joy.
817 Build this ability.
818 Build this structure.
819 Build this action.
820 Build joining release.
821 Build joining now.
822 Build joining compromise.
823 Build joining trust.
824 Build joining support.
825 Build joining acceptance.
826 Build joining joy.
827 Build joining ability.
828 Build joining structure.
829 Build joining action.
830 Build trusting self.
881 Build trusting now.
832 Build trusting compromise.
833 Build trusting blessing.
834 Build trusting support.
835 Build trusting acceptance.
836 Build trusting joy.
837 Build trusting ability.
838 Build trusting building.
839 Build trusting feelings.
840 Build supporting self.
841 Build supporting this.
842 Build supporting compromise.

Myn in Numbers

843 Build supporting trust.
844 Build supporting support.
845 Build supporting receiving.
846 Build supporting joy.
847 Build supporting ability.
848 Build supporting building.
849 Build supporting action.
850 Build accepting release.
851 Build accepting now.
852 Build accepting compromise.
853 Build accepting trust.
854 Build accepting support.
855 Build accepting acceptance.
856 Build accepting joy.
857 Build accepting ability.
858 Build accepting building.
859 Build accepting action.
860 Build serving self.
861 Build joy now.
862 Build serving compromise.
863 Build serving trusted.
864 Build serving supported.
865 Build serving acceptance.
866 Building serves joy.
867 Build joy ability.
868 Build joy structure.
869 Build joy feelings.
870 Building works self.
871 Building works now.
872 Building works friendship.
873 Building works trusted.
874 Building works supported.
875 Building works acceptance.
876 Building works joy.

877	Building works ability.
878	Building works building.
879	Building works action.
880	Building forms self.
881	Building forms now.
882	Building forms friendship.
883	Building forms trust.
884	Building forms support.
885	Building forms acceptance.
886	Building forms serving.
887	Building forms ability.
888	Build…build…build.
889	Building forms action.
890	Build active releasing.
891	Build active now.
892	Build active compromise.
893	Build active trust.
894	Build active support.
895	Build active acceptance.
896	Build active joy.
897	Build active ability.
898	Build active structure.
899	Build active feelings.

Myn in Numbers

Action

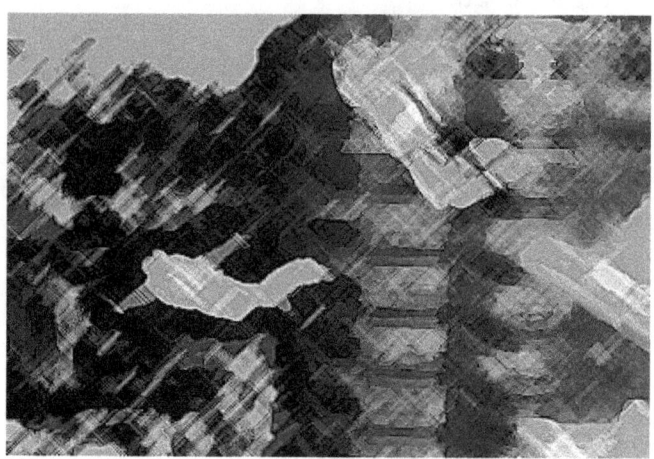

900

When "9" leads the pack your source is inviting you to "Act" as you conduct yourself in the personal moment of the trailing numbers. Weigh the points and ponder the outcome.

***

900	Action self releasing.
901	Action releases now.
902	Action releases compromise.
903	Action releases trusting.
904	Action releases support.
905	Action releases acceptance.
906	Action releases joy.
907	Action releases ability.
908	Action releases building.
909	Action releases testing.
910	Action now releasing.
911	Action is now.

912   Action now compromise.
913   Action now trusted.
914   Action now supported.
915   Action now accepted.
916   Action now joy.
917   Action now ability.
918   Action now building.
919   Action now active.
920   Action joins releasing.
921   Action joins now.
922   Action joins compromise.
923   Action joins trust.
924   Action joins support.
925   Action joins acceptance.
926   Action joins joy.
927   Action joins ability.
928   Action joins building.
929   Action joins feelings.
930   Action trust release.
931   Action trusted now.
932   Action trust compromise.
933   Action trust blessing.
934   Action trust support.
935   Action trust acceptance.
936   Action trust joy.
937   Action trust ability.
938   Action trust builds.
939   Action trusts action.
940   Action supports release.
941   Action supports now.
942   Action supports compromise.
943   Action supports trusting.
944   Action means support.
945   Action supports acceptance.

Myn in Numbers

946	Action supports joy.
947	Action supports ability.
948	Action supports building.
949	Action supports feelings.
950	Action presents release.
951	Action presents now.
952	Action presents compromise.
953	Action presents blessing.
954	Action presents support.
955	Action presents acceptance.
956	Action presents joy.
957	Action presents ability.
958	Action presents building.
959	Action presents feelings.
960	Action serves release.
961	Action serves now.
962	Action serves compromise.
963	Action serves blessing.
964	Action serves supported.
965	Action serves acceptance.
966	Action serves joy.
967	Action serves ability.
968	Action serves building.
969	Action serves feelings.
970	Action working release.
971	Action working now.
972	Action working partner.
973	Action working trust.
974	Action working support.
975	Action working acceptance.
976	Action working joy.
977	Action working ability.
978	Action working structure.
979	Action working feelings.

Kevin J. Baird

980   Action builds release.
981   Action builds now.
982   Action builds compromise.
983   Action builds trust.
984   Action builds support.
985   Action builds acceptance.
986   Action builds joy.
987   Action builds ability.
988   Action builds structure.
989   Action builds feelings.
990   Action tests release.
991   Action tests now.
992   Action tests compromise.
993   Action tests trust.
994   Action tests support.
995   Action tests acceptance.
996   Action tests joy.
997   Action tests ability.
998   Action tests building.
999   Action tests feelings.

Myn in Numbers

Now

1000-1999

When "1" leads the group your source is inviting you to "Now" as you conduct yourself in the group moment of the trailing numbers. Weigh the points and ponder the outcome.

***

1000	Now my self releases.
1001	This release self is.
1002	Is my self compromise.
1003	Is my self trust.
1004	Now my self supported.
1005	Now my self acceptance.
1006	Now my self joy.
1007	Now my self ability.
1008	Now my self building.
1009	Now my self action.
1010	Now self is releasing.

www.templeofgaia.com

Kevin J. Baird

1011   This release is now.
1012   Now release this compromise.
1013   Now self is trusting.
1014   Now self is supported.
1015   Now self is received.
1016   Now self is joy.
1017   Now self is ability.
1018   Now self is building.
1019   Now self is action.
1020   Now soul joins release.
1021   This release joins now.
1022   This my friend joins.
1023   This my joins trust.
1024   This release joins support.
1025   This release joins acceptance.
1026   This release joins joy.
1027   This release joins ability.
1028   This release joins building.
1029   This release joins action.
1030   This release myn releasing.
1031   This release trusts now.
1032   This release myn compromise.
1033   This release trust myn.
1034   This release myn supported.
1035   This release trust accepted.
1036   This release trusts joy.
1037   This release trusts ability.
1038   This release trusts building.
1039   This release trusts action.
1040   This release supports self.
1041   This release supports now.
1042   This release supports compromise.
1043   This release supports blessing.
1044   This release supports means.

Myn in Numbers

1045	This release supports acceptance.
1046	This release supports joy.
1047	This release supports ability.
1048	This release supports building.
1049	This release supports action.
1050	This release receives self.
1051	This release receives now.
1052	This release receives compromise.
1053	This release receives blessing.
1054	This release receives support.
1055	This release receives acceptance.
1056	This release receives joy.
1057	This release receives ability.
1058	This release receives building.
1059	This release receives action.
1060	Is my serving release.
1061	Is my joy now?
1062	Now my joy compromise.
1063	This release serves blessing.
1064	Now my joy supported.
1065	Now my joy received.
1066	Now release content laugh.
1067	Now my joy ability.
1068	Now my joy building.
1069	Now my joy action.
1070	Now my ability releasing.
1071	This my ability now.
1072	This my ability compromise.
1073	This my ability blesses.
1074	This my ability supports.
1075	Now my ability accepted.
1076	Now my ability serves.
1077	Now my ability enabled.
1078	Now my ability building.

1079   Now my ability active.
1080   This release building self.
1081   This release building now.
1082   This release building compromise.
1083   This release building blessing.
1084   This release building support.
1085   This release building acceptance.
1086   This release building joy.
1087   This release building ability.
1088   This release building structure.
1089   This release building action.
1090   This release tests me.
1091   This release testing now.
1092   This release tests compromise.
1093   This release tests trust.
1094   This release tests support.
1095   This release tests acceptance.
1096   This release tests joy.
1097   This release tests ability.
1098   This release tests building.
1099   This release tests action.
1100   This is my self.
1101   This is my now.
1102   This is my compromise.
1103   This is my blessing.
1104   This is my support.
1105   This is my acceptance.
1106   This is my joy.
1107   This is my ability.
1108   This is my building.
1109   This is my action.
1110   This is now released.
1111   This is is now.
1112   This is now compromise.

Myn in Numbers

1113	This is now trusted.
1114	This is now supported.
1115	This is now received.
1116	This is is joy.
1117	This is now ability.
1118	This is now building.
1119	This is now action.
1120	This is joining me.
1121	This is joining now.
1122	This is joining compromise.
1123	This is joining trust.
1124	This is joining support.
1125	This now joins acceptance.
1126	This is joining joy.
1127	This is joining ability.
1128	This is joining building.
1129	This is joining action.
1130	This is blessing self.
1131	This is trusting now.
1132	This is trusting compromise.
1133	Is now trusting prosperity.
1134	This is trusting support.
1135	This is trusting acceptance.
1136	This is trusting joy.
1137	This is trusting ability.
1138	This is trusting building.
1139	This is trusting action.
1140	This is through me.
1141	This is supported now.
1142	This is through compromise.
1143	This is through trust.
1144	This is through support.
1145	This is through receiving.
1146	This is through joy.

1147	This is through ability.
1148	This is through building.
1149	This is through action.
1150	Now this presents release.
1151	Now this acceptance is.
1152	Now is receiving compromise.
1153	Now is receiving trust.
1154	Now is accepting support.
1155	Now is receiving acceptance.
1156	Now is receiving joy.
1157	Now is receiving ability.
1158	Now is receiving building.
1159	Now is receiving action.
1160	This is joy releasing.
1161	This is joy now.
1162	This is joy compromise.
1163	This is serving trust.
1164	This is joy supported.
1165	This is joy received.
1166	This is serving joy.
1167	This is joy working.
1168	This is joy building.
1169	This is joy action.
1170	This is working release.
1171	This is working now.
1172	This is working compromise.
1173	This is working blessing.
1174	This is working support.
1175	This is working acceptance.
1176	This is working joy.
1177	This is working ability.
1178	This is working building.
1179	This is working action.
1180	This is building release.

Myn in Numbers

1181	This is building now.
1182	This is building compromise.
1183	This is building blessing.
1184	This is building support.
1185	This is building acceptance.
1186	This is building joy.
1187	This is building ability.
1188	This is building structure.
1189	This is building action.
1190	This is active release.
1191	This is active now.
1192	This is active compromise.
1193	This is active blessing.
1194	This is active support.
1195	This is active acceptance.
1196	This is active joy.
1197	This is active ability.
1198	This is active building.
1199	This is active action.
1200	This joins my release.
1201	This joins my now.
1202	This joins my compromise.
1203	This joins my blessing.
1204	This joins my support.
1205	This joins my acceptance.
1206	This joins my joy.
1207	This joins my ability.
1208	This joins my building.
1209	This joins my action.
1210	This joining is releasing.
1211	This compromise is now.
1212	This joining is compromise.
1213	This joining is blessed.
1214	This joining is supported.

Kevin J. Baird

1215   This joining is accepted.
1216   This joining is serving.
1217   This joining now tests.
1218   This joining is building.
1219   This joining is moving.
1220   This joins friend's release.
1221   This joins friend's now.
1222   This joins friend's compromise.
1223   This joins friend's blessing.
1224   This joins friend's support.
1225   This joins friend's acceptance.
1226   This joins friend's joy.
1227   This joins friend's ability.
1228   This joins friend's building.
1229   This joins friend's feelings.
1230   Now join trusting release.
1231   Now join trusting now.
1232   Now join trusting compromise.
1233   Now join trusting blessing.
1234   Now join trusting support.
1235   Now join trusting acceptance.
1236   Now join trusting joy.
1237   Now join trusting ability.
1238   Now join trusting building.
1239   Now join trusting feelings.
1240   Now join supporting release.
1241   Now join supporting this.
1242   Now join supporting compromise.
1243   Now join supporting blessing.
1244   Now join supporting means.
1245   Now join supporting acceptance.
1246   Now join supporting joy.
1247   Now join supporting ability.
1248   Now join supporting building.

Myn in Numbers

1249   Now join supporting action.
1250   Now join accepting release.
1251   Now join accepting this.
1252   Now join accepting compromise.
1253   Now join accepting blessing.
1254   Now join accepting support.
1255   Now join accepting acceptance.
1256   Now join accepting joy.
1257   Now join accepting ability.
1258   Now join accepting building.
1259   Now join accepting action.
1260   Now join serving release.
1261   Now join serving this.
1262   Now join serving friend.
1263   Now join serving blessing.
1264   Now join serving supportive.
1265   Now join serving acceptance.
1266   Now join serving joy.
1267   Now join serving ability.
1268   Now join serving building.
1269   Now join serving action.
1270   This joining works release.
1271   Is partner ability now.
1272   Is partner ability compromise.
1273   Is partner ability blessing.
1274   Now partner ability supported.
1275   Now partner ability received.
1276   Now partner ability joy.
1277   Now join working ability.
1278   Now join ability building.
1279   Now join able action.
1280   Now companion building self.
1281   Now join building this.
1282   Now join building compromise.

1283   Now join building blessing.
1284   Now join building support.
1285   Now join building acceptance.
1286   Now join building joy.
1287   Now join building ability.
1288   Now join building structure.
1289   Now join building action.
1290   Now join testing self.
1291   Now join testing this.
1292   Now join testing compromise.
1293   Now join testing blessing.
1294   Now join testing support.
1295   Now join testing acceptance.
1296   Now join testing joy.
1297   Now join testing ability.
1298   Now join testing building.
1299   Now join testing action.
1300   Now trust my self.
1301   Now trust my now.
1302   Now trust my compromise.
1303   Now trust my blessings.
1304   Now trust my support.
1305   Now trust my acceptance.
1306   Now trust my joy.
1307   Now trust my ability.
1308   Now trust my building.
1309   Now trust my feelings.
1310   Now trust this soul.
1311   Now trust this is.
1312   Now trust this compromise.
1313   Now trust this blessing.
1314   Now trust this supported.
1315   Now trust this accepted.
1316   Now trust this joy.

Myn in Numbers

1317 Now trust this ability.
1318 Now trust this building.
1319 Now trust this feeling.
1320 Now trust joining release.
1321 Now trust joining this.
1322 Now trust joining compromise.
1323 Now trust joining blessings.
1324 Now trust joining support.
1325 Now trust joining acceptance.
1326 Now trust joining joy.
1327 Now trust joining ability.
1328 Now trust joining building.
1329 Now trust joining action.
1330 Now Myn blesses release.
1331 Now Myn blesses this.
1332 Now Myn blesses compromise.
1333 Now Myn blesses prosperity.
1334 Now Myn blesses support.
1335 Now Myn blesses acceptance.
1336 Now Myn blesses joy.
1337 Now Myn blesses ability.
1338 Now Myn blesses building.
1339 Now Myn blesses action.
1340 Not trust supporting release.
1341 Now trust supporting now.
1342 Now trust supporting compromise.
1343 Now trust supporting prosperity.
1344 Now trust supporting means.
1345 Now trust supporting acceptance.
1346 Now trust supporting joy.
1347 Now trust supporting ability.
1348 Now trust supporting building.
1349 Now trust supporting feelings.
1350 Now trust accepting release.

1351   Now trust accepting this.
1352   Now trust accepting compromise.
1353   Now trust accepting blessing.
1354   Now trust accepting support.
1355   Now trust accepting acceptance.
1356   Now trust accepting joy.
1357   Now trust accepting ability.
1358   Now trust accepting building.
1359   Now trust accepting action.
1360   Now trust serving release.
1361   Now trust serving now.
1362   Now trust serving compromise.
1363   Now trust serving trust
1364   Now trust serving support.
1365   Now trust serving acceptance.
1366   Now trust serving joy.
1367   Now trust serving ability.
1368   Now trust serving building.
1369   Now trust serving feelings.
1370   Now trust working release.
1371   Now trust working this.
1372   Now trust working friendship.
1373   Now trust working prosperity.
1374   Now trust working supported.
1375   Now trust working acceptance.
1376   Now trust working joy.
1377   Now trust working ability.
1378   Now trust working building.
1379   Now trust working feelings.
1380   Now trust building release.
1381   Now trust building this.
1382   Now trust building compromise.
1383   Now trust building prosperity.
1384   Now trust building means.

Myn in Numbers

1385	Now trust building release.
1386	Now trust building joy.
1387	Now trust building ability.
1388	Now trust building structure.
1389	Now trust building feelings.
1390	Now trust active release.
1391	Now trust active this.
1392	Now trust active compromise.
1393	Now trust active blessings.
1394	Now trust active support.
1395	Now trust active acceptance.
1396	Now trust active joy.
1397	Now trust active ability.
1398	Now trust active building.
1399	Now trust active feelings.
1400	This supports my release.
1401	This supports my now.
1402	This supports my friendship.
1403	This supports my trust.
1404	This supports my means.
1405	This supports my acceptance.
1406	This supports my joy.
1407	This supports my ability.
1408	This supports my building.
1409	This supports my feelings.
1410	Now support is self.
1411	Now support this done.
1412	Now support this compromise.
1413	Now support this trusted.
1414	Now means is support.
1415	Now support this received.
1416	Now support this joy.
1417	Now support this ability.
1418	Now support this building.

1419   Now support this action.
1420   Is through joining release.
1421   Is through joining this.
1422   Is through joining compromise.
1423   Is through joining trust.
1424   Is through joining support.
1425   Is through joining acceptance.
1426   Is through joining serving.
1427   Is through joining ability.
1428   Is through joining structure.
1429   Is through joining feelings.
1430   Now support trusting release.
1431   Now support trusting this.
1432   Now support trusting compromise.
1433   Now support trusting blessing.
1434   Now support trusting means.
1435   Now support trusting acceptance.
1436   Now support trusting joy.
1437   Now support trusting ability.
1438   Now support trusting building.
1439   Now support trusting feelings.
1440   This means through release.
1441   This means through now.
1442   This means through compromise.
1443   This means through blessing.
1444   This means through conveying.
1445   This means through acceptance.
1446   This means through joy.
1447   This means through ability.
1448   This means through building.
1449   This means through feeling.
1450   Now support accepting release.
1451   Now support accepting this.
1452   Now support accepting compromise.

Myn in Numbers

1453	Now support accepting blessings.
1454	Now support accepting support.
1455	Now support accepting present.
1456	Now support accepting joy.
1457	Now support accepting ability.
1458	Now support accepting build.
1459	Now support accepting feelings.
1460	Now support serving self.
1461	Now support serving this.
1462	Now support serving friendship.
1463	Now support serving trust.
1464	Now support serving means.
1465	Now support serving acceptance.
1466	Now support serving joy.
1467	Now support serving ability.
1468	Now support serving structure.
1469	Now support serving feelings.
1470	This support working release.
1471	This support working this.
1472	This support working friendship.
1473	This support working trust.
1474	This support working means.
1475	This support working acceptance.
1476	This support working joy.
1477	This support working ability.
1478	This support working structure.
1479	This support working feelings.
1480	Is through building self.
1481	Is through building now.
1482	Is through building compromise.
1483	Is through building trust.
1484	Is through building supported.
1485	Is through building acceptance.
1486	Is through building joy.

1487	Is through building ability.
1488	Is through building structure.
1489	Is through building feelings.
1490	Is through feeling release.
1491	Is through feeling now.
1492	Is through feeling compromise.
1493	Is through feeling trusted.
1494	Is through feeling supported.
1495	Is through feeling acceptance.
1496	Is through feeling joy.
1497	Is through feeling able.
1498	Is through feelings building.
1499	Is through feelings tested.
1500	This acceptance my release.
1501	This acceptance my now.
1502	This acceptance my friendship.
1503	This acceptance my trusting.
1504	This acceptance my support.
1505	This acceptance my conveyance.
1506	This acceptance my joy.
1507	This acceptance my ability.
1508	This acceptance my building.
1509	This acceptance my action.
1510	This acceptance is releasing.
1511	This acceptance is now.
1512	This acceptance is compromise.
1513	This acceptance is trusting.
1514	This acceptance is supported.
1515	This receiving is acceptance.
1516	This acceptance now serves.
1517	This acceptance is ability.
1518	This acceptance is building.
1519	This acceptance is feeling.
1520	This acceptance joins release.

Myn in Numbers

1521	This acceptance joins now.
1522	This acceptance joins compromise.
1523	This acceptance joins trusting.
1524	This acceptance joins supported.
1525	This acceptance joins accepted.
1526	This acceptance joins joy.
1527	This acceptance joins ability.
1528	This acceptance joins building.
1529	This acceptance joins feelings.
1530	Now receive trusting self.
1531	Now receive trusting now.
1532	Now receive trusting compromise.
1533	Now receive trusting prosperity.
1534	Now receive trusting support.
1535	Now receive trusting acceptance.
1536	Now receive trusting joy.
1537	Now receive trusting ability.
1538	Now receive trusting building.
1539	Now receive trusting feelings.
1540	Is accepted through self.
1541	Is accepted supporting now.
1542	Is accepted supporting compromise.
1543	Is accepted supporting release.
1544	Is accepted supporting means.
1545	Is accepted supporting receiving.
1546	Is accepted supporting joy.
1547	Is accepted supporting ability.
1548	Is accepted supporting building.
1549	Is accepted supporting action.
1550	Now present accepting release.
1551	This acceptance receive now.
1552	This acceptance receives compromise.
1553	This acceptance receives release.
1554	This acceptance receives support.

1555   This acceptance received granted.
1556   This acceptance receives joy.
1557   This acceptance receives ability.
1558   This acceptance receives building.
1559   This acceptance receives action.
1560   Now present laughing released.
1561   Now present laughing now.
1562   Now present laughing compromise.
1563   Now present laughing blessing.
1564   Now present laugh support.
1565   Now present laughing acceptance.
1566   Now present content laugh.
1567   Now present laugh ability.
1568   Now present laugh building.
1569   Now present laughing action.
1570   Now accept working self.
1571   Now accept working this.
1572   Now accept working compromise.
1573   Now accept working blessing.
1574   Now accept working supported.
1575   Now accept working granted.
1576   Now accept working served.
1577   Now accept working ability.
1578   Now accept working structure.
1579   Now accept working feelings.
1580   Now accept building self.
1581   Now accept building this.
1582   Now accept building compromise.
1583   Now accept building trust.
1584   Now accept building support.
1585   Now accept building acceptance.
1586   Now accept building joy.
1587   Now accept building ability.
1588   Now accept building structure.

Myn in Numbers

1589	Now accept building feelings.
1590	Now receive testing release.
1591	Now receive testing this.
1592	Now receive testing compromise.
1593	Now receive testing trust.
1594	Now receive testing support.
1595	Now receive testing acceptance.
1596	Now receive testing joy.
1597	Now receive testing ability.
1598	Now receive testing structure.
1599	Now receive testing feelings.
1600	Now enjoy my release.
1601	Now enjoy my now.
1602	Now enjoy my compromise.
1603	Now enjoy my trusting.
1604	Now enjoy my support.
1605	Now enjoy my acceptance.
1606	Now enjoy my joy.
1607	Now enjoy my ability.
1608	Now enjoy my building.
1609	Now enjoy my feelings.
1610	This joy is releasing.
1611	This joy is now.
1612	This joy is compromise.
1613	This joy is blessing.
1614	This joy is supported.
1615	This joy is received.
1616	This joy now serves.
1617	Now joy is ability.
1618	Now joy is building.
1619	This joy is action.
1620	Is serving friendship release.
1621	Is serving friendship now.
1622	Is serving friendship compromise.

Kevin J. Baird

1623   Is serving friendship trust.
1624   Is serving friendship support.
1625   Is serving friendship acceptance.
1626   Is serving friendship joy.
1627   Is serving friendship ability.
1628   Is serving friendship building.
1629   Is serving friendship feelings.
1630   This serves trusting release.
1631   This serves trusting now.
1632   This serves trusting compromise.
1633   This serves trusting blessing.
1634   This serves trusting support.
1635   This serves trusting acceptance.
1636   This serves trusting joy.
1637   This serves trusting ability.
1638   Now joy myn building.
1639   This serves trusting feelings.
1640   This serves supporting release.
1641   This serves supporting done.
1642   This serves supporting friendship.
1643   This serves supporting trust.
1644   This serves supporting means.
1645   This serves supporting acceptance.
1646   This serves supporting joy.
1647   This serves supporting ability.
1648   This serves support builds.
1649   This serves supporting action.
1650   This serves receiving self.
1651   This serves receiving now.
1652   This serves receiving compromise.
1653   This serves receiving trust.
1654   This serves receiving support.
1655   This serves receiving acceptance.
1656   This serves receiving joy.

Myn in Numbers

1657	This serves receiving ability.
1658	This serves receiving building.
1659	This serves receiving action.
1660	This joy serves releasing.
1661	This joy serves now.
1662	This joy serves friendship.
1663	This joy serves trusting.
1664	This joy serves supported.
1665	This joy serves receives.
1666	This joy serves laughing.
1667	This joy serves ability.
1668	This joy serves building.
1669	This joy serves feelings.
1670	This serves working self.
1671	This serves working now.
1672	This serves working friendship.
1673	This serves working trusted.
1674	This serves working supported.
1675	This serves working acceptance.
1676	This serves working joy.
1677	This serves working ability.
1678	This serves work building.
1679	This serves working feelings.
1680	This serves building release.
1681	This serves building now.
1682	This serves building compromise.
1683	This serves building trust.
1684	This serves building support.
1685	This serves building acceptance.
1686	This serves building joy.
1687	This serves building ability.
1688	This serves building structure.
1689	This serves building feelings.
1690	This serves testing self.

1691   This serves testing now.
1692   This serves testing friendship.
1693   This serves testing trust.
1694   This serves testing means.
1695   This serves testing acceptance.
1696   This serves testing joy.
1697   This serves testing ability.
1698   This serves testing structure.
1699   This serves testing feelings.
1700   Is working my release.
1701   Is working my done.
1702   Is working my compromise.
1703   Is working my trust.
1704   Is working my support.
1705   Is working my acceptance.
1706   Is working my joy.
1707   Is working my ability.
1708   Is working my building.
1709   Is working my feelings.
1710   Is working this released.
1711   Is working this now.
1712   Is working this compromise.
1713   Is working this trust.
1714   Is working this means.
1715   Is working this acceptance.
1716   Is working this joy.
1717   Is working this ability.
1718   Is working this structure.
1719   Is working this action.
1720   This ability joins me.
1721   This ability joins now.
1722   This ability joins compromise.
1723   This ability joins trust.
1724   This ability joins support.

Myn in Numbers

1725	This ability joins accepted.
1726	This ability joins joy.
1727	This ability joins able.
1728	This ability joins building.
1729	This ability joins action.
1730	This ability trusting release.
1731	This ability trusting now.
1732	This ability trusting compromise.
1733	This ability trusting blessing.
1734	This ability trusting support.
1735	This ability trusting acceptance.
1736	This ability trusting joy.
1737	This ability trusting ability.
1738	This ability trusting building.
1739	This ability trusting feelings.
1740	This ability supporting release.
1741	This ability supporting now.
1742	This ability supporting compromise.
1743	This ability supporting trust.
1744	This ability supporting means.
1745	This ability supporting acceptance.
1746	This ability supporting joy.
1747	This ability supports working.
1748	This ability supports building.
1749	This ability supporting action.
1750	Is ability accepting release.
1751	Is ability accepting now.
1752	Is ability accepting compromise.
1753	Is ability accepting trust.
1754	Is ability accepting support.
1755	Is ability receiving acceptance.
1756	Is ability accepting joy.
1757	Is ability accepting working.
1758	Is ability accepting form.

Kevin J. Baird

1759	Is ability accepting action.
1760	Now able joy releasing.
1761	Now able joy is.
1762	Now able joy compromise.
1763	Now able joy trusts.
1764	Now able joy support.
1765	Now able joy accepted.
1766	Now able joy serves.
1767	Now able joy ability.
1768	Now able joy building.
1769	Now able joy active.
1770	This ability working release.
1771	This ability working now.
1772	This ability working compromise.
1773	This ability working trust.
1774	This ability working supported.
1775	This ability working acceptance.
1776	This ability working happiness.
1777	Is ability working ability.
1778	This ability working building.
1779	This ability working action.
1780	This ability building release.
1781	This ability building now.
1782	This ability building compromise.
1783	This ability building trust.
1784	This ability building supported.
1785	This ability building accepted.
1786	This ability building happiness.
1787	This ability building ability.
1788	This ability building structure.
1789	This ability building action.
1790	Is work testing release.
1791	Is work testing now.
1792	Is work testing compromise.

Myn in Numbers

1793	Is work testing prosperity.
1794	Is work testing support.
1795	Is work testing acceptance.
1796	Is work testing joy.
1797	Is work testing ability.
1798	Is work testing building.
1799	Is work testing feelings.
1800	Now building my releasing.
1801	Now building my now.
1802	Now building my compromise.
1803	Now building my trust.
1804	Now building my support.
1805	Now building my acceptance.
1806	Now building my joy.
1807	Now building my ability.
1808	Now building my building.
1809	Now building my action.
1810	Is forming this releasing.
1811	Is forming this now.
1812	Is forming this compromise.
1813	Is forming this trust.
1814	Is forming this support.
1815	Is forming this acceptance.
1816	Is forming this joy.
1817	Is forming this ability.
1818	Is forming this building.
1819	Is forming this action.
1820	Is building friendship release.
1821	Is building friendship now.
1822	Is building friendship compromise.
1823	Is building friendship trust.
1824	Is building friendship supported.
1825	Is building friendship present.
1826	Is building friendship happiness.

1827	Is building friendship ability.
1828	Is building friendship storage.
1829	Is building friendship action.
1830	Is building trust release.
1831	Is building trust now.
1832	Is building trust compromise.
1833	Is building trusted prosperity.
1834	Is building trusted support.
1835	Is building trusted acceptance.
1836	Is building trusted joy.
1837	Is building trusted ability.
1838	Is building trust building.
1839	Is building trusted action.
1840	Is building through release.
1841	Is storing through this.
1842	Now building through compromise.
1843	Now building through myn.
1844	Now building through support.
1845	Now building through acceptance.
1846	Now building through joy.
1847	Now building through ability.
1848	Now building through building.
1849	Now building through action.
1850	Is building accepting release.
1851	Now building receive now.
1852	Now building receiving compromise.
1853	Now building accepting trust.
1854	Now building receiving support.
1855	Is building serving acceptance.
1856	Now building receiving joy.
1857	Now building receiving ability.
1858	Now building receiving building.
1859	Now building receiving action.
1860	Is building serving release.

Myn in Numbers

1861	Is building serving now.
1862	Is building serving compromise.
1863	Is building serving trust.
1864	Is building serving support.
1865	This building serves acceptance.
1866	Is building serving joy.
1867	Is building serving ability.
1868	Is building serving structure.
1869	Is building serving action.
1870	Now build able releasing.
1871	This building works now.
1872	This building works compromise.
1873	This building works trust.
1874	This building works supported.
1875	This building works receiving.
1876	This building works joy.
1877	This building works ability.
1878	This building works building.
1879	This building works action.
1880	This form builds release.
1881	This form builds now.
1882	This form builds compromise.
1883	This form builds trust.
1884	This form builds support.
1885	This form builds acceptance.
1886	This form builds joy.
1887	This form builds ability.
1888	Now build…build…build.
1889	This form builds action.
1890	Now building active releasing.
1891	Is building action now.
1892	Now building active compromise.
1893	Now building active trust.
1894	Now building active support.

1895	Now building active acceptance.
1896	Now building active joy.
1897	Now building active ability.
1898	Now building active form.
1899	Now builds feeling active.
1900	Is testing my self.
1901	This action releasing now.
1902	This action releasing compromise.
1903	This action my trusting.
1904	Now action my support.
1905	Now action my acceptance.
1906	Now action my joy.
1907	Now action my ability.
1908	Now action my building.
1909	Now action my action.
1910	This action now releasing.
1911	This action is now.
1912	This action now compromise.
1913	This action is trust.
1914	This action now supported.
1915	This action now received.
1916	This action is joy.
1917	This action is ability.
1918	This action now building.
1919	This action is testing.
1920	This action joins releasing.
1921	This action joins now.
1922	This action joins compromise.
1923	This action joins trust.
1924	This action joins supported.
1925	This action joins acceptance.
1926	This action joins joy.
1927	This action joins ability.
1928	This action joins building.

Myn in Numbers

1929	This action joins action.
1930	Now action trusting self.
1931	This action prosperity now.
1932	This action prosperity compromise.
1933	This action prosperity myn.
1934	This action prosperity support.
1935	This action prosperity received.
1936	This action prosperity joy.
1937	This action prosperity ability.
1938	This action prosperity building.
1939	This action prosperity action.
1940	Now test supporting release.
1941	Now test supporting this.
1942	Now test supporting compromise.
1943	Now test supporting myn.
1944	Now test supporting means.
1945	Now test supporting acceptance.
1946	Now test supporting joy.
1947	Now test supporting ability.
1948	Now test supporting building.
1949	Now test supporting action.
1950	Now test accepting release.
1951	Now test accepting now.
1952	Now test accepting compromise.
1953	Now test accepting trust.
1954	Now test accepting support.
1955	Now test receiving acceptance.
1956	Now test accepting joy.
1957	Now test accepting ability.
1958	Now test accepting building.
1959	Now test accepting action.
1960	Now testing joy release.
1961	Is testing joy now.
1962	Now test joy compromise.

Kevin J. Baird

1963	Now testing joy trust.
1964	Now testing joy supported.
1965	Now test joy acceptance.
1966	Now testing content laughing.
1967	Now testing joy ability.
1968	Now testing joy building.
1969	This action serves action.
1970	Now action working self.
1971	Done testing ability now.
1972	Done testing able compromise.
1973	Done testing able trust.
1974	Done testing able support.
1975	Done testing able acceptance.
1976	Done testing able joy.
1977	Done testing able ability.
1978	Done testing able building.
1979	Done testing able action.
1980	Now action building self.
1981	Now action building this.
1982	Now action building compromise.
1983	Now action building trust.
1984	Now action building supported.
1985	Now action building acceptance.
1986	Now action building joy.
1987	Now action building ability.
1988	Now action building structure.
1989	Now feelings building action.
1990	Now action testing release.
1991	This action testing now.
1992	Now action testing compromise.
1993	Now action testing trust.
1994	Now action testing support.
1995	Now action testing acceptance.
1996	Now action testing joy.

Myn in Numbers

1997   Now action testing ability.

1998   This action testing structure.

1999   Now testing moving action.

Kevin J. Baird

Myn in Numbers

Join

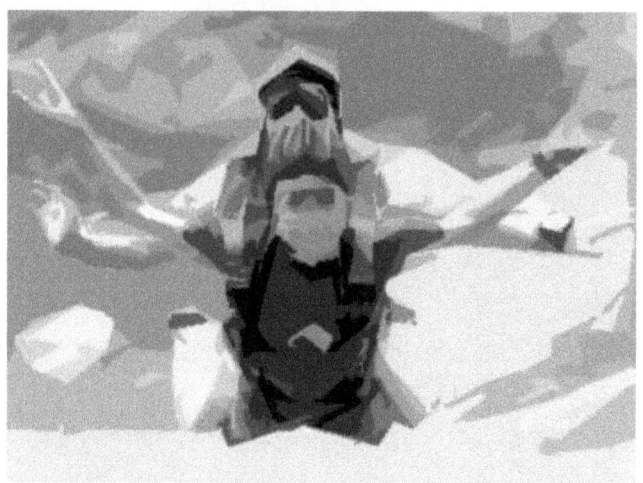

2000-2999

When "2" leads the group your source is inviting you to "Joining the group" as you conduct yourself in the group moment of the trailing numbers. Weigh the points and ponder the outcome.

***

2000	Joins my soul release.
2001	Joins my self now.
2002	Joins my self compromise.
2003	Joins my friend trust.
2004	Joins my self supported.
2005	Joins my self accepted.
2006	Partner my self joy.
2007	Partner my self ability.
2008	Partner my self building.
2009	Partner my self action.
2010	Join my now self.
2011	Partner releasing this now.
2012	Friend's release is joining.

www.templeofgaia.com

2013	Friend's release is blessed.
2014	Friend's release is supported.
2015	Friend's release is accepted.
2016	Friend's release is joy.
2017	Friend's release is working.
2018	Friend's release is building.
2019	Friend's release is action.
2020	Join self joining release.
2021	Join self joining now.
2022	Join self joining compromise.
2023	Join self joining blessing.
2024	Join self joining supported.
2025	Join self joining acceptance.
2026	Join self joining joy.
2027	Join self joining ability.
2028	Join self joining building.
2029	Join self join feelings.
2030	Join self trusting release.
2031	Join self trusting now.
2032	Join self trusting compromise.
2033	Join self trusting prosperity.
2034	Join self trusting support.
2035	Join self trusting acceptance.
2036	Join self trusting joy.
2037	Join self trusting ability.
2038	Join self trusting building.
2039	Join self trusting action.
2040	Join self through release.
2041	Join self through this.
2042	Partner self through compromise.
2043	Partner self through trusting.
2044	Partner self through support.
2045	Partner self through acceptance.
2046	Partner self through joy.

Myn in Numbers

2047	Partner self through ability.
2048	Partner self through building.
2049	Partner self through action.
2050	Partner self accepting release.
2051	Partner self accepting this.
2052	Partner self accepting compromise.
2053	Partner self accepting trust.
2054	Partner self accepting support.
2055	Join self receiving acceptance.
2056	Partner self acceptance serves.
2057	Partner self accepting ability.
2058	Partner self accepting build.
2059	Partner self accepting action.
2060	Partner release serving self.
2061	Partner release serving now.
2062	Partner release serving compromise.
2063	Partner release serving trust.
2064	Partner release serving supported.
2065	Partner release serving acceptance.
2066	Partner release serving joy.
2067	Partner release serving ability.
2068	Partner release serving building.
2069	Partner release serving action.
2070	Partner self working release.
2071	Partner my ability now.
2072	Partner my ability compromise.
2073	Partner my ability trusting.
2074	Partner my ability supported.
2075	Partner my ability accepted.
2076	Partner my ability serves.
2077	Partner my ability works.
2078	Partner my ability building.
2079	Partner my ability tested.
2080	Joining released builds self.

Kevin J. Baird

2081   Joining released builds now.
2082   Joining released builds compromise.
2083   Joining released builds trust.
2084   Joining released builds support.
2085   Joining released builds acceptance.
2086   Joining released builds joy.
2087   Joining released builds ability.
2088   Joining released builds structure.
2089   Joining released builds feelings.
2090   Friend joins active release.
2091   Friend joins active now.
2092   Friend joins active compromise.
2093   Friend joins testing trust.
2094   Friend joins active support.
2095   Friend joins active acceptance.
2096   Friend joins testing joy.
2097   Friend joins active ability.
2098   Friend joins active building.
2099   Partner my moving action.
2100   Partner is my releasing.
2101   Partner is my now.
2102   Partner is my compromise.
2103   Partner is my blessing.
2104   Partner is my support.
2105   Partner is my acceptance.
2106   Partner is my joy.
2107   Partner is my ability.
2108   Partner is my building.
2109   Partner is my action.
2110   Partner this now releasing.
2111   Partner this now done.
2112   Partner this now friendship.
2113   Partner this now trusting.
2114   Partner this now supported.

Myn in Numbers

2115   Partner this now accepted.
2116   Partner this now serving.
2117   Partner this now ability.
2118   Partner this now building.
2119   Partner this now active.
2120   Join this joins release.
2121   Join this join this.
2122   Join this joins compromise.
2123   Join this joins trusting.
2124   Join this joins supported.
2125   Join this joins acceptance.
2126   Join this joins joy.
2127   Join this joins ability.
2128   Join this joins building.
2129   Join this joins action.
2130   Partner this trusting release.
2131   Partner is trusting now.
2132   Partner is trusting compromise.
2133   Join this prosperity blessing.
2134   Join this trusting support.
2135   Join this trusting acceptance.
2136   Join this trusting joy.
2137   Join this trusting ability.
2138   Joins this trusting building.
2139   Join this trusting action.
2140   Partner this through self.
2141   Partner this means now.
2142   Partner this through compromise.
2143   Partner this through trust.
2144   Partner this through support.
2145   Partner this through acceptance.
2146   Partner this through joy.
2147   Partner this through ability.
2148   Joining this means building.

2149   Joining this means action.
2150   Join this accepting releasing.
2151   Join this accepting now.
2152   Join this accepting compromise.
2153   Join this accepting trust.
2154   Join this accepting support.
2155   Join this accepting accepted.
2156   Join this accepting joy.
2157   Join this accepting ability.
2158   Join this accepting building.
2159   Join this accepting action.
2160   Join this serving release.
2161   Join this serving now.
2162   Join this serving compromise.
2163   Join this serving trust.
2164   Join this serving means.
2165   Join this serving acceptance.
2166   Join this serving joy.
2167   Join this serving ability.
2168   Join this joy building.
2169   Join this serving action.
2170   Join this working release.
2171   Join this working now.
2172   Join this working compromise.
2173   Join this works trust.
2174   Join this working supported.
2175   Join this working acceptance.
2176   Join this working content.
2177   Join this working ability.
2178   Join this work building.
2179   Join this working action.
2180   Join this building release.
2181   Join this building now.
2182   Join this building compromise.

Myn in Numbers

2183	Join this building trust.
2184	Join this building support.
2185	Join this building acceptance.
2186	Join this building joy.
2187	Join this building ability.
2188	Join this building structure.
2189	Join this building action.
2190	Partner this action releasing.
2191	Partner this action now.
2192	Partner this active compromise.
2193	Partner this action trusting.
2194	Partner this action supported.
2195	Partner this action received.
2196	Partner this active joy.
2197	Partner this action ability.
2198	Partner this action building.
2199	Partner this testing action.
2201	Friend joins releasing now.
2202	Friend joins releasing compromise.
2203	Friend joins releasing trust.
2204	Friend joins releasing supportive.
2205	Friend joins releasing content.
2206	Friend joins releasing joy.
2207	Friend joins release ability.
2208	Friend joins self building.
2209	Friend joins my action.
2210	Friend joins this releasing.
2211	Friend joins this now.
2212	Friend joins this compromise.
2213	Friend joins this trusting.
2214	Friend joins this supportive.
2215	Friend joins this accepting.
2216	Friend joins this content.
2217	Friend joins this ability.

2218   Friend joins this building.
2219   Friend joins this action.
2220   Join friend's joining release.
2221   Partner friend's compromise now.
2222   Partner joining friendship compromise.
2223   Join friend's joining trust.
2224   Join friend's joining support.
2225   Join friend's joining acceptance.
2226   Join friend's joining joy.
2227   Join friend's joining ability.
2228   Join friend's joining building.
2229   Join friend's joining action.
2230   Join friend's trusting release.
2231   Join friend trusting now.
2232   Join friend's trusting compromise.
2233   Join friend blessing trust.
2234   Join friend trusting support.
2235   Join friend trusting acceptance.
2236   Join friend trusting joy.
2237   Join friend trusting ability.
2238   Join friend trusting building.
2239   Join friend trusting action.
2240   Join friend through releasing.
2241   Join friend supporting now.
2242   Join friend supporting compromise.
2243   Join friend supporting trust.
2244   Join friend through support.
2245   Join friend support received.
2246   Join friend supporting joy.
2247   Join friend supporting ability.
2248   Join friend supporting building.
2249   Join friend supporting action.
2250   Join friend receive releasing.
2251   Join friend receive now.

Myn in Numbers

2252   Join friend receive compromise.
2253   Join friend receive myn.
2254   Join friend receive supported.
2255   Join friend receiving acceptance.
2256   Join friend receive joy.
2257   Join friend receive ability.
2258   Join friend receive building.
2259   Join friend receive action.
2260   Join friend serves releasing.
2261   Join friend serves now.
2262   Join friend serves compromise.
2263   Join friend serves trust.
2264   Join friend serves supported.
2265   Join friend serves received.
2266   Join friend content laugh.
2267   Join friend serves ability.
2268   Join friend serves building.
2269   Join friend's joy action.
2270   Join friend ability releasing.
2271   Join friend ability now.
2272   Join friend working compromise.
2273   Join friend ability myn.
2274   Join friend ability supported.
2275   Join friend ability received.
2276   Join friend ability joy.
2277   Join friend working ability.
2278   Join friend ability building.
2279   Join friend working action.
2280   Join friend building release.
2281   Join friend building now.
2282   Join friend building compromise.
2283   Join friend building trust.
2284   Join friend building support.
2285   Join friend building acceptance.

Kevin J. Baird

2286   Join friend building joy.
2287   Join friend building ability.
2288   Join friend building structure.
2289   Join friend building action.
2290   Join friend testing release.
2291   Join friend testing now.
2292   Join friend testing compromise.
2293   Join friend testing trust.
2294   Join friend testing support.
2295   Join friend testing acceptance.
2296   Join friend testing joy.
2297   Join friend testing ability.
2298   Join friend testing structure.
2299   Join friend testing action.
2300   Join trust releasing self.
2301   Join trust releasing now.
2302   Join trust releasing compromise.
2303   Join trust releasing trust.
2304   Join trust releasing support.
2305   Join trust releasing acceptance.
2306   Join trust releasing joy.
2307   Join trust releasing ability.
2308   Join trust releasing building.
2309   Join trust releasing feelings.
2310   Join trust is releasing.
2311   Join trust is now.
2312   Join trust is compromise.
2313   Join trust is trust.
2314   Join trust is supported.
2315   Join trust is received.
2316   Join trust is joy.
2317   Join trust is ability.
2318   Join trust is building.
2319   Join trust is action.

Myn in Numbers

2320   Friend trusts joining release.
2321   Friend trusts joining now.
2322   Friend trusts joining compromise.
2323   Friend trusts joining prosperity.
2324   Friend trusts joining supported.
2325   Friend trusts joining accepted.
2326   Friend trusts joining serves.
2327   Friend trusts joining ability.
2328   Friend trusts joining building.
2329   Friend trusts joining feelings.
2330   Friend trusts blessing self.
2331   Join trusting Myn now.
2332   Join trusting Myn compromise.
2333   Join trusting Myn blessing.
2334   Join trusting Myn support.
2335   Join trusting Myn present.
2336   Join trusting Myn serves.
2337   Join trusting Myn ability.
2338   Join trusting Myn building.
2339   Join trusting Myn action.
2340   Friend trusts supporting release.
2341   Friend trusts blessing now.
2342   Friend trusts blessing compromise.
2343   Friend trusts blessing prosperity.
2344   Friend trusts blessing support.
2345   Friend trusts blessing acceptance.
2346   Friend trusts blessing joy.
2347   Friend trusts blessing ability.
2348   Friend trusts blessing building.
2349   Friend trusts blessing action.
2350   Friend trusts accepting release.
2351   Friend trusts accepting this.
2352   Friend trusts accepting compromise.
2353   Friend trusts accepting trust.

2354   Friend trusts accepting support.
2355   Friend trusts receiving acceptance.
2356   Friend trusts accepting joy.
2357   Friend trusts accepting ability.
2358   Friend trusts accepting building.
2359   Friend trusts accepting action.
2360   Join trust serving release.
2361   Join trust serving this.
2362   Join trust serving compromise.
2363   Join trust serving trust.
2364   Join trust serving supported.
2365   Join trust serving acceptance.
2366   Join trust serving joy.
2367   Join trust serving ability.
2368   Join trust serving building.
2369   Join trust serving action.
2370   Join trusting working release.
2371   Join trusting working now.
2372   Join trusting working compromise.
2373   Join trusting working blessing.
2374   Join trusting working supported.
2375   Join trusting working acceptance.
2376   Join trusting working joy.
2377   Join trusting working ability.
2378   Join trusting working form.
2379   Joining trust works feelings.
2380   Partner trust building release.
2381   Partner trust building now.
2382   Partner trust building compromise.
2383   Partner trust building prosperity.
2384   Partner trust building support.
2385   Partner trust building acceptance.
2386   Partner trust building joy.
2387   Partner trust building ability.

Myn in Numbers

2388	Partner trust building structure.
2389	Partner trust building action.
2390	Partner trust feel releasing.
2391	Partner trust feel now.
2392	Partner trust feel compromise.
2393	Partner trust feel blessing.
2394	Partner trust feel supported.
2395	Partner trust feel received.
2396	Partner trust feel joy.
2397	Partner trust feel ability.
2398	Partner trust feel building.
2399	Partner trust feel action.
2400	Join through my release.
2401	Join through my now.
2402	Join through my compromise.
2403	Join through my trust.
2404	Join through my support.
2405	Join through my receiving.
2406	Join through my joy.
2407	Join through my ability.
2408	Join through my building.
2409	Join through my action.
2410	Partner supports this release.
2411	Partner supports this now.
2412	Partner supports this compromise.
2413	Partner supports this blessing.
2414	Partner means this support.
2415	Partner supports this received.
2416	Partner supports this joy.
2417	Partner supports this ability.
2418	Partner supports this building.
2419	Partner supports this action.
2420	Compromise means joining release.
2421	Partner through compromise now.

2422   Partner through friendship compromise.
2423   Partner through compromise myn.
2424   Partner through compromise supported.
2425   Partner through compromise received.
2426   Partner through joining joy.
2427   Partner through compromise ability.
2428   Partner through compromise building.
2429   Partner through compromise action.
2430   Partner through trusting self.
2431   Partner through trust now.
2432   Join through trusting compromise.
2433   Partner through trusting blessing.
2434   Partner through trusting support.
2435   Partner through trusting acceptance.
2436   Partner through trusting joy.
2437   Partner through trusting ability.
2438   Partner through trusting building.
2439   Partner through trusting feelings.
2440   Partner through supporting release.
2441   Partner through supporting now.
2442   Partner through supporting compromise.
2443   Partner through supporting trust.
2444   Partner through supporting means.
2445   Partner through supporting acceptance.
2446   Partner through supporting joy.
2447   Partner through supporting ability.
2448   Partner through supporting building.
2449   Partner through supporting action.
2450   Joining supports accepting release.
2451   Joining supports accepting this.
2452   Joining supports accepting compromise.
2453   Joining supports accepting trust.
2454   Joining supports accepting support.
2455   Joining supports receiving acceptance.

Myn in Numbers

2456	Joining supports accepting joy.
2457	Joining supports accepting ability.
2458	Joining supports accepting building.
2459	Joining supports accepting action.
2460	Partner through joy releasing.
2461	Partner through joy now.
2462	Partner through joy compromise.
2463	Partner through joy trust.
2464	Partner through joy support.
2465	Partner through joy received.
2466	Partner through content laugh.
2467	Partner through joy ability.
2468	Partner through joy building.
2469	Partner through joy action.
2470	Partner through ability releasing.
2471	Partner through ability now.
2472	Partner through ability compromise.
2473	Partner through able trust.
2474	Partner through ability supported.
2475	Partner through ability accepted.
2476	Partner through able joy.
2477	Partner through working ability.
2478	Partner through ability building.
2479	Partner through able action.
2480	Partner through forming release.
2481	Partner through building now.
2482	Partner through building compromise.
2483	Partner through building trust.
2484	Partner through building support.
2485	Partner through building accepted.
2486	Partner through building joy.
2487	Partner through building ability.
2488	Partner through building structure.
2489	Partner through building action.

www.templeofgaia.com

2490   Partner through action releasing.
2491   Partner through action now.
2492   Partner through action compromise.
2493   Partner through active trust.
2494   Partner through action supported.
2495   Partner through action received.
2496   Partner through active joy.
2497   Partner through action ability.
2498   Partner through action building.
2499   Partner through moving action.
2500   Joining acceptance soul releases.
2501   Joining acceptance my now.
2502   Joining acceptance my compromise.
2503   Joining acceptance my trusting.
2504   Joining acceptance my support.
2505   Joining acceptance release granted.
2506   Joining acceptance my joy.
2507   Joining acceptance my ability.
2508   Joining acceptance my building.
2509   Joining acceptance my action.
2510   Joining acceptance is releasing.
2511   Joining acceptance is now.
2512   Joining acceptance is compromise.
2513   Joining acceptance is trusting.
2514   Joining acceptance is supported.
2515   Joining acceptance is received.
2516   Joining acceptance is joy.
2517   Joining acceptance is working.
2518   Joining acceptance is building.
2519   Joining acceptance is action.
2520   Friend accepts joining release.
2521   Friend accepts joining now.
2522   Friend accepts joining compromise.
2523   Friend accepts joining trust.

Myn in Numbers

2524	Friend accepts joining support.
2525	Friend accepts joining acceptance.
2526	Friend accepts joining joy.
2527	Friend receives joining ability.
2528	Friend accepts joining structure.
2529	Friend accepts joining action.
2530	Friend accepts trusting release.
2531	Friend accepts trusting now.
2532	Friend accepts trusting compromise.
2533	Friend accepts trusting blessing.
2534	Friend accepts trusting support.
2535	Friend accepts trusting contentment.
2536	Friend accepts trusting joy.
2537	Friend accepts trusting ability.
2538	Friend accepts trust building.
2539	Friend receives trusting action.
2540	Friend receives through releasing.
2541	Friend receives support now.
2542	Friend receives supporting compromise.
2543	Friend receives supporting trust.
2544	Friend receives supporting means.
2545	Friend receives supporting acceptance.
2546	Friend receives supporting joy.
2547	Friend receives supporting ability.
2548	Friend receives supporting building.
2549	Friend receives supporting action.
2550	Join accepting contentment releasing.
2551	Join accepting contentment now.
2552	Join accepting contentment friend.
2553	Join accepting contentment trust.
2554	Join accepting contentment supported.
2555	Join accepting contentment received.
2556	Join accepting content joy.
2557	Join accepting contentment ability.

2558   Join accepting contentment building.
2559   Join accepting contentment action.
2560   Join accepting joy releasing.
2561   Join accepting joy now.
2562   Join accepting joy compromise.
2563   Join accepting joy trust.
2564   Join accepting joy supported.
2565   Join accepting joy received.
2566   Join accepting content laughing.
2567   Join accepting joy ability.
2568   Join accepting joy building.
2569   Join accepting joy action.
2570   Join accepting ability releasing.
2571   Join accepting work now.
2572   Join accepting work compromise.
2573   Join accepting working trust.
2574   Join accepting work supported.
2575   Join accepting work received.
2576   Join accepting work joy.
2577   Join accepting working ability.
2578   Join accepting work building.
2579   Join accepting work action.
2580   Joining acceptance builds release.
2581   Joining acceptance builds now.
2582   Joining acceptance builds compromise.
2583   Joining acceptance builds trust.
2584   Joining acceptance builds supported.
2585   Joining acceptance builds receiving.
2586   Joining acceptance builds joy.
2587   Joining acceptance builds ability.
2588   Joining acceptance builds structure.
2589   Joining acceptance builds action.
2590   Join accepting action releasing.
2591   Join accepting action now.

Myn in Numbers

2592   Join accepting action compromise.
2593   Join accepting action trust.
2594   Join accepting action supported.
2595   Join accepting action received.
2596   Join accepting action joy.
2597   Join accepting action ability.
2598   Join accepting action building.
2599   Join accepting action action.
2600   Join joy my self.
2601   Join joy my now.
2602   Join joy my compromise.
2603   Join joy my myn.
2604   Join joy my supported.
2605   Join joy my received.
2606   Join joy my joy.
2607   Join joy my ability.
2608   Join joy my building.
2609   Join joy my action.
2610   Join serving this release.
2611   Join serving this now.
2612   Join serving this compromise.
2613   Join serving this trust.
2614   Join serving this supported.
2615   Join serving this received.
2616   Join serving this joy.
2617   Join serving this ability.
2618   Join serving this building.
2619   Join serving this action.
2620   Join joy joining release.
2621   Join joy joining now.
2622   Join joy joining compromise.
2623   Join joy joining trust.
2624   Join joy joining supported.
2625   Join joy joining acceptance.

Kevin J. Baird

2626 Join joy join laughing.
2627 Join joy joining ability.
2628 Join joy join building.
2629 Join joy joining action.
2630 Partner joy trusting release.
2631 Partner joy trusting now.
2632 Partner joy trusting compromise.
2633 Partner joy trusting prosperity.
2634 Partner joy trusting support.
2635 Partner joy trusting acceptance.
2636 Partner contentment trusting joy.
2637 Partner joy trusting ability.
2638 Partner joy trusting building.
2639 Partner joy trusting action.
2640 Join joy through release.
2641 Join joy through now.
2642 Join joy through compromise.
2643 Join joy through myn.
2644 Join joy through support.
2645 Join joy through acceptance.
2646 Join joy through joy.
2647 Join joy through ability.
2648 Join joy through building.
2649 Join joy through action.
2650 Join joy acceptance releasing.
2651 Join joy acceptance now.
2652 Join joy accepting friendship.
2653 Join joy acceptance trust.
2654 Join joy acceptance supported.
2655 Join joy acceptance received.
2656 Join joy accepting joy.
2657 Join joy acceptance ability.
2658 Join joy acceptance building.
2659 Join joy acceptance action.

Myn in Numbers

2660	Join joy laugh releasing.
2661	Join joy laugh now.
2662	Join joy laugh compromise.
2663	Join joy laugh trusting.
2664	Join joy laugh supporting.
2665	Join joy laugh accepting.
2666	Join joy laugh laugh.
2667	Join joy laugh ability.
2668	Join joy laugh building.
2669	Join joy laugh testing.
2670	Join joy ability releasing.
2671	Join joy ability now.
2672	Join joy ability compromise.
2673	Join joy ability trusting.
2674	Join joy ability supported.
2675	Join joy ability received.
2676	Join joy working contentment.
2677	Join joy working ability.
2678	Join joy ability building.
2679	Partner joy ability active.
2680	Partner joy building releasing.
2681	Partner joy building now.
2682	Partner joy building compromise.
2683	Partner joy building trust.
2684	Partner joy building support.
2685	Partner joy building acceptance.
2686	Partner contentment building joy.
2687	Partner joy building ability.
2688	Partner joy building structure.
2689	Partner joy building action.
2690	Join joy testing release.
2691	Join joy testing now.
2692	Join joy testing compromise.
2693	Join joy testing trust.

Kevin J. Baird

2694   Join joy testing support.
2695   Join joy testing acceptance.
2696   Join joy testing joy.
2697   Join joy testing ability.
2698   Join joy testing builds.
2699   Join joy move feelings.
2700   Partner works self releasing.
2701   Partner works self now.
2702   Partner works self compromise.
2703   Partner works self trust.
2704   Partner works self support.
2705   Partner works self acceptance.
2706   Partner works self joy.
2707   Partner works self ability.
2708   Partner works self building.
2709   Partner works self test.
2710   Partner works this release.
2711   Partner works this now.
2712   Partner works this compromise.
2713   Partner works this trust.
2714   Partner works this support.
2715   Partner works this received.
2716   Partner works this joy.
2717   Partner works this ability.
2718   Partner works this building.
2719   Partner works this action.
2720   Partner works compromise releasing.
2721   Partner works compromise now.
2722   Partner works friendship compromise.
2723   Partner works compromise trust.
2724   Partner works compromise supported.
2725   Partner works compromise received.
2726   Partner works compromise joy.
2727   Partner works compromise ability.

Myn in Numbers

2728	Partner works compromise building.
2729	Partner works compromise action.
2730	Joining works trusting releasing.
2731	Joining works trusting now.
2732	Joining works trusting compromise.
2733	Joining works trusting prosperity.
2734	Joining works trusting support.
2735	Joining works trusting acceptance.
2736	Joining works trusting joy.
2737	Joining works trusting ability.
2738	Joining works trusting building.
2739	Joining works trusting action.
2740	Joining works supporting release.
2741	Joining works supporting now.
2742	Joining works supporting compromise.
2743	Joining works supporting trust.
2744	Joining works through support.
2745	Joining works supporting acceptance.
2746	Joining works supporting joy.
2747	Joining works supporting ability.
2748	Joining works supporting building.
2749	Joining works supporting action.
2750	Joining works acceptance releasing.
2751	Joining works acceptance now.
2752	Joining works acceptance friendship.
2753	Joining works acceptance trust.
2754	Joining works acceptance supported.
2755	Joining works acceptance received.
2756	Joining works accepting contentment.
2757	Joining works acceptance ability.
2758	Joining works acceptance building.
2759	Joining works acceptance action.
2760	Joining works joy releasing.
2761	Joining works joy now.

2762	Joining works joy compromise.
2763	Joining works joy trust.
2764	Joining works joy supported.
2765	Joining works joy received.
2766	Joining works content laugh.
2767	Joining works joy ability.
2768	Joining works joy building.
2769	Joining works joy action.
2770	Joining works ability releasing.
2771	Joining works ability now.
2772	Joining works ability compromise.
2773	Joining works ability myn.
2774	Joining works ability supported.
2775	Joining works ability received.
2776	Joining works able joy.
2777	Joining works working ability.
2778	Joining works ability building.
2779	Joining works ability action.
2780	Joining works building release.
2781	Join ability building now.
2782	Join ability building compromise.
2783	Join ability building myn.
2784	Join ability building supported.
2785	Join ability building received.
2786	Join ability building joy.
2787	Join ability building ability.
2788	Join ability building structure.
2789	Join ability building action.
2790	Join ability testing release.
2791	Join ability testing now.
2792	Join ability testing compromise.
2793	Join ability testing myn.
2794	Join ability testing supported.
2795	Join ability testing received.

Myn in Numbers

2796	Join ability testing joy.
2797	Join ability testing ability.
2798	Join ability testing building.
2799	Partner working moving action.
2800	Friend builds my release.
2801	Friend builds my now.
2802	Friend builds my compromise.
2803	Friend builds my trust.
2804	Friend builds my support.
2805	Friend builds my acceptance.
2806	Friend builds my joy.
2807	Friend builds my ability.
2808	Friend builds my structure.
2809	Friend builds my activities.
2810	Join building this release.
2811	Join building this now.
2812	Join building this compromise.
2813	Join building this trust.
2814	Join building this supported.
2815	Join building this received.
2816	Join building this joy.
2817	Join building this ability.
2818	Join building this structure.
2819	Join building this action.
2820	Join building friend's release.
2821	Join building friend's now.
2822	Join building friend's compromise.
2823	Join building friend's trust.
2824	Join building friend's support.
2825	Join building compromise receiving.
2826	Join building friend's joy.
2827	Join building friend's ability.
2828	Join building friend's building.
2829	Join building friend's action.

2830	Join building trusting self.
2831	Join building trusting now.
2832	Join building trusting compromise.
2833	Join building trusting prosperity.
2834	Join building trusting support.
2835	Join building trusting acceptance.
2836	Join building trusting joy.
2837	Join building trusting ability.
2838	Join building trusting form.
2839	Join building trusting action.
2840	Friendship builds through releasing.
2841	Friendship builds through this.
2842	Friendship builds through compromise.
2843	Friendship builds through trust.
2844	Friendship builds through support.
2845	Friendship builds through acceptance.
2846	Friendship builds through joy.
2847	Friendship builds through ability.
2848	Friendship builds through structuring.
2849	Friendship builds through action.
2850	Friendship builds accepting self.
2851	Friendship builds acceptance now.
2852	Friendship builds acceptance compromise.
2853	Friendship builds accepting trust.
2854	Friendship builds acceptance supported.
2855	Friendship builds acceptance received.
2856	Friendship builds accepting joy.
2857	Friendship builds acceptance ability.
2858	Friendship builds accepting structure.
2859	Friendship builds acceptance action.
2860	Friendship builds joy release.
2861	Friendship builds joy now.
2862	Friendship builds joy compromise.
2863	Friendship builds joy trust.

Myn in Numbers

2864 Friendship builds joy support.
2865 Friendship builds joy received.
2866 Friendship builds content laugh.
2867 Friendship builds joy ability.
2868 Friendship builds joy structure.
2869 Friendship builds joy action.
2870 Friendship builds working release.
2871 Friendship builds working now.
2872 Friendship builds working compromise.
2873 Friendship builds working trust.
2874 Friendship builds working support.
2875 Friendship builds working acceptance.
2876 Friendship builds working joy.
2877 Friendship builds working ability.
2878 Friendship builds working form.
2879 Friendship builds working action.
2880 Friendship structure builds release.
2881 Friendship structure builds now.
2882 Friendship structure builds compromise.
2883 Friendship structure builds trust.
2884 Friendship structure builds support.
2885 Friendship structure builds acceptance.
2886 Friendship structure builds joy.
2887 Friendship structure builds ability.
2888 Friendship structure builds form.
2889 Friendship structure builds feelings.
2890 Friendship builds testing soul.
2891 Friendship builds testing now.
2892 Friendship builds testing compromise.
2893 Friendship builds testing trust.
2894 Friendship builds testing support.
2895 Friendship builds testing acceptance.
2896 Friendship builds testing joy.
2897 Friendship builds testing ability.

Kevin J. Baird

2898   Friendship builds testing structure.
2899   Friendship builds testing feelings.
2900   Friend tests my soul.
2901   Friend tests releasing this.
2902   Friend tests releasing compromise.
2903   Friend tests releasing trust.
2904   Friend tests releasing support.
2905   Friend tests releasing acceptance.
2906   Friend tests releasing joy.
2907   Friend tests releasing ability.
2908   Friend tests releasing building.
2909   Friend tests releasing action.
2910   Friend tests this release.
2911   Friend tests this now.
2912   Friend tests this compromise.
2913   Friend tests this trust.
2914   Friend tests this support.
2915   Friend tests this acceptance.
2916   Friend tests this joy.
2917   Friend tests this ability.
2918   Friend tests this building.
2919   Friend tests this action.
2920   Friend tests friend release.
2921   Friend tests friend now.
2922   Friend tests friend compromise.
2923   Friend tests friend trust.
2924   Friend tests friend support.
2925   Friend tests friend acceptance.
2926   Friend tests friend serves.
2927   Friend tests friend ability.
2928   Friend tests friend building.
2929   Friend tests friend action.
2930   Friend tests trusting release.
2931   Friend tests trusting now.

Myn in Numbers

2932 Friend tests trusting compromise.
2933 Friend tests trusting blessing.
2934 Friend tests trusting support.
2935 Friend tests trusting acceptance.
2936 Friend tests trusting joy.
2937 Friend tests trusting ability.
2938 Friend tests trusting structure.
2939 Friend tests trusting action.
2940 Friend's test means release.
2941 Friend's test means now.
2942 Friend's test means compromise.
2943 Friend's test means trust.
2944 Friend's test means support.
2945 Friend's test means acceptance.
2946 Friend's test means joy.
2947 Friend's test means ability.
2948 Friend's test means building.
2949 Friend's test means action.
2950 Friend tests granting self.
2951 Friend tests granting now.
2952 Friend tests granting compromise.
2953 Friend tests granting trust.
2954 Friend tests granting support.
2955 Friend tests granting acceptance.
2956 Friend tests granting joy.
2957 Friend tests granting ability.
2958 Friend tests granting building.
2959 Friend tests granting action.
2960 Friend feels joy releasing.
2961 Friend feels joy now.
2962 Friend feels joy compromise.
2963 Friend feels joy trust.
2964 Friend feels joy supported.
2965 Friend feels joy received.

2966 Friend feels content laugh.
2967 Friend feels joy ability.
2968 Friend feels joy building.
2969 Friend feels joy action. ☺
2970 Friend feels ability releasing.
2971 Friend feels able now.
2972 Friend feels able compromise.
2973 Friend feels able trust.
2974 Friend feels able support.
2975 Friend feels able acceptance.
2976 Friend feels able joy.
2977 Friend feels able ability.
2978 Friend feels able building.
2979 Friend feels able action.
2980 Friend feels building release.
2981 Friend feels building now.
2982 Friend feels building compromise.
2983 Friend feels building trust.
2984 Friend feels building supported.
2985 Friend feels building received.
2986 Friend feels building joy.
2987 Friend feels building ability.
2988 Friend feels building structure.
2989 Friend feels building action.
2990 Friend feels action releasing.
2991 Friend feels action now.
2992 Friend feels action compromise.
2993 Friend feels active trust.
2994 Friend feels action supported.
2995 Friend feels action received.
2996 Friend feels active joy.
2997 Friend feels active ability.
2998 Friend feels action building.
2999 Friend feels moving action.

Myn in Numbers

Trust

3000-3999

When "3" leads the group your source is inviting you to "Look upward" as you conduct yourself in the group moment of the trailing numbers. Weigh the points and ponder the outcome.

***

3000	Trust releasing my self.
3001	Trust my self now.
3002	Trust my self joins.
3003	Trust my self trust.
3004	Trust my self supports.
3005	Trust my self accepted.
3006	Trust my self joy.
3007	Trust my self ability.
3008	Trust my self building.
3009	Trust my self feelings.
3010	Trusting self is releasing.
3011	Trust releasing this now.
3012	Trust releasing this compromise.
3013	Trust releasing this blessing.

3014	Trust releasing this support.
3015	Trust releasing this accepted.
3016	Trust releasing this joy.
3017	Trust releasing this ability.
3018	Trust releasing this building.
3019	Trust releasing this action.
3020	Trust my compromise releasing.
3021	Trust my compromise now.
3022	Trust my friendship compromise.
3023	Trust my joining trust.
3024	Trust my joining supported.
3025	Trust my joining accepted.
3026	Trust my joining joy.
3027	Trust my joining ability.
3028	Trust my joining building.
3029	Trust my joining action.
3030	Trust releasing trust releasing.
3031	Trust my prosperity now.
3032	Trust my prosperity compromise.
3033	Trust my prosperity blessing.
3034	Trust my prosperity supported.
3035	Trust my prosperity granted.
3036	Trust my prosperity serves.
3037	Trust my trust ability.
3038	Trust my trust building.
3039	Trust my trust action.
3040	Trust releasing through releasing.
3041	Trust self supporting this.
3042	Trust self through compromise.
3043	Trust self through blessing.
3044	Trust self through support.
3045	Trust self through acceptance.
3046	Trust self through joy.
3047	Trust self through ability.

Myn in Numbers

3048	Trust self through building.
3049	Trust self through action.
3050	Trusting self acceptance releases.
3051	Trust self acceptance now.
3052	Trust self accepting compromise.
3053	Trust self acceptance blesses.
3054	Trust self acceptance supported.
3055	Trust self acceptance received.
3056	Trust self acceptance content.
3057	Trust self accepting ability.
3058	Trust self acceptance building.
3059	Trust self acceptance action.
3060	Trust self joy release.
3061	Trust my joy now.
3062	Trust my joy compromise.
3063	Trust my joy blessing.
3064	Trust my joy supported.
3065	Trust my joy received.
3066	Trust my joy laughing.
3067	Trust my joy ability.
3068	Trust my joy building.
3069	Trust my joy feeling.
3070	Trust my ability releasing.
3071	Trust my ability now.
3072	Trust my ability compromise.
3073	Trust my ability trusting.
3074	Trust my ability supported.
3075	Trust my ability received.
3076	Trust my ability joy.
3077	Trust my working ability.
3078	Trust my ability building.
3079	Trust my ability action.
3080	Trust releasing building release.
3081	Trust my building now.

Kevin J. Baird

3082	Trust my building compromise.
3083	Trust my building trust.
3084	Trust my building supported.
3085	Trust my building accepted.
3086	Trust my building joy.
3087	Trust my building ability.
3088	Trust my building structure.
3089	Trust my building action.
3090	Trust my action release.
3091	Trust my action now.
3092	Trust my action joining.
3093	Trust my testing trust.
3094	Trust my action support.
3095	Trust my action accepted.
3096	Trust my action content.
3097	Trust my action ability.
3098	Trust my action building.
3099	Trust my testing action.
3100	Trust is my self.
3101	Trust is my now.
3102	Trust is my compromise.
3103	Trust is my trust.
3104	Trust is my support.
3105	Trust is my acceptance.
3106	Trust is my joy.
3107	Trust is my ability.
3108	Trust is my building.
3109	Trust is my action.
3110	Trust is now releasing.
3111	Trust is now done.
3112	Trust is now compromise.
3113	Trust is now trusted.
3114	Trust is now supported.
3115	Trust is now received.

Myn in Numbers

3116	Trust is now joy.
3117	Trust is now ability.
3118	Trust is now building.
3119	Trust is now testing.
3120	Trust is compromise releasing.
3121	Trust is compromise now.
3122	Trust is friendship compromise.
3123	Trust is joining trust.
3124	Trust is compromise supported.
3125	Trust is compromise acceptance.
3126	Trust now joining joy.
3127	Trust is compromise ability.
3128	Trust is compromise building.
3129	Trust is compromise action.
3130	Trust this trust releasing.
3131	Trust this trusts now.
3132	Trusting this trusts compromise.
3133	Trust this prosperity blessing.
3134	Trust this trust support.
3135	Trust this trust accepted.
3136	Trusting this trusts joy.
3137	Trust this trusts ability.
3138	Trust this trust building.
3139	Trust this trust action.
3140	Trust is through releasing.
3141	Trust is through now.
3142	Trust is through compromise.
3143	Trust is through blessings.
3144	Trust is through support.
3145	Trust is through acceptance.
3146	Trust is through joy.
3147	Trust is through ability.
3148	Trust is through building.
3149	Trust is through action.

3150	Trust this accepting release.
3151	Trust is received now.
3152	Trust is receiving compromise.
3153	Trust is receiving blessing.
3154	Trust this receiving support.
3155	Trust this receiving acceptance.
3156	Trust this receiving joy.
3157	Trust this receiving ability.
3158	Trust this receiving building.
3159	Trust this receiving action.
3160	Trust this serving release.
3161	Trust this serving now.
3162	Trust this serving compromise.
3163	Trust this serving trust.
3164	Trust this serving supported.
3165	Trust this serving accepted.
3166	Trust this serving joy.
3167	Trust this serving ability.
3168	Trust this serving building.
3169	Trust this serving action.
3170	Trust now work releasing.
3171	Trust now work now.
3172	Trust now work compromise.
3173	Trust now work blessing.
3174	Trust now work supported.
3175	Trust now work received.
3176	Trust now work joy.
3177	Trust now work ability.
3178	Trust now work building.
3179	Prosperity is able action.
3180	Prosperity is building me.
3181	Prosperity is building now.
3182	Prosperity is building compromise.
3183	Prosperity is building blessings.

Myn in Numbers

3184	Prosperity is building support.
3185	Prosperity is building acceptance.
3186	Prosperity is building joy.
3187	Prosperity is building ability.
3188	Prosperity is building structure.
3189	Prosperity is building action.
3190	Prosperity is testing release.
3191	Trust is active now.
3192	Trust is testing compromise.
3193	Trust is testing blessing.
3194	Trust this feeling supported.
3195	Prosperity is feeling accepted.
3196	Prosperity is active joy.
3197	Prosperity is testing ability.
3198	Prosperity is actively building.
3199	Trust is active feelings.
3200	Trust joining my self.
3201	Trust befriending self now.
3202	Trust joining self compromise.
3203	Trust joining self blessing.
3204	Trust joining self support.
3205	Trust joining self acceptance.
3206	Trust joining self joy.
3207	Trust joining self ability.
3208	Trust joining self building.
3209	Trust joining self action.
3210	Trust joining this release.
3211	Trust joining this now.
3212	Trust joining this compromise.
3213	Trust joining this blessing.
3214	Trust joining this supported.
3215	Trust joining this acceptance.
3216	Trust joining this joy.
3217	Trust joining this work.

Kevin J. Baird

3218   Trust joining this building.
3219   Trust joining this feeling.
3220   Trust joining friend release.
3221   Trust joining friend now.
3222   Trust joining friend compromise.
3223   Trust joining friend blessing.
3224   Trust joining friend support.
3225   Trust joining friendship accepted.
3226   Trust joining friend serves.
3227   Trust joining friend ability.
3228   Trust joining friend building.
3229   Trust joining friend action.
3230   Trust friend trusting release.
3231   Trust friend trusting now.
3232   Trust friend trusting compromise.
3233   Trust friend trusting blessing.
3234   Trust friend trusting support.
3235   Trust friend trusting acceptance.
3236   Trust friend trusting joy.
3237   Trust friend trusting ability.
3238   Trust friend trusting building.
3239   Trust friend trusting action.
3240   Trust joining supporting release.
3241   Trust joining supporting now.
3242   Trust joining supporting compromise.
3243   Trust joining supporting blessing.
3244   Trust joining supporting means.
3245   Trust joining supporting acceptance.
3246   Trust joining supporting joy.
3247   Trust joining supporting ability.
3248   Trust joining supporting building.
3249   Trust joining supporting action.
3250   Trust joining accepting release.
3251   Trust joining accepting this.

Myn in Numbers

3252	Trust joining accepting compromise.
3253	Trust joining accepting blessing.
3254	Trust joining accepting support.
3255	Trust joining receiving acceptance.
3256	Trust joining accepting joy.
3257	Trust joining accepting ability.
3258	Trust joining accepting structure.
3259	Trust joining accepting action.
3260	Trust joining serving release.
3261	Trust joining serving now.
3262	Trust joining serving compromise.
3263	Trust joining serving trust.
3264	Trust joining serving support.
3265	Trust joining serving accepted.
3266	Trust joining content laugh.
3267	Trust joining serving ability.
3268	Trust joining serving form.
3269	Trust joining serving action.
3270	Trust joining ability releasing.
3271	Trust joining ability now.
3272	Trust joining ability compromise.
3273	Trust joining ability myn.
3274	Trust joining ability supported.
3275	Trust joining ability received.
3276	Trust joining ability content.
3277	Trust joining working ability.
3278	Trust joining ability building.
3279	Trust joining able action.
3280	Trust joins building releasing.
3281	Trust joins building now.
3282	Trust joins building compromise.
3283	Trust joins building blessings.
3284	Trust joins building supported.
3285	Trust joins building received.

3286	Trust joins building joy.
3287	Trust joins building ability.
3288	Trust joins building structure.
3289	Trust joins building action.
3290	Trust joins action releasing.
3291	Trust joins action now.
3292	Trust joins action compromise.
3293	Trust joins action blessed.
3294	Trust joins action supported.
3295	Trust joins action received.
3296	Trust joins action joy.
3297	Trust joins action ability.
3298	Trust joins active building.
3299	Trust partner active moving.
3300	Trusting trust my self.
3301	Trusting trust releasing now.
3302	Trusting trust releasing compromise.
3303	Trusting trust releases myn.
3304	Trusting trust releasing support.
3305	Trusting trust releases acceptance.
3306	Trusting trust releases joy.
3307	Trusting trust releases ability.
3308	Trusting trust releases building.
3309	Trusting trust releases action.
3310	Trusting blessing is releasing.
3311	Prosperity blesses this now.
3312	Trusting blessing is compromise.
3313	Prosperity blessing is trust.
3314	Prosperity blessing this supported.
3315	Prosperity blessing this acceptance.
3316	Prosperity blessing this joy.
3317	Prosperity blessing this ability.
3318	Prosperity blessing this building.
3319	Prosperity blessing this action.

Myn in Numbers

3320	Trust blessing partners release.
3321	Trust blessing joins now.
3322	Trust blessing joins friends.
3323	Trust blessing joins myn.
3324	Trust blessing joins supported.
3325	Trust blessing joins acceptance.
3326	Trust blessing joins joy.
3327	Trust blessing joins ability.
3328	Trust blessing joining builds.
3329	Trust blessing joins action.
3330	Trust blessing myn releases.
3331	Trust blessing myn now.
3332	Trust blessing myn compromise.
3333	Trust myn blessing prosperity.
3334	Trust blessing myn support.
3335	Trust blessing myn acceptance.
3336	Trust blessing myn joy.
3337	Trust blessing myn ability.
3338	Trust blessing myn building.
3339	Trust blessing myn action.
3340	Trust blessings through release.
3341	Trusting blessings supported now.
3342	Trust blessing through compromise.
3343	Trust blessing through blessing.
3344	Trust blessing through support.
3345	Trust blessing through acceptance.
3346	Trusting blessing supports joy.
3347	Trust blessings through ability.
3348	Trust blessing through building.
3349	Trust blessing through action.
3350	Trust blessing accepting self.
3351	Trust blessing present now.
3352	Trust blessing receive compromise.
3353	Trusting blessing accept prosperity.

3354	Trust blessing receive support.
3355	Trust blessing receiving acceptance.
3356	Trust blessing receive joy.
3357	Trust blessing receive ability.
3358	Trust blessing receive building.
3359	Trust blessing accept action.
3360	Trust blessed serving self.
3361	Trust blesses joy now.
3362	Trust blesses joy compromise.
3363	Trust blesses joy blessing.
3364	Trust blesses joy support.
3365	Trust blesses joy acceptance.
3366	Trust blesses laughing content.
3367	Trust blesses joy ability.
3368	Trust blesses joy building.
3369	Trust blesses joy action.
3370	Trust blesses able releasing.
3371	Trust blesses ability now.
3372	Trust blesses ability compromise.
3373	Trust blesses able trusting.
3374	Trust blesses ability supported.
3375	Trust blesses ability received.
3376	Trust blesses ability joy.
3377	Trust blesses working ability.
3378	Trust blesses work building.
3379	Trust blesses ability test.
3380	Trust blesses building release.
3381	Trust blesses building now.
3382	Trust blesses building compromise.
3383	Trust blesses building myn.
3384	Trust blesses building supported.
3385	Trust blesses building acceptance.
3386	Trust blesses building joy.
3387	Trust blesses building ability.

Myn in Numbers

3388	Trust blesses building structure.
3389	Trust blesses building action.
3390	Myn trust tests releasing.
3391	Myn trust tests now.
3392	Myn trust tests compromise.
3393	Myn trust tests blessings.
3394	Myn trust tests means.
3395	Myn trust tests acceptance.
3396	Myn trust tests joy.
3397	Myn trust tests ability.
3398	Myn trust tests structure.
3399	Myn trust tests action.
3400	Myn supports my soul.
3401	Myn supports me now.
3402	Myn supports my compromise.
3403	Myn supports my trust.
3404	Myn supports my support.
3405	Myn supports my acceptance.
3406	Myn supports my joy.
3407	Myn supports my ability.
3408	Myn supports my building.
3409	Myn supports my action.
3410	Myn supports this release.
3411	Myn supports this now.
3412	Myn supports this compromise.
3413	Myn supports this blessing.
3414	Myn supports this means.
3415	Myn supports this acceptance.
3416	Myn supports this joy.
3417	Myn supports this ability.
3418	Myn supports this building.
3419	Myn supports this action.
3420	Myn supports compromise releasing.
3421	Myn supports compromise now.

3422   Myn supports friendship compromise.
3423   Myn supports compromise trust.
3424   Myn supports compromise supported.
3425   Myn supports compromise received.
3426   Myn supports compromise joy.
3427   Myn supports compromise ability.
3428   Myn supports compromise building.
3429   Myn supports compromise action.
3430   Myn supports myn releasing.
3431   Myn supports myn now.
3432   Myn supports myn compromise.
3433   Myn supports trust myn.
3434   Myn supports myn supported.
3435   Myn supports myn received.
3436   Myn supports myn joy.
3437   Myn supports myn ability.
3438   Myn supports myn building.
3439   Myn supports myn action.
3440   Myn supports through releasing.
3441   Myn supports through now.
3442   Myn supports through compromise.
3443   Myn supports through myn.
3444   Myn supports through support.
3445   Myn supports through acceptance.
3446   Myn supports through joy.
3447   Myn supports through ability.
3448   Myn supports through building.
3449   Myn supports through action.
3450   Myn supports accepting releasing.
3451   Myn supports accepting now.
3452   Myn supports accepting compromise.
3453   Myn supports accepting trust.
3454   Myn supports accepting support.
3455   Myn supports accepting present.

Myn in Numbers

3456	Myn supports accepting joy.
3457	Myn supports accepting ability.
3458	Myn supports accepting building.
3459	Myn supports accepting action.
3460	Myn supports joy releasing.
3461	Myn supports joy now.
3462	Myn supports joy compromise.
3463	Myn supports joy trust.
3464	Myn supports joy supported.
3465	Myn supports joy received.
3466	Myn supports content laugh.
3467	Myn supports joy ability.
3468	Myn supports joy building.
3469	Myn supports joy action.
3470	Myn supports ability releasing.
3471	Myn supports ability now.
3472	Myn supports ability compromise.
3473	Myn supports ability trusting.
3474	Myn supports ability supported.
3475	Myn supports ability received.
3476	Myn supports ability joy.
3477	Myn supports working ability.
3478	Myn supports ability building.
3479	Myn supports ability action.
3480	Myn supports building release.
3481	Myn supports building now.
3482	Myn supports building compromise.
3483	Myn supports building trust.
3484	Myn supports building supported.
3485	Myn supports building acceptance.
3486	Myn supports building joy.
3487	Myn supports building ability.
3488	Myn supports building structure.
3489	Myn supports building action.

3490 Myn supports action releasing.
3491 Myn supports action now.
3492 Myn supports action compromise.
3493 Myn supports active trust.
3494 Myn supports action supported.
3495 Myn supports action received.
3496 Myn supports action joy.
3497 Myn supports action ability.
3498 Myn supports action building.
3499 Myn supports moving action.
3500 Trust accepting soul releases.
3501 Trust accepting my now.
3502 Trust accepting my compromise.
3503 Trust accepting my myn.
3504 Trust accepting my support.
3505 Trust accepting my received.
3506 Trust accepting my joy.
3507 Trust accepting my ability.
3508 Trust accepting my building.
3509 Trust accepting my action.
3510 Trust accepting now releasing.
3511 Trust accepting is now.
3512 Trust accepting now compromise.
3513 Trust accepting now myn.
3514 Trust accepting now supported.
3515 Trust accepting now received.
3516 Trust accepting now joy.
3517 Trust accepting now ability.
3518 Trust accepting now building.
3519 Trust accepting now action.
3520 Trust accepting compromise releasing.
3521 Trust accepting compromise now.
3522 Trust accepting friendship compromise.
3523 Trust accepting compromise blessing.

Myn in Numbers

3524	Trust accepting compromise supported.
3525	Trust accepting compromise received.
3526	Trust accepting compromise joy.
3527	Trust accepting compromise ability.
3528	Trust accepting compromise building.
3529	Trust accepting compromise action.
3530	Trust accepting myn releasing.
3531	Trust accepting myn now.
3532	Trust accepting myn compromise.
3533	Trust accepting trust myn.
3534	Trust accepting myn supported.
3535	Trust accepting myn received.
3536	Trust accepting myn joy.
3537	Trust accepting myn ability.
3538	Trust accepting myn building.
3539	Trust accepting myn action.
3540	Trust accepting through releasing.
3541	Trust accepting through now.
3542	Trust accepting through compromise.
3543	Trust accepting through myn.
3544	Trust accepting through support.
3545	Trust accepting through received.
3546	Trust accepting through joy.
3547	Trust accepting through ability.
3548	Trust accepting through building.
3549	Trust accepting through action.
3550	Trust accepting receive releasing.
3551	Trust accepting receive now.
3552	Trust accepting receive compromise.
3553	Trust accepting receive myn.
3554	Trust accepting receive supported.
3555	Trust accepting receive acceptance.
3556	Trust accepting receive joy.
3557	Trust accepting receive ability.

3558	Trust accepting receive building.
3559	Trust accepting receive action.
3560	Trust accepting joy releasing.
3561	Trust accepting joy now.
3562	Trust accepting joy compromise.
3563	Trust accepting joy blessing.
3564	Trust accepting joy supported.
3565	Trust accepting joy received.
3566	Trust accepting content laugh.
3567	Trust accepting joy ability.
3568	Trust accepting joy building.
3569	Trust accepting joy action.
3570	Trust accepting ability releasing.
3571	Trust accepting ability now.
3572	Trust accepting ability compromise.
3573	Trust accepting ability myn.
3574	Trust accepting ability supported.
3575	Trust accepting ability received.
3576	Trust accepting ability joy.
3577	Trust accepting working ability.
3578	Trust accepting ability building.
3579	Trust accepting ability action.
3580	Trust accepting building releasing.
3581	Trust accepting building now.
3582	Trust accepting building compromise.
3583	Trust accepting building trust.
3584	Trust accepting building supported.
3585	Trust accepting building received.
3586	Trust accepting building joy.
3587	Trust accepting building ability.
3588	Trust accepting building structure.
3589	Trust accepting building action.
3590	Trust accepting action releasing.
3591	Trust accepting action now.

Myn in Numbers

3592	Trust accepting action compromise.
3593	Trust accepting action myn.
3594	Trust accepting action supported.
3595	Trust accepting action received.
3596	Trust accepting action joy.
3597	Trust accepting action ability.
3598	Trust accepting action building.
3599	Trust accepting moving action.
3600	Trusting joy soul releases.
3601	Trusting joy my now.
3602	Trusting joy my compromise.
3603	Trusting joy my myn.
3604	Trusting joy my supported.
3605	Trusting joy my received.
3606	Trusting joy my joy.
3607	Trusting joy my ability.
3608	Trusting joy my building.
3609	Trusting joy my action.
3610	Trusting joy now releasing.
3611	Trusting joy is now.
3612	Trusting joy now compromise.
3613	Trusting joy now myn.
3614	Trusting joy now supported.
3615	Trusting joy now received.
3616	Trusting joy now joy.
3617	Trusting joy now ability.
3618	Trusting joy now building.
3619	Trusting joy now action.
3620	Trusting joy compromise releasing.
3621	Trusting joy compromise now.
3622	Trusting joy friendship compromise.
3623	Trusting joy compromise myn.
3624	Trusting joy compromise supported.
3625	Trusting joy compromise received.

3626   Trusting joy compromise joy.
3627   Trusting joy compromise ability.
3628   Trusting joy compromise building.
3629   Trusting joy compromise action.
3630   Trusting joy myn releasing.
3631   Trusting joy myn now.
3632   Trusting joy myn compromise.
3633   Trusting joy trust myn.
3634   Trusting joy myn supported.
3635   Trusting joy myn received.
3636   Trusting joy myn joy.
3637   Trusting joy myn ability.
3638   Trusting joy myn building.
3639   Trusting joy myn action.
3640   Trusting joy through releasing.
3641   Trusting joy through now.
3642   Trusting joy through compromise.
3643   Trusting joy through myn.
3644   Trusting joy through support.
3645   Trusting joy through receiving.
3646   Trusting joy through joy.
3647   Trusting joy through ability.
3648   Trusting joy through building.
3649   Trusting joy through action.
3650   Trusting joy receive releasing.
3651   Trusting joy receive now.
3652   Trusting joy receive compromise.
3653   Trusting joy receive myn.
3654   Trusting joy receive supported.
3655   Trusting joy receive present.
3656   Trusting joy receive joy.
3657   Trusting joy receive ability.
3658   Trusting joy receive building.
3659   Trusting joy receive action.

Myn in Numbers

3660	Trusting joy joy releasing.
3661	Trusting joy joy now.
3662	Trusting joy joy compromise.
3663	Trusting joy joy myn.
3664	Trusting joy joy supported.
3665	Trusting joy joy received.
3666	Trusting joy content laugh.
3667	Trusting joy joy ability.
3668	Trusting joy joy building.
3669	Trusting joy joy action.
3670	Trusting joy ability releasing.
3671	Trusting joy ability now.
3672	Trusting joy ability compromise.
3673	Trusting joy ability myn.
3674	Trusting joy ability supported.
3675	Trusting joy ability received.
3676	Trusting joy enables joy.
3677	Trusting joy working ability.
3678	Trusting joy ability building.
3679	Trusting joy ability action.
3680	Trusting joy building release.
3681	Trusting joy building now.
3682	Trusting joy building compromise.
3683	Trusting joy building myn.
3684	Trusting joy building supported.
3685	Trusting joy building received.
3686	Trusting joy building joy.
3687	Trusting joy building ability.
3688	Trusting joy building structure.
3689	Trusting joy building action.
3690	Trust joy action releasing.
3691	Trust joy action now.
3692	Trust joy action compromise.
3693	Trust joy action myn.

3694	Trust joy action supported.
3695	Trust joy action received.
3696	Trust joy action joy.
3697	Trust joy action ability.
3698	Trust joy action building.
3699	Trust joy moving action.
3700	Trust ability soul releases.
3701	Trust ability my now.
3702	Trust ability my compromise.
3703	Trust ability my myn.
3704	Trust ability my supported.
3705	Trust ability my received.
3706	Trust ability my joy.
3707	Trust ability my ability.
3708	Trust ability my building.
3709	Trust ability my action.
3710	Trust ability now releasing.
3711	Trust ability is now.
3712	Trust ability is compromise.
3713	Trust ability is myn.
3714	Trust ability now supported.
3715	Myn ability now granted.
3716	Trust ability now joy.
3717	Trust ability now ability.
3718	Trust ability now building.
3719	Trust ability is action.
3720	Trust ability partners me.
3721	Trust ability compromise now.
3722	Trust works friendship compromise.
3723	Trust works friendship blessing.
3724	Trust works friendship support.
3725	Trust works friend's compromise.
3726	Trust works friend's joy.
3727	Trust works friend's ability.

Myn in Numbers

3728	Trust works friend's building.
3729	Trust works friend's move.
3730	Trust works blessing me.
3731	Trust works blessing now.
3732	Trust works blessing compromise.
3733	Trust works blessing prosperity.
3734	Trust works blessing support.
3735	Trust works myn acceptance.
3736	Trust works trusting joy.
3737	Trust works blessing ability.
3738	Trust works blessing building.
3739	Trust works blessing action.
3740	Trust ability through me.
3741	Trust ability support now.
3742	Trust ability through compromise.
3743	Trust ability through myn.
3744	Trust ability through support.
3745	Trust ability through acceptance.
3746	Trust ability through joy.
3747	Trust ability through ability.
3748	Trust ability through building.
3749	Trust ability through action.
3750	Trust work accepting me.
3751	Trust ability received now.
3752	Trust ability accepts compromise.
3753	Trust ability presents myn.
3754	Trust ability acceptance supported.
3755	Trust work receives acceptance.
3756	Trust ability presents joy.
3757	Trust work presents ability.
3758	Trust ability receive building.
3759	Trust ability receive action.
3760	Trust ability joy releasing.
3761	Trust ability joy now.

www.templeofgaia.com

3762	Trust ability joy compromise.
3763	Trust ability joy myn.
3764	Trust ability joy supported.
3765	Trust ability joy received.
3766	Trust ability content laugh.
3767	Trust ability joy ability.
3768	Trust ability joy building.
3769	Trust ability joy action.
3770	Trust ability working releasing.
3771	Trust ability working now.
3772	Trust ability working compromise.
3773	Trust ability working myn.
3774	Trust ability working supported.
3775	Trust ability working received.
3776	Trust ability working joy.
3777	Trust ability working ability.
3778	Trust ability working building.
3779	Trust ability working action.
3780	Trust ability building release.
3781	Trust ability building now.
3782	Trust ability building compromise.
3783	Trust ability building myn.
3784	Trust ability building supported.
3785	Trust ability building received.
3786	Trust ability building joy.
3787	Trust ability building ability.
3788	Trust ability building structure.
3789	Trust ability building action.
3790	Trust ability action releasing.
3791	Trust ability action now.
3792	Trust ability action compromise.
3793	Trust ability action trusting.
3794	Trust ability action support.
3795	Trust ability action received.

Myn in Numbers

3796	Trust ability action joy.
3797	Trust ability action working.
3798	Trust ability action building.
3799	Trust ability moving action.
3800	Trust building soul releases.
3801	Trust building my now.
3802	Trust building my compromise.
3803	Trust building my blessings.
3804	Trust building my support.
3805	Trust building my acceptance.
3806	Trust building my joy.
3807	Trust building my ability.
3808	Trust building my building.
3809	Trust building my action.
3810	Trust building now releasing.
3811	Trust building this now.
3812	Trust building this compromise.
3813	Trust building this blessing.
3814	Trust building this supported.
3815	Trust building this accepted.
3816	Trust building this joy.
3817	Trust building this ability.
3818	Trust building this structure.
3819	Trust building this action.
3820	Trust building compromise releasing.
3821	Trust building compromise now.
3822	Trust building friendship compromise.
3823	Trust building compromise trusting.
3824	Trust building compromise supported.
3825	Trust building compromise received.
3826	Trust building compromise joy.
3827	Trust building compromise ability.
3828	Trust building compromise building.
3829	Trust building compromise action.

3830   Trust building trust releasing.
3831   Trust building trust now.
3832   Trust building trust compromise.
3833   Trust building trust myn.
3834   Trust building trust supported.
3835   Trust building trust received.
3836   Trust building trust joy.
3837   Trust building trust ability.
3838   Trust building trust building.
3839   Trust building trust action.
3840   Trust building through releasing.
3841   Trust building through now.
3842   Trust building through compromise.
3843   Trust building through trust.
3844   Trust building through support.
3845   Trust building through acceptance.
3846   Trust building through joy.
3847   Trust building through ability.
3848   Trust building through building.
3849   Trust building through action.
3850   Trust building receive releasing.
3851   Trust building receive now.
3852   Trust building receive compromise.
3853   Trust building receive trust.
3854   Trust building receive supported.
3855   Trust building receive received.
3856   Trust building receive joy.
3857   Trust building receive ability.
3858   Trust building receive building.
3859   Trust building receive action.
3860   Trust building joy releasing.
3861   Trust building joy now.
3862   Trust building joy compromise.
3863   Trust building joy blessing.

Myn in Numbers

3864	Trust building joy supported.
3865	Trust building joy received.
3866	Trust building laughing content.
3867	Trust building joy ability.
3868	Trust building joy structure.
3869	Trust building joy action.
3870	Trust building ability releasing.
3871	Trust building ability now.
3872	Trust building ability compromise.
3873	Trust building ability trusting.
3874	Trust building ability supported.
3875	Trust building ability received.
3876	Trust building ability joy.
3877	Trust building working ability.
3878	Trust building ability building.
3879	Trust building ability action.
3880	Trust building forms releasing.
3881	Trust building structure now.
3882	Trust building structured compromise.
3883	Trust building forms myn.
3884	Trust building forms support.
3885	Trust building forms acceptance.
3886	Trust building forms joy.
3887	Trust building forms ability.
3888	Trust building forms structure.
3889	Trust building forms action.
3890	Trust building action releasing.
3891	Trust building action now.
3892	Trust building action compromise.
3893	Trust building action myn.
3894	Trust building action supported.
3895	Trust building action received.
3896	Trust building action joy.
3897	Trust building action ability.

3898   Trust building action building.
3899   Trust building moving action.
3900   Prosperity tests soul releases.
3901   Prosperity tests my now.
3902   Prosperity tests my compromise.
3903   Prosperity tests my myn.
3904   Prosperity tests my supported.
3905   Prosperity tests my received.
3906   Prosperity tests my joy.
3907   Prosperity tests my ability.
3908   Prosperity tests my building.
3909   Prosperity tests my action.
3910   Prosperity tests now releasing.
3911   Prosperity tests is now.
3912   Prosperity tests now compromise.
3913   Prosperity tests now myn.
3914   Prosperity tests now supported.
3915   Prosperity tests now received.
3916   Prosperity tests now joy.
3917   Prosperity tests now ability.
3918   Prosperity tests now building.
3919   Prosperity tests now action.
3920   Prosperity tests compromise releasing.
3921   Prosperity tests compromise now.
3922   Prosperity tests friendship compromise.
3923   Prosperity tests compromise myn.
3924   Prosperity tests compromise supported.
3925   Prosperity tests compromise received.
3926   Prosperity tests compromise joy.
3927   Prosperity tests compromise ability.
3928   Prosperity tests compromise building.
3929   Prosperity tests compromise action.
3930   Prosperity tests myn releasing.
3931   Prosperity tests myn now.

Myn in Numbers

3932	Prosperity tests myn compromise.
3933	Prosperity tests trust myn.
3934	Prosperity tests myn supported.
3935	Prosperity tests myn received.
3936	Prosperity tests myn joy.
3937	Prosperity tests myn ability.
3938	Prosperity tests myn building.
3939	Prosperity tests myn action.
3940	Prosperity tests through releasing.
3941	Prosperity tests through now.
3942	Prosperity tests through compromise.
3943	Prosperity tests through myn.
3944	Prosperity tests through support.
3945	Prosperity tests through acceptance.
3946	Prosperity tests through joy.
3947	Prosperity tests through ability.
3948	Prosperity tests through building.
3949	Prosperity tests through action.
3950	Prosperity tests receive releasing.
3951	Prosperity tests receive now.
3952	Prosperity tests receive compromise.
3953	Prosperity tests receive myn.
3954	Prosperity tests receive supported.
3955	Prosperity tests receiving acceptance.
3956	Prosperity tests receive joy.
3957	Prosperity tests receive ability.
3958	Prosperity tests receive building.
3959	Prosperity tests receive action.
3960	Prosperity tests joy releasing.
3961	Prosperity tests joy now.
3962	Prosperity tests joy compromise.
3963	Prosperity tests joy myn.
3964	Prosperity tests joy supported.
3965	Prosperity tests joy received.

3966	Prosperity tests content laugh.
3967	Prosperity tests joy ability.
3968	Prosperity tests joy building.
3969	Prosperity tests joy action.
3970	Prosperity tests ability releasing.
3971	Prosperity tests ability now.
3972	Prosperity tests ability compromise.
3973	Prosperity tests ability myn.
3974	Prosperity tests ability supported.
3975	Prosperity tests ability received.
3976	Prosperity tests ability joy.
3977	Prosperity tests working ability.
3978	Prosperity tests ability building.
3979	Prosperity tests ability action.
3980	Prosperity tests building releasing.
3981	Prosperity tests building now.
3982	Prosperity tests building compromise.
3983	Prosperity tests building trust.
3984	Prosperity tests building supported.
3985	Prosperity tests building received.
3986	Prosperity tests building joy.
3987	Prosperity tests building ability.
3988	Prosperity tests building structure.
3989	Prosperity tests building action.
3990	Prosperity tests action releasing.
3991	Prosperity tests action now.
3992	Prosperity tests action compromise.
3993	Prosperity tests active trust.
3994	Prosperity tests action supported.
3995	Prosperity tests active acceptance.
3996	Prosperity tests active joy.
3997	Prosperity tests action ability.
3998	Prosperity tests active building.
3999	Prosperity tests moving action.

Myn in Numbers

Support

4000-4999

When "4" leads the group your source is inviting you to "Support the group" as you conduct yourself in the group moment of the trailing numbers. Weigh the points and ponder the outcome.

***

4000	Through my soul self.
4001	Through my self now.
4002	Through my self compromise.
4003	Through my self trust.
4004	Through my self supported.
4005	Through my self acceptance.
4006	Through my self contentment.
4007	Through my self ability.
4008	Through my self building.
4009	Through my self action.
4010	Through me is me.
4011	Through me this is.
4012	Through me is compromise.
4013	Through me is trust.
4014	Through me is supported.

4015	Through me now acceptance.
4016	Through me is joy.
4017	Through me is ability.
4018	Through me is building.
4019	Through me is action.
4020	Through me partner me.
4021	Through my partner this.
4022	Through me partner compromise.
4023	Through my friendship trust.
4024	Through me compromise supported.
4025	Through me compromise accepted.
4026	Through my partner joy.
4027	Through my friendship ability.
4028	Through my friendship building.
4029	Through my friend's action.
4030	Through me myn releasing.
4031	Through self myn now.
4032	Through self myn compromise.
4033	Through self trust myn.
4034	Through self myn supported.
4035	Through self myn received.
4036	Through self myn joy.
4037	Through self myn ability.
4038	Through self myn building.
4039	Through self myn action.
4040	Through self through releasing.
4041	Through self through now.
4042	Through self through compromise.
4043	Through self through myn.
4044	Through self through support.
4045	Through self through acceptance.
4046	Through self through joy.
4047	Through self through ability.
4048	Through self through building.

Myn in Numbers

4049	Through self through action.
4050	Through self receive releasing.
4051	Through self receive now.
4052	Through self receive compromise.
4053	Through self receive myn.
4054	Through self receive supported.
4055	Through self receive acceptance.
4056	Through self receive joy.
4057	Through self receive ability.
4058	Through self receive building.
4059	Through self receive action.
4060	Through self joy releasing.
4061	Through self joy now.
4062	Through self joy compromise.
4063	Through self joy myn.
4064	Through self joy supported.
4065	Through self joy received.
4066	Through self content laugh.
4067	Through self joy ability.
4068	Through self joy building.
4069	Through self joy action.
4070	Through self ability releasing.
4071	Through self ability now.
4072	Through self ability compromise.
4073	Through self ability myn.
4074	Through self ability supported.
4075	Through self ability received.
4076	Through self ability joy.
4077	Through self working ability.
4078	Through self ability building.
4079	Through self ability action.
4080	Through self building releasing.
4081	Through self building now.
4082	Through self building compromise.

4083 Through self building myn.
4084 Through self building supported.
4085 Through self building received.
4086 Through self building joy.
4087 Through self building ability.
4088 Through self building structure.
4089 Through self building action.
4090 Through self action releasing.
4091 Through self action now.
4092 Through self action compromise.
4093 Through self testing myn.
4094 Through self action supported.
4095 Through self action accepted.
4096 Through self action joy.
4097 Through self action ability.
4098 Through self action building.
4099 Through self moving action.
4100 Support is my self.
4101 Support is my now.
4102 Support is self compromise.
4103 Support is self myn.
4104 Support is self supported.
4105 Support is self received.
4106 Support is self joy.
4107 Support is self ability.
4108 Support is self building.
4109 Support is self action.
4110 Support is now releasing.
4111 Support is now done.
4112 Support is now compromise.
4113 Support is now trust.
4114 Support is now supported.
4115 Support is now received.
4116 Support is now joy.

Myn in Numbers

4117	Support is now ability.
4118	Support is now building.
4119	Support is now action.
4120	Support is compromise releasing.
4121	Support is compromise now.
4122	Support is joining compromise.
4123	Support is compromise myn.
4124	Support is compromise supported.
4125	Support this compromise received.
4126	Support this compromise joy.
4127	Support this compromise ability.
4128	Support this compromise building.
4129	Support this compromise action.
4130	Support this myn releasing.
4131	Support this myn now.
4132	Support this myn compromise.
4133	Support this trust myn.
4134	Support this myn supported.
4135	Support this myn received.
4136	Support this trusting joy.
4137	Support this myn ability.
4138	Support this myn building.
4139	Support this myn action.
4140	Support this through releasing.
4141	Support this through now.
4142	Support this through compromise.
4143	Support this through myn.
4144	Support this through support.
4145	Support this through acceptance.
4146	Support this through joy.
4147	Support this through ability.
4148	Support this through building.
4149	Support this through action.
4150	Support this receive releasing.

Kevin J. Baird

4151   Support this receive now.
4152   Support this receive compromise.
4153   Support this receive myn.
4154   Support this receive supported.
4155   Support this receive acceptance.
4156   Support this receive joy.
4157   Support this receive ability.
4158   Support this receive building.
4159   Support this receive action.
4160   Support this joy releasing.
4161   Support this joy now.
4162   Support this joy compromise.
4163   Support this joy myn.
4164   Support this joy supported.
4165   Support this joy received.
4166   Support this content laugh.
4167   Support this joy ability.
4168   Support this joy building.
4169   Support this joy action.
4170   Support this work releasing.
4171   Support this work now.
4172   Support this work compromise.
4173   Support this work myn.
4174   Support this work supported.
4175   Support this work received.
4176   Support this work joy.
4177   Support this work ability.
4178   Support this work building.
4179   Support this work action.
4180   Support is building releasing.
4181   Support is building now.
4182   Support is building compromise.
4183   Support is building myn.
4184   Support is building supported.

Myn in Numbers

4185	Support is building received.
4186	Support is building joy.
4187	Support is building ability.
4188	Support is building structure.
4189	Support is building action.
4190	Support is action releasing.
4191	Support is action now.
4192	Support is action compromise.
4193	Support is action myn.
4194	Support is action supported.
4195	Support is action received.
4196	Support is active joy.
4197	Support is action ability.
4198	Support is action building.
4199	Support is moving action.
4200	Support joins my self.
4201	Through partner self now.
4202	Through partner self compromise.
4203	Through partner self myn.
4204	Through partner self supported.
4205	Through partner self received.
4206	Through partner self joy.
4207	Through partner self ability.
4208	Through partner self building.
4209	Through partner self action.
4210	Through partner now releasing.
4211	Through partner this now.
4212	Through partner now compromise.
4213	Through partner now myn.
4214	Through partner now supported.
4215	Through partner now received.
4216	Through partner now joy.
4217	Through partner now ability.
4218	Through partner now building.

4219	Through partner now action.
4220	Through partner compromise releasing.
4221	Through partner compromise now.
4222	Through partner friendship compromise.
4223	Through partner join trust.
4224	Through partner compromise supported.
4225	Through partner compromise received.
4226	Through partner compromise joy.
4227	Through partner compromise ability.
4228	Through partner compromise building.
4229	Through partner compromise action.
4230	Through partner myn releasing.
4231	Through partner myn now.
4232	Through partner myn compromise.
4233	Through partner trust myn.
4234	Through partner myn supported.
4235	Through partner myn received.
4236	Through partner myn joy.
4237	Through partner myn ability.
4238	Through partner myn building.
4239	Through partner myn action.
4240	Through partner through releasing.
4241	Through partner through now.
4242	Through partner through compromise.
4243	Through partner through myn.
4244	Through partner through support.
4245	Through partner through acceptance.
4246	Through partner through joy.
4247	Through partner through ability.
4248	Through partner through building.
4249	Through partner through action.
4250	Through partner receive releasing.
4251	Through partner receive now.
4252	Through partner receive compromise.

Myn in Numbers

4253	Through partner receive myn.
4254	Through partner receive supported.
4255	Through partner receive received.
4256	Through partner receive joy.
4257	Through partner receive ability.
4258	Through partner receive building.
4259	Through partner receive action.
4260	Through partner joy releasing.
4261	Through partner joy now.
4262	Through partner joy compromise.
4263	Through partner joy myn.
4264	Through partner joy supported.
4265	Through partner joy received.
4266	Through partner content laugh.
4267	Through partner joy ability.
4268	Through partner joy building.
4269	Through partner joy action.
4270	Through partner ability releasing.
4271	Through partner ability now.
4272	Through partner ability compromise.
4273	Through partner ability myn.
4274	Through partner ability supported.
4275	Through partner ability received.
4276	Through partner ability joy.
4277	Through partner working ability.
4278	Through partner ability building.
4279	Through partner ability action.
4280	Supporting friend building releasing.
4281	Supporting friend building now.
4282	Supporting friend building compromise.
4283	Supporting friend building myn.
4284	Supporting friend building supported.
4285	Supporting friend building received.
4286	Supporting friend building joy.

4287	Supporting friend building ability.	
4288	Supporting friend building structure.	
4289	Supporting friend building action.	
4290	Through partner action releasing.	
4291	Through partner action now.	
4292	Through partner action compromise.	
4293	Through partner action myn.	
4294	Through partner action supported.	
4295	Through partner action received.	
4296	Through partner action joy.	
4297	Through partner action ability.	
4298	Through partner action building.	
4299	Through partner moving action.	
4300	Through trust self releasing.	
4301	Through trust releases this.	
4302	Through trust releases compromise.	
4303	Through trust releases trust.	
4304	Through trust releases supported.	
4305	Through trust releases received.	
4306	Through trust releases joy.	
4307	Through trust releases ability.	
4308	Through trust releases building.	
4309	Through trust releases action.	
4310	Through trust now releasing.	
4311	Through trust is now.	
4312	Through trust now compromise.	
4313	Through trust now myn.	
4314	Through trust now supported.	
4315	Through trust now received.	
4316	Through trust now joy.	
4317	Through trust now ability.	
4318	Through trust now building.	
4319	Through trust now action.	
4320	Through trust compromise releasing.	

Myn in Numbers

4321	Through trust compromise now.
4322	Through trust friendship compromise.
4323	Through trust compromise myn.
4324	Through trust compromise supported.
4325	Through trust compromise received.
4326	Through trust compromise joy.
4327	Through trust compromise ability.
4328	Through trust compromise building.
4329	Through trust compromise action.
4330	Through blessing trust releasing.
4331	Through blessing trust now.
4332	Through blessing trust compromise.
4333	Through myn trust myn.
4334	Through blessing trust supported.
4335	Through blessing trust received.
4336	Through blessing trust joy.
4337	Through blessing trust ability.
4338	Through blessing trust building.
4339	Through blessing trust action.
4340	Support trust through releasing.
4341	Support trust through now.
4342	Support trust through compromise.
4343	Support trust through trust.
4344	Through myn through support.
4345	Through myn support acceptance.
4346	Through myn through joy.
4347	Through myn through ability.
4348	Through myn through building.
4349	Through myn through action.
4350	Through myn receive releasing.
4351	Through myn receive now.
4352	Through myn receive compromise.
4353	Through myn receive myn.
4354	Through myn receive supported.

4355   Through myn receive acceptance.
4356   Through myn receive joy.
4357   Through myn receive ability.
4358   Through myn receive building.
4359   Through myn receive action.
4360   Through myn joy releasing.
4361   Through myn joy now.
4362   Through myn joy compromise.
4363   Through myn joy myn.
4364   Through myn joy supported.
4365   Through myn joy received.
4366   Through myn content laugh.
4367   Through myn joy ability.
4368   Through myn joy building.
4369   Through myn joy action.
4370   Through myn ability releasing.
4371   Through myn ability now.
4372   Through myn ability compromise.
4373   Through myn ability myn.
4374   Through myn ability supported.
4375   Through myn ability received.
4376   Through myn ability joy.
4377   Through myn working ability.
4378   Through myn ability building.
4379   Through myn ability action.
4380   Through myn build releasing.
4381   Through myn build now.
4382   Through myn build compromise.
4383   Through myn build myn.
4384   Through myn build supported.
4385   Through myn build received.
4386   Through myn build joy.
4387   Through myn build ability.
4388   Through myn build structure.

Myn in Numbers

4389	Through myn build action.
4390	Through myn action releasing.
4391	Through myn action now.
4392	Through myn action compromise.
4393	Through myn action trust.
4394	Through myn action supported.
4395	Through myn action received.
4396	Through myn action joy.
4397	Through myn action ability.
4398	Through myn action building.
4399	Through myn moving feelings.
4400	Supported through my soul.
4401	Supported through my now.
4402	Supported through my compromise.
4403	Supported through my myn.
4404	Supported through my means.
4405	Supported through my receiving.
4406	Supported through my joy.
4407	Supported through my ability.
4408	Supported through my building.
4409	Supported through my action.
4410	Supported through this released.
4411	Supported support this now.
4412	Supported support is compromise.
4413	Supported support is blessing.
4414	Supported support is conduit.
4415	Supported through this received.
4416	Supported through this joy.
4417	Supported through this ability.
4418	Supported through this building.
4419	Supported through this action.
4420	Supported through joining releasing.
4421	Supported through joining now.
4422	Supported through friendship compromise.

4423   Supported through joining myn.
4424   Supported through joining support.
4425   Supported through joining acceptance.
4426   Supported through joining joy.
4427   Supported through joining ability.
4428   Supported through joining building.
4429   Supported through joining action.
4430   Supported through trusting releasing.
4431   Supported through trusting now.
4432   Supported through trusting compromise.
4433   Supported through trust myn.
4434   Supported through trusting supported.
4435   Supported through trusting received.
4436   Supported through trusting joy.
4437   Supported through trusting ability.
4438   Supported through trusting building.
4439   Supported through trusting action.
4440   Convey means supporting release.
4441   Convey means supporting now.
4442   Convey means supporting compromise.
4443   Convey means supporting trust.
4444   Convey means through support.
4445   Convey means supporting acceptance.
4446   Convey means supporting joy.
4447   Convey means supporting ability.
4448   Convey means supporting building.
4449   Convey means supporting action.
4450   Supported through receiving releasing.
4451   Supported through receiving now.
4452   Supported through receiving compromise.
4453   Supported through receiving trust.
4454   Supported through receiving means.
4455   Supported through receiving acceptance.
4456   Supported through receiving joy.

Myn in Numbers

4457	Supported through receiving ability.
4458	Supported through receiving building.
4459	Supported through receiving action.
4460	Supported through joy releasing.
4461	Supported through joy now.
4462	Supported through joy compromise.
4463	Supported through joy trust.
4464	Supported through joy supported.
4465	Supported through joy received.
4466	Supported through content laugh.
4467	Supported through joy ability.
4468	Supported through joy building.
4469	Supported through joy action.
4470	Supported through ability releasing.
4471	Supported through ability now.
4472	Supported through ability compromise.
4473	Supported through able trust.
4474	Supported through able means.
4475	Supported through ability received.
4476	Supported through able joy.
4477	Supported through working ability.
4478	Supported through ability building.
4479	Supported through ability testing.
4480	Supported through building release.
4481	Supported through building now.
4482	Supported through building compromise.
4483	Supported through building trust.
4484	Supported through building supported.
4485	Supported through building received.
4486	Supported through building joy.
4487	Supported through building ability.
4488	Supported through building structure.
4489	Supported through building action.
4490	Supported through action releasing.

4491	Supported through action now.
4492	Supported through action compromise.
4493	Supported through active trust.
4494	Supported through active means.
4495	Supported through action received.
4496	Supported through action joy.
4497	Supported through action ability.
4498	Supported through action building.
4499	Supported through moving action.
4500	Support receiving self releasing.
4501	Support receiving self now.
4502	Support receiving self compromise.
4503	Support receiving self trust.
4504	Through receiving self supported.
4505	Through receiving self received.
4506	Through receiving self joy.
4507	Through receiving self ability.
4508	Through receiving self building.
4509	Through receiving self action.
4510	Through receiving now releasing.
4511	Through receiving is now.
4512	Through receiving now compromise.
4513	Through receiving now myn.
4514	Through receiving now supported.
4515	Through receiving now received.
4516	Through receiving now joy.
4517	Through receiving now ability.
4518	Through receiving now building.
4519	Through receiving now action.
4520	Through receiving compromise releasing.
4521	Through receiving compromise now.
4522	Through receiving friendship compromise.
4523	Through receiving compromise myn.
4524	Through receiving compromise supported.

Myn in Numbers

4525	Through receiving compromise received.
4526	Through receiving compromise joy.
4527	Through receiving compromise ability.
4528	Through receiving compromise building.
4529	Through receiving compromise action.
4530	Through receiving myn releasing.
4531	Through receiving myn now.
4532	Through receiving myn compromise.
4533	Through receiving trust myn.
4534	Through receiving myn supported.
4535	Through receiving myn received.
4536	Through receiving myn joy.
4537	Through receiving myn ability.
4538	Through receiving myn building.
4539	Through receiving myn action.
4540	Through receiving means releasing.
4541	Through receiving means now.
4542	Through receiving means compromise.
4543	Through receiving means myn.
4544	Through receiving means support.
4545	Through receiving means acceptance .
4546	Through receiving means joy.
4547	Through receiving means ability.
4548	Through receiving means building.
4549	Through receiving means action.
4550	Through receiving receive releasing.
4551	Through receiving acceptance now.
4552	Through receiving acceptance compromise.
4553	Through receiving acceptance trust.
4554	Through receiving acceptance supported.
4555	Through receiving acceptance receive.
4556	Through receiving acceptance joy.
4557	Through receiving acceptance ability.
4558	Through receiving acceptance building.

4559	Through receiving acceptance action.
4560	Through receive joy releasing.
4561	Support accepting joy now.
4562	Support accepting joy compromise.
4563	Support accepting joy myn.
4564	Support accepting joy supported.
4565	Support accepting joy received.
4566	Support accepting content laugh.
4567	Support accepting joy ability.
4568	Support accepting joy building.
4569	Support accepting joy action.
4570	Support accepting ability releasing.
4571	Support accepting ability now.
4572	Support accepting ability compromise.
4573	Support accepting ability myn.
4574	Support accepting ability supported.
4575	Support accepting ability received.
4576	Support accepting ability joy.
4577	Support accepting working ability.
4578	Support accepting ability building.
4579	Support accepting ability action.
4580	Support accepting building releasing.
4581	Support accepting building now.
4582	Support accepting building compromise.
4583	Support accepting building myn.
4584	Support accepting building supported.
4585	Support accepting building received.
4586	Support accepting building joy.
4587	Support accepting building ability.
4588	Support accepting building structure.
4589	Support accepting building action.
4590	Support accepting action releasing.
4591	Support accepting action now.
4592	Support accepting action compromise.

Myn in Numbers

4593	Support accepting action myn.
4594	Support accepting action supported.
4595	Support accepting action received.
4596	Support accepting action joy.
4597	Support accepting action ability.
4598	Support accepting action building.
4599	Support accepting moving action.
4600	Through joy soul releases.
4601	Through joy my now.
4602	Through joy my compromise.
4603	Through joy my myn.
4604	Through joy my supported.
4605	Through joy my received.
4606	Through joy my joy.
4607	Through joy my ability.
4608	Through joy my building.
4609	Through joy my action.
4610	Through joy now releasing.
4611	Through joy is now.
4612	Through joy now compromise.
4613	Through joy now myn.
4614	Through joy now supported.
4615	Through joy now received.
4616	Through joy now joy.
4617	Through joy now ability.
4618	Through joy now building.
4619	Through joy now action.
4620	Through joy compromise releasing.
4621	Through joy compromise now.
4622	Through joy friendship compromise.
4623	Through joy compromise myn.
4624	Through joy compromise supported.
4625	Through joy compromise received.
4626	Through joy compromise joy.

4627   Through joy compromise ability.
4628   Through joy compromise building.
4629   Through joy compromise action.
4630   Through joy myn releasing.
4631   Through joy myn now.
4632   Through joy myn compromise.
4633   Through joy trust myn.
4634   Through joy myn supported.
4635   Through joy myn received.
4636   Through joy myn joy.
4637   Through joy myn ability.
4638   Through joy myn building.
4639   Through joy myn action.
4640   Through joy means releasing.
4641   Through joy means now.
4642   Through joy means compromise.
4643   Through joy means myn.
4644   Through joy means support.
4645   Through joy means received.
4646   Through joy means joy.
4647   Through joy means ability.
4648   Through joy means building.
4649   Through joy means action.
4650   Through joy receive releasing.
4651   Through joy receive now.
4652   Through joy receive compromise.
4653   Through joy receive myn.
4654   Through joy receive supported.
4655   Through joy receive received.
4656   Through joy receive joy.
4657   Through joy receive ability.
4658   Through joy receive building.
4659   Through joy receive action.
4660   Through joy joy releases.

Myn in Numbers

4661	Through joy joy now.
4662	Through joy joy compromise.
4663	Through joy joy trust.
4664	Through joy joy supported.
4665	Through joy joy received.
4666	Through joy content laugh.
4667	Through joy joy ability.
4668	Through joy joy building.
4669	Through joy joy action.
4670	Through joy ability releasing.
4671	Through joy ability now.
4672	Through joy ability compromise.
4673	Through joy enables trust.
4674	Through joy ability supported.
4675	Through joy ability received.
4676	Through joy enables joy.
4677	Through joy works ability.
4678	Through joy ability building.
4679	Through joy ability action.
4680	Through joy builds releasing.
4681	Through joy building now.
4682	Through joy building compromise.
4683	Through joy building trust.
4684	Through joy builds supported.
4685	Through joy builds acceptance.
4686	Through joy builds joy.
4687	Through joy builds ability.
4688	Through joy builds structure.
4689	Through joy builds action.
4690	Through joy works releasing.
4691	Through joy works now.
4692	Through joy works compromise.
4693	Through joy works trust.
4694	Through joy works supported.

4695 Through joy works acceptance.
4696 Through joy works joy.
4697 Through joy works ability.
4698 Through joy works building.
4699 Through joy moving action.
4700 Through ability soul releases.
4701 Through ability my now.
4702 Through ability my compromise.
4703 Through ability my myn.
4704 Through ability my supported.
4705 Through ability my received.
4706 Through ability my joy.
4707 Through ability my ability.
4708 Through ability my building.
4709 Through ability release works.
4710 Through ability now releasing.
4711 Through ability is now.
4712 Through ability now compromise.
4713 Through ability now myn.
4714 Through ability now supported.
4715 Through ability now received.
4716 Through ability now joy.
4717 Through ability now ability.
4718 Through ability now building.
4719 Through ability now works.
4720 Through ability compromise releases.
4721 Through ability compromise now.
4722 Through ability friendship compromise.
4723 Through ability compromise myn.
4724 Through ability compromise supported.
4725 Through ability compromise received.
4726 Through ability compromise joy.
4727 Through ability compromise ability.
4728 Through ability compromise building.

Myn in Numbers

4729	Through ability compromise works .
4730	Through ability trust releasing.
4731	Through ability trust now.
4732	Through ability trust compromise.
4733	Through ability trust myn.
4734	Through ability trust supported.
4735	Through ability trust received.
4736	Through ability trust joy.
4737	Through ability trust ability.
4738	Through ability trust building.
4739	Through ability trust works .
4740	Through ability supports releasing.
4741	Through ability supports now.
4742	Through ability supports compromise.
4743	Through ability supports myn.
4744	Through ability through support.
4745	Through ability supports acceptance.
4746	Through ability supports joy.
4747	Through ability supports ability.
4748	Through ability supports building.
4749	Through ability supports works .
4750	Through ability receive releasing.
4751	Through ability receive now.
4752	Through ability receive compromise.
4753	Through ability receive myn.
4754	Through ability receive supported.
4755	Through ability receive received.
4756	Through ability receive joy.
4757	Through ability receive ability.
4758	Through ability receive building.
4759	Through ability receive action.
4760	Through ability joy releasing.
4761	Through ability joy now.
4762	Through ability joy compromise.

4763	Through ability joy myn.
4764	Through ability joy supported.
4765	Through ability joy received.
4766	Through ability content laugh.
4767	Through ability joy ability.
4768	Through ability joy building.
4769	Through ability joy action.
4770	Through ability works releasing.
4771	Through ability works now.
4772	Through ability works compromise.
4773	Through ability works myn.
4774	Through ability works supported.
4775	Through ability works acceptance.
4776	Through ability works joy.
4777	Through ability working ability.
4778	Through ability works building.
4779	Through ability works action.
4780	Support ability building releasing.
4781	Support ability building now.
4782	Support ability building compromise.
4783	Support ability building myn.
4784	Support ability building supported.
4785	Support ability building received.
4786	Support ability building joy.
4787	Support ability building ability.
4788	Support ability building structure.
4789	Support ability building action.
4790	Support ability action releasing.
4791	Support ability action now.
4792	Support ability action compromise.
4793	Support ability action myn.
4794	Support ability action supported.
4795	Through ability action received.
4796	Through ability action joy.

Myn in Numbers

4797	Through ability action ability.
4798	Through ability action building.
4799	Through ability moving action.
4800	Through building soul releases.
4801	Support building release now.
4802	Support building release compromise.
4803	Support building release myn.
4804	Support building release supported.
4805	Support building release received.
4806	Support building release joy.
4807	Support building release ability.
4808	Support building release building.
4809	Support building release action.
4810	Support building now releasing.
4811	Support building is this.
4812	Support building this compromise.
4813	Support building this trust.
4814	Support building this supported.
4815	Support building this received.
4816	Support building this joy.
4817	Support building this ability.
4818	Support building this building.
4819	Support building this action.
4820	Support building compromise releases.
4821	Support building compromise this.
4822	Support building friendship compromise.
4823	Support building compromise trust.
4824	Support building compromise supported.
4825	Support building compromise received.
4826	Support building compromise joy.
4827	Support building compromise ability.
4828	Support building compromise building.
4829	Support building compromise action.
4830	Support building trust releasing.

4831   Support building trust this.
4832   Support building trust compromise.
4833   Support building trust myn.
4834   Support building trust supported.
4835   Support building trust received.
4836   Support building trust joy.
4837   Support building trust ability.
4838   Support building trust building.
4839   Support building trust action.
4840   Through building through releasing.
4841   Through building through now.
4842   Through building through compromise.
4843   Through building through myn.
4844   Through building through support.
4845   Through building through acceptance.
4846   Through building through joy.
4847   Through building through ability.
4848   Through building through building.
4849   Through building through action.
4850   Through building receive releasing.
4851   Through building receive now.
4852   Through building receive compromise.
4853   Through building receive myn.
4854   Through building receive supported.
4855   Through building receive received.
4856   Through building receive joy.
4857   Through building receive ability.
4858   Through building receive building.
4859   Through building receive action.
4860   Through building joy releasing.
4861   Through building joy is.
4862   Through building joy compromise.
4863   Through building joy trust.
4864   Through building joy supported.

Myn in Numbers

4865	Through building joy received.
4866	Through building content laugh.
4867	Through building joy ability.
4868	Through building joy building.
4869	Through building joy action.
4870	Through building ability releasing.
4871	Through building ability now.
4872	Through building ability compromise.
4873	Through building ability myn.
4874	Through building ability supported.
4875	Through building ability received.
4876	Through building ability joy.
4877	Through building working ability.
4878	Through building ability building.
4879	Through building ability action.
4880	Through building form releasing.
4881	Through building structure now.
4882	Through building structured compromise.
4883	Through building form trust.
4884	Through building forms support.
4885	Through building form acceptance.
4886	Through building form joy.
4887	Through building form ability.
4888	Through building form structure.
4889	Through building form action.
4890	Through building action releasing.
4891	Through building action now.
4892	Through building action compromise.
4893	Through building action myn.
4894	Through building action supported.
4895	Through building action received.
4896	Through building action joy.
4897	Through building action ability.
4898	Through building action building.

4899 Through building moving action.
4900 Through action soul releases.
4901 Through action my now.
4902 Support action releases compromise.
4903 Support action releases myn.
4904 Support action releases supported.
4905 Support action releases received.
4906 Support action releases joy.
4907 Support action releases ability.
4908 Support action releases building.
4909 Support action releases action.
4910 Support activating this releasing.
4911 Support activating this now.
4912 Support activating this compromise.
4913 Support activating this trust.
4914 Support activating this supported.
4915 Support activating this received.
4916 Support activating this joy.
4917 Support activating this ability.
4918 Support activating this building.
4919 Support activating this action.
4920 Through action compromise releases.
4921 Through action compromise now.
4922 Through action join friendship.
4923 Through action join trust.
4924 Through action join supporting.
4925 Through action join acceptance.
4926 Through action join joy.
4927 Through action join ability.
4928 Through action join building.
4929 Through action join action.
4930 Through action trust releases.
4931 Through action trust now.
4932 Through action trust compromise.

Myn in Numbers

4933	Through action trust blessing.
4934	Through action trust supporting.
4935	Through action trust acceptance.
4936	Through action trust joy.
4937	Through action trust ability.
4938	Through action trust building.
4939	Through action trust action.
4940	Through action support releasing.
4941	Through action support this.
4942	Through action support compromise.
4943	Through action support myn.
4944	Through action through support.
4945	Through action support acceptance.
4946	Through action support joy.
4947	Through action support ability.
4948	Through action support building.
4949	Through action support action.
4950	Through action receive releasing.
4951	Through action receive now.
4952	Through action receive compromise.
4953	Through action receive trust.
4954	Through action receive supported.
4955	Through action receive acceptance.
4956	Through action receive joy.
4957	Through action receive ability.
4958	Through action receive building.
4959	Through action receive action.
4960	Through action joy releases.
4961	Through action joy now.
4962	Through action joy compromise.
4963	Through action enjoy trust.
4964	Through action joy supported.
4965	Through action joy received.
4966	Through action content laugh.

4967	Through action joy ability.
4968	Through action joy building.
4969	Through action joy action.
4970	Through action works releasing.
4971	Through action works now.
4972	Through action works compromise.
4973	Through action works myn.
4974	Through action works supported.
4975	Through action works received.
4976	Through action works joy.
4977	Through action working ability.
4978	Through action works building.
4979	Through action works action.
4980	Support action building releasing.
4981	Support action building now.
4982	Support action building compromise.
4983	Support action building myn.
4984	Support action building means.
4985	Support action building acceptance.
4986	Support action building joy.
4987	Support action building ability.
4988	Support action building structure.
4989	Support action building action.
4990	Support action testing self.
4991	Support action testing now.
4992	Support action testing compromise.
4993	Support action testing trust.
4994	Support action testing supported.
4995	Support action testing received.
4996	Support action testing joy.
4997	Support action testing ability.
4998	Support action testing building.
4999	Support action testing feelings.

Myn in Numbers

Accept

5000-5999

When "5" leads the group your source is inviting you to "Receive or accept" as you conduct yourself in the group moment of the trailing numbers. Weigh the points and ponder the outcome.

***

5000	Present my self release.
5001	Accept my self now.
5002	Accept my self compromise.
5003	Accept my self trust.
5004	Accept my self supported.
5005	Accept my self received.
5006	Accept my self content.
5007	Accept my self ability.
5008	Accept my self building.
5009	Accept my self action.
5010	Accepting self is releasing.
5011	Accepting self is now.
5012	Accepting self is compromise.
5013	Accepting self is trust.
5014	Accepting self is supported.
5015	Accepting self is received.

www.templeofgaia.com

5016	Accepting self is joy.
5017	Accepting self is ability.
5018	Accepting self is building.
5019	Accepting self is action.
5020	Accepting self joins releasing.
5021	Accepting self joins now.
5022	Accepting self friend joins.
5023	Accepting self joins trust.
5024	Accepting self joins supported.
5025	Accepting self joins received.
5026	Accepting self joins joy.
5027	Accepting self joins ability.
5028	Accepting self joins building.
5029	Accepting self joins action.
5030	Accepting self trust release.
5031	Accepting self trust now.
5032	Accepting self trust joining.
5033	Accepting self trust blessed.
5034	Accepting self trust supported.
5035	Accepting self trust received.
5036	Accepting self trust joy.
5037	Accepting self trust ability.
5038	Accepting self trust building.
5039	Accepting self trust action.
5040	Accepting self through releasing.
5041	Accepting self through this.
5042	Accepting self through compromise.
5043	Accepting self through trust.
5044	Accepting self through support.
5045	Accepting self through acceptance.
5046	Accepting self through joy.
5047	Accepting self through ability.
5048	Accepting self through building.
5049	Accepting self through action.

Myn in Numbers

5050	Accepting self receive releasing.
5051	Accepting self receive now.
5052	Accepting self receive compromise.
5053	Accepting self receive trust.
5054	Accepting self receive supported.
5055	Accepting self receive received.
5056	Accepting self receive joy.
5057	Accepting self receive ability.
5058	Accepting self receive building.
5059	Accepting self receive action.
5060	Accepting self serves releasing.
5061	Accepting self serves now.
5062	Accepting self serves compromise.
5063	Accepting self serves myn.
5064	Accepting self serves supported.
5065	Accepting self serves received.
5066	Accepting self serves laughing.
5067	Accepting self serves ability.
5068	Accepting self serves building.
5069	Accepting self serves action.
5070	Accepting self ability releasing.
5071	Accepting self ability now.
5072	Accepting self ability compromise.
5073	Accepting self ability trusting.
5074	Accepting self ability supported.
5075	Accepting self ability received.
5076	Accepting self ability joy.
5077	Accepting self working ability.
5078	Accepting self ability building.
5079	Accepting self ability action.
5080	Accepting self building releasing.
5081	Accepting self building now.
5082	Accepting self building compromise.
5083	Accepting self building myn.

5084	Accepting self building supported.
5085	Accepting self building received.
5086	Accepting self building joy.
5087	Accepting self building ability.
5088	Accepting self building structure.
5089	Accepting self building action.
5090	Accepting self tests releasing.
5091	Accepting self tests now.
5092	Accepting self tests compromise.
5093	Accepting self tests trust.
5094	Accepting self tests supported.
5095	Accepting self tests accepted.
5096	Accepting self tests joy.
5097	Accepting self tests ability.
5098	Accepting self tests building.
5099	Accepting self tests feelings.
5100	Accepting self soul releases.
5101	Accepting self releases now.
5102	Accepting self releases compromise.
5103	Accepting self releases trust.
5104	Accepting self releases supported.
5105	Accepting self releases content.
5106	Accepting self releases joy.
5107	Accepting self releases ability.
5108	Accepting self releases building.
5109	Accepting self releases action.
5110	Accept this is releasing.
5111	Accept this now done.
5112	Accept this is compromise.
5113	Accept this is trust.
5114	Accept this is supported.
5115	Accept this is received.
5116	Accept this is joy.
5117	Accept this is ability.

Myn in Numbers

5118	Accept this is building.
5119	Accept this is action.
5120	Accept this compromise releasing.
5121	Accept this compromise now.
5122	Accept this friendship compromise.
5123	Accept this compromise trusting.
5124	Accept this compromise supported.
5125	Accept this compromise received.
5126	Accept this compromise joy.
5127	Accept this compromise ability.
5128	Accept this compromise building.
5129	Accept this compromise action.
5130	Accept this trusting release.
5131	Accept this trusting now.
5132	Accept this trusting compromise.
5133	Accept this trusting blessing.
5134	Accept this trusting support.
5135	Accept this trusting content.
5136	Acceptance is trusting joy.
5137	Accept this trusting ability.
5138	Accept this trusting building.
5139	Accept this trusting action.
5140	Accept this through releasing.
5141	Accept this through now.
5142	Accept this through compromise.
5143	Accept this through trust.
5144	Accept this through support.
5145	Accept this through acceptance.
5146	Accept this through joy.
5147	Accept this through ability.
5148	Accept this through building.
5149	Accept this through action.
5150	Accepting this receive releasing.
5151	Accepting this receive now.

5152	Accepting this receive compromise.
5153	Accepting this receive trust.
5154	Accepting this receive supported.
5155	Accepting this receive present.
5156	Accepting this receive joy.
5157	Accepting this receive ability.
5158	Accepting this receive building.
5159	Accepting this receive action.
5160	Accepting this joy releasing.
5161	Accepting this joy now.
5162	Accepting this joy compromise.
5163	Accepting this joy trust.
5164	Accepting this joy supported.
5165	Accepting this joy received.
5166	Accepting this content laugh.
5167	Accepting this joy ability.
5168	Accepting this joy building.
5169	Accepting this joy action.
5170	Accept this works releasing.
5171	Accept this works now.
5172	Accept this works compromise.
5173	Accept this works trust.
5174	Accept this works supported.
5175	Accept this works received.
5176	Accept this works joy.
5177	Accept this works ability.
5178	Accept this works building.
5179	Accept this works action.
5180	Accept this building release.
5181	Accept this building now.
5182	Accept this building compromise.
5183	Accept this building trust.
5184	Accept this building supported.
5185	Accept this building received.

Myn in Numbers

5186	Accept this building joy.
5187	Accept this building ability.
5188	Accept this building structure.
5189	Accept this building action.
5190	Accept this action releasing.
5191	Accept this action now.
5192	Accept this action compromise.
5193	Accept this action trust.
5194	Accept this action supported.
5195	Accept this action received.
5196	Accept this action joy.
5197	Accept this action ability.
5198	Accept this action building.
5199	Accept this moving action.
5201	Accept friend releasing now.
5202	Accept friend releasing compromise.
5203	Accept friend releasing trust.
5204	Accept friend releasing supported.
5205	Accept friend releasing received.
5206	Accept friend releasing joy.
5207	Accept friend releasing ability.
5208	Accept friend releasing building.
5209	Accept friend releasing action.
5210	Accept joining this release.
5211	Accept joining this now.
5212	Accept joining this compromise.
5213	Accept joining this myn.
5214	Accept joining this supported.
5215	Accept joining this received.
5216	Accept joining this joy.
5217	Accept joining this ability.
5218	Accept joining this building.
5219	Accept joining this action.
5220	Receive friend joining releasing.

5221	Receive friend joining now.
5222	Receive friend joining compromise.
5223	Receive friend joining trust.
5224	Receive friend joining supported.
5225	Receive friend joining received.
5226	Receive friend joining joy.
5227	Receive friend joining ability.
5228	Receive friend joining building.
5229	Receive friend joining action.
5230	Receive joining trusting release.
5231	Receive joining trusting now.
5232	Receive joining trusting compromise.
5233	Receive joining trusting blessing.
5234	Receive joining trusting support.
5235	Receive joining trusting acceptance.
5236	Receive joining trusting joy.
5237	Receive joining trusting ability.
5238	Receive joining trusting building.
5239	Receive joining trusting action.
5240	Receive joining supporting release.
5241	Receive joining supporting now.
5242	Receive joining supporting compromise.
5243	Receive joining supporting trust.
5244	Receive joining supporting support.
5245	Receive joining supporting acceptance.
5246	Receive joining supporting joy.
5247	Receive joining supporting ability.
5248	Receive joining supporting structure.
5249	Receive joining supporting action.
5250	Receive joining accepting release.
5251	Receive joining accepting now.
5252	Receive joining accepting compromise.
5253	Receive joining accepting trust.
5254	Receive joining accepting support.

Myn in Numbers

5255	Receive joining accepting present.
5256	Receive joining accepting joy.
5257	Receive joining accepting ability.
5258	Receive joining accepting building.
5259	Receive joining accepting action.
5260	Receive joining serves releasing.
5261	Receive joining serves now.
5262	Receive joining serves compromise.
5263	Receive joining serves trust.
5264	Receive joining serves supported.
5265	Receive joining serves received.
5266	Receive joining serves joy.
5267	Receive joining serves ability.
5268	Receive joining serves building.
5269	Receive joining serves action.
5270	Receive joining works releasing.
5271	Receive joining works now.
5272	Receive joining works compromise.
5273	Receive joining works trust.
5274	Receive joining works supported.
5275	Receive joining works received.
5276	Receive joining works joy.
5277	Receive joining works ability.
5278	Receive joining works building.
5279	Receive joining works action.
5280	Receive compromise building releasing.
5281	Receive compromise building now.
5282	Receive compromise building compromise.
5283	Receive compromise building myn.
5284	Receive compromise building supported.
5285	Receive compromise building received.
5286	Receive compromise building joy.
5287	Receive compromise building ability.
5288	Receive compromise building structure.

5289	Receive compromise building action.
5290	Accept compromise testing releasing.
5291	Accept compromise testing now.
5292	Accept compromise testing friendship.
5293	Accept compromise testing trust.
5294	Accept compromise testing supported.
5295	Accept compromise testing received.
5296	Accept compromise testing joy.
5297	Accept compromise testing ability.
5298	Accept compromise testing structure.
5299	Receive partner testing feelings.
5300	Accepting trust soul release.
5301	Present trust releasing now.
5302	Present trust releasing compromise.
5303	Present trust releasing myn.
5304	Present trust releasing supported.
5305	Present trust releasing received.
5306	Present trust releasing joy.
5307	Present trust releasing ability.
5308	Present trust releasing building.
5309	Present trust releasing action.
5310	Present trust now releasing.
5311	Present trust is now.
5312	Present trust now compromise.
5313	Present trust now myn.
5314	Present trust now supported.
5315	Present trust now received.
5316	Present trust now joy.
5317	Present trust now ability.
5318	Present trust now building.
5319	Present trust now action.
5320	Present trust compromise releasing.
5321	Present trust compromise now.
5322	Present trust friendship compromise.

Myn in Numbers

5323	Present trust compromise myn.
5324	Present trust compromise supported.
5325	Present trust compromise received.
5326	Present trust compromise joy.
5327	Present trust compromise ability.
5328	Present trust compromise building.
5329	Present trust compromise action.
5330	Present trusting prosperity releasing.
5331	Present trusting prosperity now.
5332	Present trusting prosperity compromise.
5333	Present trusting prosperity blessing.
5334	Present trusting prosperity supported.
5335	Present trusting prosperity received.
5336	Present trusting prosperity joy.
5337	Present trusting prosperity ability.
5338	Present trusting prosperity building.
5339	Present trusting prosperity action.
5340	Present trust supporting releasing.
5341	Present trust supporting now.
5342	Present trust supporting compromise.
5343	Present trust supporting blessing.
5344	Present trust supporting support.
5345	Present trust supporting received.
5346	Present trust supporting joy.
5347	Present trust supporting ability.
5348	Present trust supporting building.
5349	Present trust supporting action.
5350	Present trust receiving releasing.
5351	Present trust receiving now.
5352	Present trust receiving compromise.
5353	Present trust receiving blessing.
5354	Present trust receiving supported.
5355	Present trust receiving acceptance.
5356	Present trust receiving joy.

5357   Present trust receiving ability.
5358   Present trust receiving building.
5359   Present trust receiving action.
5360   Presenting trust serves releasing.
5361   Presenting trust serves now.
5362   Presenting trust serves compromise.
5363   Presenting trust serves myn.
5364   Presenting trust serves supported.
5365   Presenting trust serves received.
5366   Presenting trust serves joy.
5367   Presenting trust serves ability.
5368   Presenting trust serves building.
5369   Presenting trust serves action.
5370   Present trust works release.
5371   Present trust works now.
5372   Present trust works compromise.
5373   Present trust works blesses.
5374   Present trust works supported.
5375   Present trust works received.
5376   Present trust works joy.
5377   Present trust works ability.
5378   Present trust works building.
5379   Present trust works action.
5380   Presenting trust builds releasing.
5381   Presenting trust builds now.
5382   Presenting trust builds compromise.
5383   Presenting trust builds myn.
5384   Presenting trust builds supported.
5385   Presenting trust builds received.
5386   Presenting trust builds joy.
5387   Presenting trust builds ability.
5388   Presenting trust builds structure.
5389   Presenting trust builds action.
5390   Presenting trust tests releasing.

Myn in Numbers

5391	Presenting trust tests now.
5392	Presenting trust tests compromise.
5393	Presenting trust tests blessing.
5394	Presenting trust tests supported.
5395	Presenting trust tests received.
5396	Presenting trust tests joy.
5397	Presenting trust tests ability.
5398	Presenting trust tests building.
5399	Presenting trust tests action.
5400	Accepting support soul releases.
5401	Accepting support releases now.
5402	Accepting support releases compromise.
5403	Accepting support releases myn.
5404	Accepting support releases supported.
5405	Accepting support releases receiving.
5406	Accepting support releases joy.
5407	Accepting support releases ability.
5408	Accepting support releases building.
5409	Accepting support releases action.
5410	Accept through this soul.
5411	Accept supporting this now.
5412	Accept supporting this compromise.
5413	Accept supporting this blessing.
5414	Accept supporting this means.
5415	Accept supporting this received.
5416	Accept supporting this joy.
5417	Accept supporting this ability.
5418	Accept supporting this building.
5419	Accept supporting this action.
5420	Accept support joining release.
5421	Accept support joining now.
5422	Accept through friendship compromise.
5423	Accept support joining myn.
5424	Accept support joining supported.

5425   Accept support joining granted.
5426   Accept support joining joy.
5427   Accept support joining ability.
5428   Accept support joining building.
5429   Accept support joining action.
5430   Receiving means trusting releasing.
5431   Receiving means trusting now.
5432   Receiving means trusting friendship.
5433   Receiving means trusting blessings.
5434   Receiving means trusting supported.
5435   Receiving means trusting received.
5436   Receiving means trusting joy.
5437   Receiving means trusting ability.
5438   Receiving means trusting building.
5439   Receiving means trusting action.
5440   Receiving means through releasing.
5441   Receiving means through this.
5442   Receiving means through compromise.
5443   Receiving means through trust.
5444   Receiving means through support.
5445   Receiving means through acceptance.
5446   Receiving means through joy.
5447   Receiving means through ability.
5448   Receiving means through building.
5449   Receiving means through action.
5450   Present support granting release.
5451   Present support granting now.
5452   Present support granting compromise.
5453   Present support granting trust.
5454   Present support granting support.
5455   Present support granting received.
5456   Present support granting joy.
5457   Present support granting ability.
5458   Present support granting building.

Myn in Numbers

5459	Present support granting action.
5460	Present support serving releasing.
5461	Present support serving now.
5462	Present support serving compromise.
5463	Present support serving trust.
5464	Present support serving supported.
5465	Present support serving acceptance.
5466	Present support serving joy.
5467	Present support serving ability.
5468	Presenting support serves building.
5469	Present support serving action.
5470	Presenting support works releasing.
5471	Presenting support works now.
5472	Presenting support works compromise.
5473	Presenting support works trust.
5474	Presenting support works supported.
5475	Presenting support works received.
5476	Presenting support works joy.
5477	Presenting support works ability.
5478	Presenting support works building.
5479	Presenting support works action.
5480	Acceptance support builds releasing.
5481	Acceptance support builds now.
5482	Acceptance support builds compromise.
5483	Acceptance support builds trust.
5484	Acceptance support builds supported.
5485	Acceptance support builds received.
5486	Acceptance support builds joy.
5487	Acceptance support builds ability.
5488	Acceptance support builds structure.
5489	Acceptance support builds feelings.
5490	Acceptance supports testing releasing.
5491	Acceptance supports testing now.
5492	Acceptance supports testing compromise.

5493   Acceptance supports testing trust.
5494   Acceptance supports testing means.
5495   Acceptance supports testing received.
5496   Acceptance supports testing joy.
5497   Acceptance supports testing ability.
5498   Acceptance supports testing building.
5499   Acceptance supports testing feelings.
5500   Present acceptance releases soul.
5501   Present acceptance releases now.
5502   Present acceptance releases compromise.
5503   Present acceptance releases myn.
5504   Present acceptance releases supported.
5505   Present acceptance releases received.
5506   Present acceptance releases joy.
5507   Present acceptance releases ability.
5508   Present acceptance releases building.
5509   Present acceptance releases action.
5510   Present accepting this releasing.
5511   Present accepting this now.
5512   Present accepting this compromise.
5513   Present accepting this trust.
5514   Present accepting this supported.
5515   Present accepting this received.
5516   Present accepting this joy.
5517   Present accepting this ability.
5518   Present accepting this building.
5519   Present accepting this action.
5520   Present accepting compromise releasing.
5521   Present accepting compromise now.
5522   Present accepting friendship compromise.
5523   Present accepting joins trust.
5524   Present accepting compromise supported.
5525   Present accepting compromise received.
5526   Present accepting compromise joy.

Myn in Numbers

5527	Present accepting compromise ability.
5528	Present accepting compromise building.
5529	Present accepting compromise action.
5530	Present accepting myn releasing.
5531	Present accepting myn now.
5532	Present accepting myn compromise.
5533	Present accepting trust myn.
5534	Present accepting myn supported.
5535	Present accepting myn received.
5536	Present accepting trust joy.
5537	Present accepting trust ability.
5538	Present accepting trust building.
5539	Present accepting trust action.
5540	Present accepting through releasing.
5541	Present accepting through now.
5542	Present accepting through compromise.
5543	Present accepting through trust.
5544	Present accepting through support.
5545	Present accepting through received.
5546	Present accepting through joy.
5547	Present accepting through ability.
5548	Present accepting through building.
5549	Present accepting through action.
5550	Present accepting receive releasing.
5551	Present accepting receive now.
5552	Present accepting receive compromise.
5553	Present accepting receive trust.
5554	Present accepting receive supported.
5555	Present accepting receive granted.
5556	Present accepting receive joy.
5557	Present accepting receive ability.
5558	Present accepting receive building.
5559	Present accepting receive action.
5560	Present accepting joy releasing.

5561   Present accepting joy now.
5562   Present accepting joy compromise.
5563   Present accepting joy blessing.
5564   Present accepting joy supported.
5565   Present accepting joy received.
5566   Present accepting laugh content.
5567   Present accepting joy ability.
5568   Present accepting joy building.
5569   Present accepting joy action.
5570   Present accepting working release.
5571   Present accepting ability now.
5572   Present accepting ability compromise.
5573   Present accepting ability myn.
5574   Present accepting ability supported.
5575   Present accepting ability received.
5576   Present accepting works joy.
5577   Present accepting working ability.
5578   Present accepting ability building.
5579   Present accepting ability action.
5580   Present accepting building releasing.
5581   Present accepting building now.
5582   Present accepting building compromise.
5583   Present accepting building trust.
5584   Present accepting building supported.
5585   Present accepting building received.
5586   Present accepting building joy.
5587   Present accepting building ability.
5588   Present accepting building structure.
5589   Present accepting building action.
5590   Present accepting action release.
5591   Present accepting action now.
5592   Present accepting action compromise.
5593   Present accepting tests trust.
5594   Present accepting action supported.

Myn in Numbers

5595	Present accepting action received.
5596	Present accepting action joy.
5597	Present accepting action ability.
5598	Present accepting action building.
5599	Present accepting feelings tested.
5600	Receive joy soul releases.
5601	Present serving my now.
5602	Present serving my compromise.
5603	Present serving my trust.
5604	Present serving my supported.
5605	Present serving my received.
5606	Present serving my joy.
5607	Present serving my ability.
5608	Present serving my building.
5609	Present serving my action.
5610	Present serving this releasing.
5611	Present serving this now.
5612	Present serving this compromise.
5613	Present serving this trusted.
5614	Present serving this supported.
5615	Present serving this accepted.
5616	Present serving this joy.
5617	Present serving this ability.
5618	Present serving this building.
5619	Present serving this action.
5620	Present serving joins releasing.
5621	Present serving joins now.
5622	Present serving joins compromise.
5623	Present serving joins trust.
5624	Present serving joins supported.
5625	Present serving joins received.
5626	Present serving joins joy.
5627	Present serving joins ability.
5628	Present serving joins building.

5629   Present serving joins action.
5630   Present serving trust release.
5631   Present serving trust now.
5632   Present serving trust compromise.
5633   Present serving trust myn.
5634   Present serving trust supported.
5635   Present serving trust received.
5636   Present serving trust joy.
5637   Present serving trust ability.
5638   Present serving trust building.
5639   Present serving trust action.
5640   Present serving means releasing.
5641   Present serving means now.
5642   Present serving means compromise.
5643   Present serving means trust.
5644   Present serving means support.
5645   Present serving means received.
5646   Present serving means joy.
5647   Present serving means ability.
5648   Present serving means building.
5649   Present serving means action.
5650   Present serving receive releasing.
5651   Present serving receive now.
5652   Present serving receive compromise.
5653   Present serving receive trust.
5654   Present serving receive supported.
5655   Present serving receive received.
5656   Present serving receive joy.
5657   Present serving receive ability.
5658   Present serving receive building.
5659   Present serving receive action.
5660   Present serving laugh releasing.
5661   Present serving joy now.
5662   Present serving joy compromise.

Myn in Numbers

5663   Present serving joy trusting.
5664   Present serving joy supported.
5665   Present serving joy accepted.
5666   Present serving laugh content.
5667   Present serving joy ability.
5668   Present serving joy building.
5669   Present serving joy action.
5670   Present serving works release.
5671   Present serving works now.
5672   Present serving works compromise.
5673   Present serving works trust.
5674   Present serving works supported.
5675   Present serving works acceptance.
5676   Present serving works joy.
5677   Present serving working ability.
5678   Present serving works building.
5679   Present serving works action.
5680   Present serving builds releasing.
5681   Present serving builds now.
5682   Present serving builds compromise.
5683   Present serving builds trust.
5684   Present serving builds supported.
5685   Present serving builds received.
5686   Present serving builds joy.
5687   Present serving builds ability.
5688   Present serving builds structure.
5689   Present serving builds action.
5690   Present serving action releasing.
5691   Present serving action now.
5692   Present serving action compromise.
5693   Present serving action trust.
5694   Present serving action supported.
5695   Present serving action received.
5696   Present serving action joy.

5697	Present serving action ability.
5698	Present serving action building.
5699	Present serving tests feelings.
5700	Acceptance works soul release.
5701	Acceptance works my now.
5702	Acceptance works my compromise.
5703	Acceptance works my trust.
5704	Acceptance works my supported.
5705	Acceptance works my received.
5706	Acceptance works my joy.
5707	Acceptance works my ability.
5708	Acceptance works my building.
5709	Acceptance works my action.
5710	Acceptance works this release.
5711	Acceptance works this now.
5712	Acceptance works this compromise.
5713	Acceptance works this myn.
5714	Acceptance works this supported.
5715	Acceptance works this received.
5716	Acceptance works this joy.
5717	Acceptance works this ability.
5718	Acceptance works this building.
5719	Acceptance works this action.
5720	Acceptance works compromise release.
5721	Acceptance works friendship now.
5722	Acceptance works friendship compromise.
5723	Acceptance works friendship trust.
5724	Acceptance works friendship supported.
5725	Acceptance works friendship received.
5726	Acceptance works friendship joy.
5727	Acceptance works friendship ability.
5728	Acceptance works friendship building.
5729	Acceptance works friendship action.
5730	Acceptance works trust releasing.

Myn in Numbers

5731	Acceptance works trust now.
5732	Acceptance works trust compromise.
5733	Acceptance works trust myn.
5734	Acceptance works trust supported.
5735	Acceptance works trust received.
5736	Acceptance works trust joy.
5737	Acceptance works trust ability.
5738	Acceptance works trust building.
5739	Acceptance works trust action.
5740	Acceptance works through releasing.
5741	Acceptance works through now.
5742	Acceptance works through compromise.
5743	Acceptance works through trust.
5744	Acceptance works through support.
5745	Acceptance works through received.
5746	Acceptance works through joy.
5747	Acceptance works through ability.
5748	Acceptance works through building.
5749	Acceptance works through action.
5750	Acceptance works receiving release.
5751	Acceptance works granting now.
5752	Acceptance works granting compromise.
5753	Acceptance works granting trust.
5754	Acceptance works granting supported.
5755	Acceptance works granting received.
5756	Acceptance works granting joy.
5757	Acceptance works granting ability.
5758	Acceptance works granting building.
5759	Acceptance works granting action.
5760	Acceptance works joy releasing.
5761	Acceptance works joy now.
5762	Acceptance works joy compromise.
5763	Acceptance works joy myn.
5764	Acceptance works joy supported.

5765   Acceptance works joy received.
5766   Acceptance works content laugh.
5767   Acceptance works joy ability.
5768   Acceptance works joy building.
5769   Acceptance works joy action.
5770   Acceptance works capable releasing.
5771   Acceptance works capable now.
5772   Acceptance works capable compromise.
5773   Acceptance works capable myn.
5774   Acceptance works capable supported.
5775   Acceptance works capable received.
5776   Acceptance works capable joy.
5777   Acceptance works working capable.
5778   Acceptance works capable building.
5779   Acceptance works capable action.
5780   Acceptance works building release.
5781   Acceptance works building now.
5782   Acceptance works building compromise.
5783   Acceptance works building myn.
5784   Acceptance works building supported.
5785   Acceptance works building received.
5786   Acceptance works building joy.
5787   Acceptance works building ability.
5788   Acceptance works building structure.
5789   Acceptance works building action.
5790   Acceptance works action releasing.
5791   Acceptance works action now.
5792   Acceptance works action compromise.
5793   Acceptance works action myn.
5794   Acceptance works action supported.
5795   Acceptance works action received.
5796   Acceptance works action joy.
5797   Acceptance works action ability.
5798   Acceptance works action building.

Myn in Numbers

5799	Acceptance works testing feelings.
5800	Acceptance builds soul releases.
5801	Acceptance builds my now.
5802	Acceptance builds my compromise.
5803	Acceptance builds my myn.
5804	Acceptance builds my supported.
5805	Acceptance builds my received.
5806	Acceptance builds my joy.
5807	Acceptance builds my ability.
5808	Acceptance builds my building.
5809	Acceptance builds my action.
5810	Acceptance builds this release.
5811	Acceptance builds this now.
5812	Acceptance builds this compromise.
5813	Acceptance builds this trust.
5814	Acceptance builds this supported.
5815	Acceptance builds this received.
5816	Acceptance builds this joy.
5817	Acceptance builds this ability.
5818	Acceptance builds this building.
5819	Acceptance builds this action.
5820	Acceptance builds friendship releasing.
5821	Acceptance builds friendship now.
5822	Acceptance builds friendship compromise.
5823	Acceptance builds friendship trust.
5824	Acceptance builds friendship supported.
5825	Acceptance builds friendship received.
5826	Acceptance builds friendship joy.
5827	Acceptance builds friendship ability.
5828	Acceptance builds friendship building.
5829	Acceptance builds friendship action.
5830	Acceptance builds trust releasing.
5831	Acceptance builds trusting now.
5832	Acceptance builds trusting compromise.

Kevin J. Baird

5833   Acceptance builds trusting myn.
5834   Acceptance builds trusting supported.
5835   Acceptance builds trusting received.
5836   Acceptance builds trusting joy.
5837   Acceptance builds trusting ability.
5838   Acceptance builds trusting building.
5839   Acceptance builds trusting action.
5840   Acceptance builds through releasing.
5841   Acceptance builds supporting now.
5842   Acceptance builds supporting compromise.
5843   Acceptance builds supporting trust.
5844   Acceptance builds through support.
5845   Acceptance builds supporting received.
5846   Acceptance builds supporting joy.
5847   Acceptance builds supporting ability.
5848   Acceptance builds supporting building.
5849   Acceptance builds supporting action.
5850   Acceptance builds receiving releasing.
5851   Acceptance builds receiving now.
5852   Acceptance builds receiving compromise.
5853   Acceptance builds receiving trust.
5854   Acceptance builds receiving supported.
5855   Acceptance builds receiving received.
5856   Acceptance builds receiving joy.
5857   Acceptance builds receiving ability.
5858   Acceptance builds receiving building.
5859   Acceptance builds receiving action.
5860   Acceptance builds joy releasing.
5861   Acceptance builds joy now.
5862   Acceptance builds joy compromise.
5863   Acceptance builds joy myn.
5864   Acceptance builds joy supported.
5865   Acceptance builds joy receiving.
5866   Acceptance builds content laugh.

Myn in Numbers

5867 Acceptance builds joy ability.
5868 Acceptance builds joy structure.
5869 Acceptance builds joy action.
5870 Acceptance builds working release.
5871 Acceptance builds working now.
5872 Acceptance builds working compromise.
5873 Acceptance builds working myn.
5874 Acceptance builds working supported.
5875 Acceptance builds working received.
5876 Acceptance builds working joy.
5877 Acceptance builds working ability.
5878 Acceptance builds capable structure.
5879 Acceptance builds working action.
5880 Acceptance builds building release.
5881 Acceptance builds structure now.
5882 Acceptance builds structured compromise.
5883 Acceptance builds building trust.
5884 Acceptance builds building means.
5885 Acceptance builds building presence.
5886 Acceptance builds building joy.
5887 Acceptance builds building ability.
5888 Acceptance builds building structure.
5889 Acceptance builds building action.
5890 Acceptance builds action releasing.
5891 Acceptance builds action now.
5892 Acceptance builds action compromise.
5893 Acceptance builds action myn.
5894 Acceptance builds action supported.
5895 Acceptance builds action received.
5896 Acceptance builds action joy.
5897 Acceptance builds action ability.
5898 Acceptance builds action building.
5899 Acceptance builds testing feelings.
5900 Acceptance tests soul's release.

5901	Acceptance tests releasing this.
5902	Acceptance tests my compromise.
5903	Acceptance tests my trust.
5904	Acceptance tests my support.
5905	Acceptance tests my presence.
5906	Acceptance tests my joy.
5907	Acceptance tests my ability.
5908	Acceptance tests my building.
5909	Acceptance tests my action.
5910	Acceptance tests this release.
5911	Acceptance tests this now.
5912	Acceptance tests this compromise.
5913	Acceptance tests this trust.
5914	Acceptance tests this supported.
5915	Acceptance tests this received.
5916	Acceptance tests this joy.
5917	Acceptance tests this ability.
5918	Acceptance tests this building.
5919	Acceptance tests this action.
5920	Acceptance tests friendship soul.
5921	Acceptance tests friendship now.
5922	Acceptance tests friendship compromise.
5923	Acceptance tests friendship trust.
5924	Acceptance tests friendship supported.
5925	Acceptance tests friendship received.
5926	Acceptance tests friendship joy.
5927	Acceptance tests friendship ability.
5928	Acceptance tests friendship building.
5929	Acceptance tests friendship action.
5930	Acceptance tests trusting self.
5931	Acceptance tests trusting now.
5932	Acceptance tests trusting compromise.
5933	Acceptance tests trust myn.
5934	Acceptance tests trusting supported.

Myn in Numbers

5935	Acceptance tests trusting received.
5936	Acceptance tests trusting joy.
5937	Acceptance tests trusting ability.
5938	Acceptance tests trusting building.
5939	Acceptance tests trusting action.
5940	Acceptance tests supporting releasing.
5941	Acceptance tests supporting now.
5942	Acceptance tests supporting compromise.
5943	Acceptance tests supporting trusting.
5944	Acceptance tests through support.
5945	Acceptance tests supporting received.
5946	Acceptance tests supporting joy.
5947	Acceptance tests supporting ability.
5948	Acceptance tests supporting building.
5949	Acceptance tests supporting action.
5950	Acceptance tests receiving releasing.
5951	Acceptance tests receiving now.
5952	Acceptance tests receiving compromise.
5953	Acceptance tests receiving trust.
5954	Acceptance tests receiving supported.
5955	Acceptance tests receiving received.
5956	Acceptance tests receiving joy.
5957	Acceptance tests receiving ability.
5958	Acceptance tests receiving building.
5959	Acceptance tests receiving action.
5960	Acceptance tests joy releasing.
5961	Acceptance tests joy now.
5962	Acceptance tests joy compromise.
5963	Acceptance tests joy trust.
5964	Acceptance tests joy supported.
5965	Acceptance tests joy received.
5966	Acceptance tests content laugh.
5967	Acceptance tests joy working.
5968	Acceptance tests joy building.

5969   Acceptance tests joy action.
5970   Acceptance tests working release.
5971   Acceptance tests working this.
5972   Acceptance tests working compromise.
5973   Acceptance tests working trust.
5974   Acceptance tests working supported.
5975   Acceptance tests working received.
5976   Acceptance tests working joy.
5977   Acceptance tests working ability.
5978   Acceptance tests working form.
5979   Acceptance tests working action.
5980   Acceptance tests building release.
5981   Acceptance tests building this.
5982   Acceptance tests structured compromise.
5983   Acceptance tests structured trust.
5984   Acceptance tests structure supported.
5985   Acceptance tests structure received.
5986   Acceptance tests structured joy.
5987   Acceptance tests structure ability.
5988   Acceptance tests forming structure.
5989   Acceptance tests structured action.
5990   Acceptance test feels releasing.
5991   Acceptance tests active now.
5992   Acceptance tests active compromise.
5993   Acceptance tests active trust.
5994   Acceptance tests active support.
5995   Acceptance tests active receiving.
5996   Acceptance tests active joy.
5997   Acceptance tests active ability.
5998   Acceptance tests active building.
5999   Acceptance tests moving action.

Myn in Numbers

Joy

6000-6999

When "6" leads the group your source is inviting you to "Smile" as you conduct yourself in the group moment of the trailing numbers. Weigh the points and ponder the outcome.

***

6000	Enjoy my soul self.
6001	Serving my self now.
6002	Serving my self compromise.
6003	Serving my self myn.
6004	Serving my self supported.
6005	Serving my self received.
6006	Serving my self joy.
6007	Serving my self ability.
6008	Serving my self building.
6009	Serving my self action.
6010	Serving self is releasing.
6011	Serving self is now.
6012	Serving self is compromise.

www.templeofgaia.com

6013	Serving self is myn.
6014	Serving self is supported.
6015	Serving self is received.
6016	Serving self is joy.
6017	Serving self is ability.
6018	Serving self is building.
6019	Serving self is action.
6020	Serving self joins releasing.
6021	Serving self joins now.
6022	Serving self joins compromise.
6023	Serving self joins myn.
6024	Serving self joins supported.
6025	Serving self joins received.
6026	Serving self joins joy.
6027	Serving self joins ability.
6028	Serving self joins building.
6029	Serving self joins action.
6030	Serving self trusts releasing.
6031	Serving self trusts now.
6032	Serving self trusts compromise.
6033	Serving self trusts myn.
6034	Serving self trusting support.
6035	Serving self trusts receiving.
6036	Serving self trusts joy.
6037	Serving self trusts ability.
6038	Serving self trusts building.
6039	Serving self trusts action.
6040	Serving self through releasing.
6041	Serving self through now.
6042	Serving self through compromise.
6043	Serving self through myn.
6044	Serving self through support.
6045	Serving self through acceptance.
6046	Serving self through joy.

Myn in Numbers

6047	Serving self through ability.
6048	Serving self through building.
6049	Serving self through action.
6050	Serving self receives releasing.
6051	Serving self receives now.
6052	Serving self receives compromise.
6053	Serving self receives myn.
6054	Serving self receives support.
6055	Serving self receives acceptance.
6056	Serving self receives joy.
6057	Serving self receives ability.
6058	Serving self receives building.
6059	Serving self receives action.
6060	Serving self joy releases.
6061	Serving self joy now.
6062	Serving self joy compromise.
6063	Serving self serves trust.
6064	Serving self serves support.
6065	Serving self serves acceptance.
6066	Serving self serves laughing.
6067	Serving self serves ability.
6068	Serving self serves building.
6069	Serving self serves action.
6070	Serving self enables releasing.
6071	Serving self enables this.
6072	Serving self enables compromise.
6073	Serving self enables myn.
6074	Serving self enables support.
6075	Serving self enables acceptance.
6076	Serving self enables joy.
6077	Serving self enables ability.
6078	Serving self enables building.
6079	Serving self enables action.
6080	Serving self builds release.

6081	Serving self builds now.
6082	Serving self builds compromise.
6083	Serving self builds myn.
6084	Serving self builds supported.
6085	Serving self builds acceptance.
6086	Serving self builds joy.
6087	Serving self builds ability.
6088	Serving self builds form.
6089	Serving self builds action.
6090	Serving self testing release.
6091	Serving self testing now.
6092	Serving self testing compromise.
6093	Serving self testing myn.
6094	Serving self testing support.
6095	Serving self testing acceptance.
6096	Serving self testing joy.
6097	Serving self testing ability.
6098	Serving self testing building.
6099	Serving self testing action.
6100	Content is my release.
6101	Content is my now.
6102	Content is my compromise.
6103	Content is my myn.
6104	Content is my support.
6105	Content is my received.
6106	Content is my joy.
6107	Content is my ability.
6108	Content is my building.
6109	Content is my action.
6110	Laughing is now releasing.
6111	Laughing this is now.
6112	Laughing is now compromise.
6113	Laughing is now myn.
6114	Laughing is now supported.

Myn in Numbers

6115	Laughing is now received.
6116	Laughing is now joy.
6117	Laughing is now ability.
6118	Laughing is now building.
6119	Laughing is now action.
6120	Serve this joining release.
6121	Serve this joining now.
6122	Serve this joining compromise.
6123	Serve this joining myn.
6124	Serve this joining support.
6125	Serve this joining acceptance.
6126	Serve this joining joy.
6127	Serve this joining ability.
6128	Serve this joining building.
6129	Serve this joining action.
6130	Serve this trusting release.
6131	Serve this trusting now.
6132	Serve this trusting compromise.
6133	Serve this trusting myn.
6134	Serve this trusting support.
6135	Serve this trusting acceptance.
6136	Serve this trusting joy.
6137	Serve this trusting ability.
6138	Serve this trusting building.
6139	Serve this trusting action.
6140	Joy is through releasing.
6141	Joy is through now.
6142	Joy is through compromise.
6143	Joy is through myn.
6144	Joy is through support.
6145	Laughing is supporting receiving.
6146	Laughing is supporting joy.
6147	Laughing is supporting ability.
6148	Laughing is supporting building.

www.templeofgaia.com

6149 Laughing is supporting action.
6150 Laughing is receiving releasing.
6151 Laughing is receiving now.
6152 Laughing is receiving compromise.
6153 Laughing is receiving myn.
6154 Laughing is receiving support.
6155 Laughing is receiving acceptance.
6156 Laughing is receiving joy.
6157 Laughing is receiving ability.
6158 Laughing is receiving building.
6159 Laughing is receiving action.
6160 Serving is joy releasing.
6161 Serving is joy now.
6162 Serving is joy compromise.
6163 Serving is joy myn.
6164 Serving is joy supported.
6165 Serving is joy received.
6166 Serving is content laugh.
6167 Serving is joy work.
6168 Serving is joy building.
6169 Serve this joy action.
6170 Serving this works releasing.
6171 Serving this works now.
6172 Serving this works compromise.
6173 Serving this works myn.
6174 Serving this works supported.
6175 Serving this works granted.
6176 Serving this works joy.
6177 Serving this works ability.
6178 Serving this works building.
6179 Serving this works action.
6180 Serving this builds releasing.
6181 Serving this builds now.
6182 Serving this builds compromise.

Myn in Numbers

6183	Serving this builds myn.
6184	Serving this builds supported.
6185	Serving this builds acceptance.
6186	Serving this builds joy.
6187	Serving this builds ability.
6188	Serving this builds form.
6189	Serving this builds action.
6190	Laughing is active releasing.
6191	Laughing is active now.
6192	Laughing is active compromise.
6193	Laughing is active myn.
6194	Laughing is active support.
6195	Laughing is active acceptance.
6196	Laughing is active joy.
6197	Laughing is active ability.
6198	Laughing is active building.
6199	Laughing is active feelings.
6201	Serving joins my now.
6202	Serving joins my compromise.
6203	Serving joins my trust.
6204	Serving joins my support.
6205	Serving joins my acceptance.
6206	Serving joins my joy.
6207	Serving joins my ability.
6208	Serving joins my building.
6209	Serving joins my action.
6210	Serving joins now releasing.
6211	Serving friend is now.
6212	Serving friend is compromise.
6213	Serving friend is myn.
6214	Serving friend is supported.
6215	Serving friend is received.
6216	Serving friend is joy.
6217	Serving friend is ability.

6218	Serving friend is building.
6219	Serving friend is action.
6220	Serving friend joins releasing.
6221	Serving friend joins now.
6222	Serving friend joins compromise.
6223	Serving friend joins trust.
6224	Serving friend joins support.
6225	Serving friend joins received.
6226	Serving friend joins joy.
6227	Serving friend joins ability.
6228	Serving friend joins building.
6229	Serving friend joins action.
6230	Laugh joins trusting release.
6231	Laugh joins trusting now.
6232	Laugh joins trusting compromise.
6233	Laugh joins trusting myn.
6234	Laugh joins trusting supported.
6235	Laugh joins trusting received.
6236	Laugh joins trusting joy.
6237	Laugh joins trusting ability.
6238	Laugh joins trust building.
6239	Laugh joins trusting action.
6240	Serve partnership through release.
6241	Serve partnership through this.
6242	Serve partnership through compromise.
6243	Serve partnership through myn.
6244	Serve partnership through support.
6245	Serve partnership through acceptance.
6246	Serve partnership through joy.
6247	Serve partnership through ability.
6248	Serve partnership through building.
6249	Serve partnership through action.
6250	Joy joins receiving release.
6251	Joy joins receiving now.

Myn in Numbers

6252 Joy joins receiving compromise.
6253 Joy joins presenting trust.
6254 Joy joins receiving support.
6255 Joy joins receiving acceptance.
6256 Joy joins receiving joy.
6257 Joy joins accepting ability.
6258 Joy joins accepting form.
6259 Joy joins receiving action.
6260 Content partner serves releasing.
6261 Content partner serves now.
6262 Content partner serves compromise.
6263 Content partner serves trust.
6264 Content partner serves supportive.
6265 Content partner serves accepting.
6266 Content partner serves joy.
6267 Content partner serves ability.
6268 Content partner serves building.
6269 Content partner serves action.
6270 Content partner works releasing.
6271 Content partner works now.
6272 Content partner works compromise.
6273 Content partner works myn.
6274 Content partner works supported.
6275 Content partner works received.
6276 Content partner works joy.
6277 Content partner works ability.
6278 Content partner works building.
6279 Content partner works action.
6280 Content partnership builds releasing.
6281 Content partnership builds now.
6282 Content partnership builds compromise.
6283 Content partnership builds trust.
6284 Content partnership builds support.
6285 Content partnership builds presence.

6286	Content partnership builds joy.
6287	Content partnership builds ability.
6288	Content partnership builds structure.
6289	Content partnership builds feelings.
6290	Content partnership tests releasing.
6291	Content partnership tests now.
6292	Content partnership tests compromise.
6293	Content partnership tests trust.
6294	Content partnership tests support.
6295	Content partnership tests acceptance.
6296	Content partnership tests joy.
6297	Content partnership tests ability.
6298	Content partnership tests form.
6299	Content partnership tests action.
6300	Serve trust my self.
6301	Serve trust self done.
6302	Serve trust my compromise.
6303	Serve trust my blessing.
6304	Serve trust soul supported.
6305	Serve trust self acceptance.
6306	Serve trust self joy.
6307	Serve trust self ability.
6308	Serve trust self building.
6309	Serve trust self action.
6310	Serving trust is releasing.
6311	Serving trust is now.
6312	Serving trust is compromise.
6313	Serving trust is blessing.
6314	Serving trust is supported.
6315	Serving trust is received.
6316	Serving trust is joy.
6317	Serving trust is ability.
6318	Serving trust is building.
6319	Serving trust is action.

Myn in Numbers

6320	Serving trust joins releasing.
6321	Serving trust joins now.
6322	Serving trust joins compromise.
6323	Serving trust joins trust.
6324	Serving trust joins supported.
6325	Serving trust joins received.
6326	Serving trust joins joy.
6327	Serving trust joins ability.
6328	Serving trust joins building.
6329	Serving trust joins action.
6330	Content trust blessing releasing.
6331	Content trust blessing now.
6332	Content trust blessing compromise.
6333	Content trust blessing prosperity.
6334	Content trust blessing support.
6335	Content trust blessing acceptance.
6336	Content trust blessing joy.
6337	Content trust blessing ability.
6338	Content trust blessing building.
6339	Content trust blessing action.
6340	Serve trust supporting self.
6341	Serve trust supporting now.
6342	Serve trust supporting compromise.
6343	Serve trust supporting myn.
6344	Serve trust supporting means.
6345	Serve trust supporting acceptance.
6346	Serve trust supporting joy.
6347	Serve trust supporting ability.
6348	Serve trust supporting structure.
6349	Serve trust supporting action.
6350	Serve trust accepting release.
6351	Serve trust accepting now.
6352	Serve trust accepting compromise.
6353	Serve trust accepting myn.

6354	Serve trust accepting support.
6355	Serve trust receiving acceptance.
6356	Serve trust accepting joy.
6357	Serve trust accepting ability.
6358	Serve trust accepting form.
6359	Serve trust accepting action.
6360	Serve trust laugh releasing.
6361	Serve trust laugh now.
6362	Serve trust laugh joining.
6363	Serve trust laugh trusting.
6364	Serve trust laugh supporting.
6365	Serve trust laugh accepting.
6366	Serve trust laugh laugh.
6367	Serve trust laugh able.
6368	Serve trust laugh building.
6369	Serve trust laugh moving.
6370	Serve trust working releasing.
6371	Serve trust working now.
6372	Serve trust working compromise.
6373	Serve trust working blessing.
6374	Serve trust working supported.
6375	Serve trust working accepted.
6376	Serve trust working joy.
6377	Serve trust working ability.
6378	Serve trust work building.
6379	Serve trust working action.
6380	Serve trust building release.
6381	Serve trust building now.
6382	Serve trust building compromise.
6383	Serve trust building blessing.
6384	Serve trust building support.
6385	Serve trust building acceptance.
6386	Serve trust building joy.
6387	Serve trust building ability.

Myn in Numbers

6388	Serve trust building structure.
6389	Serve trust building action.
6390	Serving trust moves releasing.
6391	Serving trust moves now.
6392	Serving trust moves compromise.
6393	Serving trust moves blessing.
6394	Serving trust moves supported.
6395	Serving trust moves acceptance.
6396	Serving trust moves joy.
6397	Serving trust moves ability.
6398	Serving trust moves building.
6399	Serving trust moves feelings.
6400	Laughing means my soul.
6401	Laughing means me done.
6402	Laughing means my compromise.
6403	Laughing means my trust.
6404	Laughing means my support.
6405	Laughing means my receiving.
6406	Laughing means my joy.
6407	Laughing means my ability.
6408	Laughing means my building.
6409	Laughing means my feelings.
6410	Laugh supporting this soul.
6411	Laugh supporting this now.
6412	Laugh supporting this compromise.
6413	Laugh supporting this blessing.
6414	Laugh supporting this means.
6415	Laugh supporting this acceptance.
6416	Laugh supporting this joy.
6417	Laugh supporting this ability.
6418	Laugh supporting this building.
6419	Laugh supporting this action.
6420	Laugh through joining release.
6421	Laugh through joining now.

6422 Laugh through joining compromise.
6423 Laugh through joining trust.
6424 Laugh through joining supported.
6425 Laugh through joining received.
6426 Laugh through joining joy.
6427 Laugh through joining ability.
6428 Laugh through joining building.
6429 Laugh through joining action.
6430 Content through trusting release.
6431 Content through trusting now.
6432 Content through trusting compromise.
6433 Content through trusting myn.
6434 Content through trusting supported.
6435 Content through trusting acceptance.
6436 Content through trusting joy.
6437 Content through trusting ability.
6438 Content through trusting building.
6439 Content through trusting action.
6440 Content through supporting release.
6441 Content through supporting this.
6442 Content through supporting compromise.
6443 Content through supporting trust.
6444 Content through supporting means.
6445 Content through supporting acceptance.
6446 Content through supporting joy.
6447 Content through supporting ability.
6448 Content through supporting building.
6449 Content through supporting action.
6450 Content through accepting release.
6451 Content through accepting now.
6452 Content through accepting compromise.
6453 Content through accepting trust.
6454 Content through accepting supported.
6455 Content through accepting granted.

Myn in Numbers

6456	Content through accepting joy.
6457	Content through accepting ability.
6458	Content through accepting building.
6459	Content through accepting action.
6460	Content through joy releasing.
6461	Content through joy now.
6462	Content through joy compromise.
6463	Content through enjoying trust.
6464	Content through joy supported.
6465	Content through joy received.
6466	Content through content laugh.
6467	Content through joy ability.
6468	Content through joy building.
6469	Content through joy action.
6470	Content through ability releasing.
6471	Content through ability now.
6472	Content through ability compromise.
6473	Content through ability trust.
6474	Content through ability supported.
6475	Content through ability received.
6476	Content through able laughing.
6477	Content through work ability.
6478	Content through ability building.
6479	Content through working action.
6480	Content through building release.
6481	Content through building now.
6482	Content through building compromise.
6483	Content through building myn.
6484	Content through building supported.
6485	Content through building acceptance.
6486	Content through building joy.
6487	Content through building ability.
6488	Content through building structure.
6489	Content through building action.

6490 Content through action releasing.
6491 Content through action now.
6492 Content through action compromise.
6493 Content through action myn.
6494 Content through action supported.
6495 Content through action received.
6496 Content through action joy.
6497 Content through action ability.
6498 Content through action building.
6499 Content through moving action.
6500 Content accepting soul releases.
6501 Content accepting my now.
6502 Content accepting my compromise.
6503 Content accepting my myn.
6504 Content accepting my support.
6505 Content accepting my received.
6506 Content accepting my joy.
6507 Content accepting my ability.
6508 Content accepting my building.
6509 Content accepting my action.
6510 Content acceptance is releasing.
6511 Content accepting is now.
6512 Content acceptance is compromise.
6513 Content acceptance is myn.
6514 Content acceptance is supported.
6515 Content acceptance is received.
6516 Content acceptance is joy.
6517 Content acceptance is ability.
6518 Content acceptance is building.
6519 Content acceptance is action.
6520 Content acceptance joins releasing.
6521 Content acceptance joins now.
6522 Content acceptance joins compromise.
6523 Content acceptance joins myn.

Myn in Numbers

6524	Content acceptance joins supported.
6525	Content acceptance joins received.
6526	Content acceptance joins joy.
6527	Content acceptance joins ability.
6528	Content acceptance joins building.
6529	Content acceptance joins action.
6530	Content accepting trust releasing.
6531	Content accepting trust now.
6532	Content accepting trust compromise.
6533	Content accepting trusting myn.
6534	Content accepting trust supported.
6535	Content accepting trust received.
6536	Content accepting trust joy.
6537	Content accepting trust ability.
6538	Content accepting trust building.
6539	Content accepting trust action.
6540	Content acceptance means releasing.
6541	Content acceptance means now.
6542	Content acceptance means compromise.
6543	Content acceptance means myn.
6544	Content acceptance means support.
6545	Content acceptance means received.
6546	Content acceptance means joy.
6547	Content acceptance means ability.
6548	Content acceptance means building.
6549	Content acceptance means action.
6550	Content acceptance receives releasing.
6551	Content acceptance received now.
6552	Content acceptance receives compromise.
6553	Content acceptance receives myn.
6554	Content acceptance receives supported.
6555	Content acceptance receives accepted.
6556	Content acceptance receives joy.
6557	Content acceptance receives ability.

6558   Content acceptance receives building.
6559   Content acceptance receives action.
6560   Content accepting joy releasing.
6561   Content accepting joy now.
6562   Content accepting joy compromise.
6563   Content accepting joy myn.
6564   Content accepting joy supported.
6565   Content accepting joy received.
6566   Content accepting content laugh.
6567   Content accepting joy ability.
6568   Content accepting joy building.
6569   Content accepting joy action.
6570   Content accepting ability releasing.
6571   Content accepting ability now.
6572   Content accepting ability compromise.
6573   Content accepting ability myn.
6574   Content accepting ability supported.
6575   Content accepting ability received.
6576   Content accepting ability joy.
6577   Content accepting working ability.
6578   Content accepting ability building.
6579   Content accepting ability action.
6580   Content accepting building release.
6581   Content acceptance building now.
6582   Content accepting builds compromise.
6583   Content accepting builds trust.
6584   Content accepting builds support.
6585   Content accepting builds received.
6586   Content accepting builds joy.
6587   Content accepting builds ability.
6588   Content accepting builds structure.
6589   Content accepting builds action.
6590   Joyful acceptance action releases.
6591   Joyful acceptance action now.

Myn in Numbers

6592	Joyful acceptance action joining.
6593	Joyful acceptance action trust.
6594	Joyful acceptance action support.
6595	Joyful acceptance action received.
6596	Joyful acceptance action joy.
6597	Joyful acceptance action able.
6598	Joyful acceptance action builds.
6599	Joy receives moving action.
6600	Laughing laughing soul releases.
6601	Laughing laughing my now.
6602	Laughing laughing my compromise.
6603	Laughing laughing my trust.
6604	Laughing laughing my support.
6605	Laughing laughing my receiving.
6606	Laughing laughing my joy.
6607	Laughing laughing my ability.
6608	Laughing laughing my building.
6609	Laughing laughing my action.
6610	Laughing laughing now releasing.
6611	Laughing laughing is now.
6612	Laughing laughing is friendship.
6613	Laughing laughing is trust.
6614	Laughing laughing is supported.
6615	Laughing laughing is receiving.
6616	Laughing laughing is joy.
6617	Laughing laughing is ability.
6618	Laughing laughing is building.
6619	Laughing laughing is action.
6620	Laughing laughing compromise releases.
6621	Laughing laughing compromise now.
6622	Laughing laughing friendship compromise.
6623	Laughing laughing joins trust.
6624	Laughing laughing compromise supported.
6625	Laughing laughing compromise received.

Kevin J. Baird

6626 Laughing laughing compromise joy.
6627 Laughing laughing compromise ability.
6628 Laughing laughing compromise building.
6629 Laughing laughing compromise action.
6630 Laughing laughing trust releasing.
6631 Laughing laughing trust now.
6632 Laughing laughing trust compromise.
6633 Laughing laughing trust trusting.
6634 Laughing laughing trust supported.
6635 Laughing laughing trust received.
6636 Laughing laughing trust joy.
6637 Laughing laughing trust ability.
6638 Laughing laughing trust building.
6639 Laughing laughing trust action.
6640 Laughing laughing through releasing.
6641 Laughing laughing through now.
6642 Laughing laughing through compromise.
6643 Laughing laughing through trust.
6644 Laughing laughing through support.
6645 Laughing laughing through acceptance.
6646 Laughing laughing through joy.
6647 Laughing laughing through ability.
6648 Laughing laughing through building.
6649 Laughing laughing through action.
6650 Laughing laughing receive releasing.
6651 Laughing laughing receive now.
6652 Laughing laughing receive compromise.
6653 Laughing laughing receive trust.
6654 Laughing laughing receive supported.
6655 Laughing laughing receives accepting.
6656 Laughing laughing receive joy.
6657 Laughing laughing receive ability.
6658 Laughing laughing receive building.
6659 Laughing laughing receive action.

Myn in Numbers

6660	Laughing laughing joy releasing.
6661	Laughing laughing serves now.
6662	Laughing laughing serves compromise.
6663	Laughing laughing serves myn.
6664	Laughing laughing serves supported.
6665	Laughing laughing serves received.
6666	Laugh laugh laugh laugh.
6667	Laughing laughing serves ability.
6668	Laughing laughing serves building.
6669	Laughing laughing serves action.
6670	Laughing laughing ability release.
6671	Laughing laughing ability now.
6672	Laughing laughing works friendship.
6673	Laughing laughing working trust.
6674	Laughing laughing ability supported.
6675	Laughing laughing ability received.
6676	Laughing laughing enables joy.
6677	Laughing laughing working ability.
6678	Laughing laughing ability building.
6679	Laughing laughing works active.
6680	Laughing laughing building release.
6681	Laughing laughing building now.
6682	Laughing laughing building friendship.
6683	Laughing laughing building myn.
6684	Laughing laughing builds support.
6685	Laughing laughing building acceptance.
6686	Laughing laughing builds joy.
6687	Laughing laughing building ability.
6688	Laughing laughing building structure.
6689	Laughing laughing building action.
6690	Laughing laughing activates release.
6691	Laughing laughing testing now.
6692	Laughing laughing testing friendship.
6693	Laughing laughing testing trust.

6694　Laughing laughing testing support.
6695　Laughing laughing testing received.
6696　Laughing laughing testing joy.
6697　Laughing laughing testing ability.
6698　Laughing laughing testing building.
6699　Laughing laughing testing feelings.
6700　Serves working my release.
6701　Serves working my now.
6702　Serves working my compromise.
6703　Serves working my trust.
6704　Serves working my support.
6705　Serves working my acceptance.
6706　Serves working my joy.
6707　Serves working my ability.
6708　Serves working my building.
6709　Serves working my feelings.
6710　Serves working this soul.
6711　Serves working this now.
6712　Serves working this compromise.
6713　Serves working this trust.
6714　Serves working this supported.
6715　Serves working this acceptance.
6716　Serves working this content.
6717　Serves working this ability.
6718　Serves working this building.
6719　Serves working this action.
6720　Serves working friend's soul.
6721　Serves working companionship now.
6722　Serves working companionship compromise.
6723　Serves working companionship trust.
6724　Serves working companionship supported.
6725　Serves working companionship received.
6726　Serves working companionship joy.
6727　Serves working companionship ability.

Myn in Numbers

6728	Serves working companionship building.
6729	Serves working companionship action.
6730	Serves working trusting self.
6731	Serves working trusting this.
6732	Serves working trusting compromise.
6733	Serves working trust prosperity.
6734	Serves working trust supported.
6735	Serves working trust received.
6736	Serves working trusting joy.
6737	Serves working trusting ability.
6738	Serves working trusting building.
6739	Serves working trusting action.
6740	Serves working supported releasing.
6741	Serves working supported now.
6742	Serves working supported compromise.
6743	Serves working supported myn.
6744	Serves working through support.
6745	Serves working supported acceptance.
6746	Serves working supported joy.
6747	Serves working supported ability.
6748	Serves working supported building.
6749	Serves working supportive feelings.
6750	Serves working accepting self.
6751	Serves working accepting this.
6752	Serves working acceptance compromise.
6753	Serves working accepting prosperity.
6754	Serves working acceptance support.
6755	Serves working acceptance receiving.
6756	Serves working acceptance content.
6757	Serves working acceptance ability.
6758	Serves working acceptance building.
6759	Serves working acceptance feelings.
6760	Serves working joy release.
6761	Serves working joy now.

6762 Serves working joy compromise.
6763 Serves working joy trust.
6764 Serves working joy supported.
6765 Serves working joy received.
6766 Serves working content laugh.
6767 Serves working joy ability.
6768 Serves working joy building.
6769 Serves working joy action.
6770 Serves working capable releasing.
6771 Serves working capable now.
6772 Serves working capable compromise.
6773 Serves working capable myn.
6774 Serves working capable supported.
6775 Serves working capable received.
6776 Serves working capable joy.
6777 Serves working capable ability.
6778 Serves working capable structure.
6779 Serves working capable action.
6780 Serves working building release.
6781 Serves working building now.
6782 Serves working building compromise.
6783 Serves working building trust.
6784 Serves working building support.
6785 Serves working building acceptance.
6786 Serves working building joy.
6787 Serves working building ability.
6788 Serves working building structure.
6789 Serves working building action.
6790 Serves working active release.
6791 Serves working action now.
6792 Serves working active compromise.
6793 Serves working active trust.
6794 Serves working active support.
6795 Serves working active acceptance.

Myn in Numbers

6796	Serves working active joy.
6797	Serves working active ability.
6798	Serves working active building.
6799	Serves working moving feelings.
6800	Serves building my release.
6801	Serves building my now.
6802	Serves building my compromise.
6803	Serves building my trust.
6804	Serves building my support.
6805	Serves building my acceptance.
6806	Serves building my joy.
6807	Serves building my ability.
6808	Serves building my building.
6809	Serves building my feelings.
6810	Serves building this release.
6811	Serves building this now.
6812	Serves building this compromise.
6813	Serves building this myn.
6814	Serves building this supported.
6815	Serves building this received.
6816	Serves building this joy.
6817	Serves building this ability.
6818	Serves building this form.
6819	Serves building this action.
6820	Serves building joining release.
6821	Serves building joining now.
6822	Serves building friendship compromise.
6823	Serves building joining trust.
6824	Serves building joining support.
6825	Serves building joining acceptance.
6826	Serves building joining joy.
6827	Serves building joining ability.
6828	Serves building joining building.
6829	Serves building joining action.

Kevin J. Baird

6830   Serves building trusting release.
6831   Serves building trust now.
6832   Serves building trusting compromise.
6833   Serves building trusting blessing.
6834   Serves building trusting support.
6835   Serves building trusting acceptance.
6836   Serves building trusting joy.
6837   Serves building trusting ability.
6838   Serves building trusting building.
6839   Serves building trusting action.
6840   Serves building through releasing.
6841   Serves building support now.
6842   Serves building support compromise.
6843   Serves building supporting trust.
6844   Serves building means support.
6845   Serves building supporting acceptance.
6846   Serves building supporting joy.
6847   Serves building supporting ability.
6848   Serves building supporting structure.
6849   Serves building support action.
6850   Serves building acceptance releasing.
6851   Serves building acceptance now.
6852   Serves building acceptance compromise.
6853   Serves building acceptance trust.
6854   Serves building acceptance supported.
6855   Serves building acceptance received.
6856   Serves building acceptance joy.
6857   Serves building acceptance ability.
6858   Serves building acceptance storage.
6859   Serves building acceptance action.
6860   Serves building joy releasing.
6861   Serves building joy now.
6862   Serves building joy compromise.
6863   Serves building joy trust.

Myn in Numbers

6864	Serves building joy support.
6865	Serves building joy acceptance.
6866	Serves building content laugh.
6867	Serves building joy ability.
6868	Serves building joy building.
6869	Serves building joy action.
6870	Serves building able release.
6871	Serves building able now.
6872	Serves building able compromise.
6873	Serves building able trust.
6874	Serves building able supported.
6875	Serves building able received.
6876	Serves building able joy.
6877	Serves building working ability.
6878	Serves building able building.
6879	Serves building able action.
6880	Serves building building release.
6881	Serves building structure now.
6882	Serves building structured compromise.
6883	Serves building building trust.
6884	Serves building building support.
6885	Serves building building acceptance.
6886	Serves building building joy.
6887	Serves building building able.
6888	Serves building building structure.
6889	Serves building building feelings.
6890	Serves building active release.
6891	Serves building activity done.
6892	Serves building active compromise.
6893	Serves building active trust.
6894	Serves building active support.
6895	Serves building active acceptance.
6896	Serves building active joy.
6897	Serves building active ability.

6898 Serves building active building.
6899 Serves building testing feelings.
6900 Joy action soul releases.
6901 Joy action releases now.
6902 Joy action releases compromise.
6903 Joy action releases trusting.
6904 Joy action releases support.
6905 Joy action releases acceptance.
6906 Joy action releases joy.
6907 Joy action releases capable.
6908 Joy action release builds.
6909 Joy action releases feelings.
6910 Joy action is releasing.
6911 Joy action is now.
6912 Joy action is friendship.
6913 Joy action is blessing.
6914 Joy action is supported.
6915 Joy action now received.
6916 Joy active is joy.
6917 Joy active is ability.
6918 Joy action is building.
6919 Joy action now feels.
6920 Joy action friend releases.
6921 Joy action friendship now.
6922 Joy action companions friendship.
6923 Joy action companions trust.
6924 Joy action companions supported.
6925 Joy action companions received.
6926 Joy action companions joy.
6927 Joy action companions ability.
6928 Joy action companions building.
6929 Joy action companions action.
6930 Joy action myn releasing.
6931 Joy action blesses now.

Myn in Numbers

6932	Joy action blesses compromise.
6933	Joy action trust blessing.
6934	Joy action blesses supported.
6935	Joy action blesses received.
6936	Joy action blesses joy.
6937	Joy action blesses ability.
6938	Joy action blesses building.
6939	Joy action blesses action.
6940	Joy action through release.
6941	Joy action support now.
6942	Joy action through compromise.
6943	Joy action through trust.
6944	Joy action through support.
6945	Joy action through acceptance.
6946	Joy action through joy.
6947	Joy action through ability.
6948	Joy action supports building.
6949	Joy action through feelings.
6950	Joy action receive release.
6951	Joy action receive now.
6952	Joy action receive friendship.
6953	Joy action receive trust.
6954	Joy action receive support.
6955	Joy action receive receive.
6956	Joy action receive joy.
6957	Joy action acceptance working.
6958	Joy action acceptance building.
6959	Joy action acceptance action.
6960	Joy active joy releasing.
6961	Joy action joy now.
6962	Joy action joy compromise.
6963	Joy action joy myn.
6964	Joy action joy supported.
6965	Joy action joy received.

6966	Joy action joy joy.
6967	Joy action joy working.
6968	Joy action joy building.
6969	Joy action enjoy feelings.
6970	Joy action working releasing.
6971	Joy action working now.
6972	Joy action working compromise.
6973	Joy action working trust.
6974	Joy action working support.
6975	Joy action working acceptance.
6976	Joy action working joy.
6977	Joy action working ability.
6978	Joy action works building.
6979	Joy action works active.
6980	Joy action building release.
6981	Joy action building now.
6982	Joy action building compromise.
6983	Joy action building trusted.
6984	Joy action building support.
6985	Joy action building acceptance.
6986	Joy action building joy.
6987	Joy action builds ability.
6988	Joy action builds structure.
6989	Joy action builds feelings.
6990	Joy action active releasing.
6991	Joy action feelings now.
6992	Joy action feelings joining.
6993	Joy action feelings trusted.
6994	Joy action feelings supported.
6995	Joy action feelings received.
6996	Joy action feelings serve.
6997	Joy action feelings able.
6998	Joy action feelings building.
6999	Joy action testing feelings.

Myn in Numbers

Work

7000-7999

When "7" leads the group your source is inviting you to "Work-it," as you conduct yourself in the group moment of the trailing numbers. Weigh the points and ponder the outcome.

***

7000	Work my soul self.
7001	Work my self now.
7002	Work my self compromise.
7003	Work my self trust.
7004	Work my self support.
7005	Work my self acceptance.
7006	Work my self joy.
7007	Work my self ability.
7008	Work my self building.
7009	Work my self action.
7010	Working self is releasing.

www.templeofgaia.com

Kevin J. Baird

7011	Working release is now.
7012	Working release is compromise.
7013	Working release is trust.
7014	Working release is supported.
7015	Working release is received.
7016	Working release is joy.
7017	Working release is ability.
7018	Working release is building.
7019	Working release is action.
7020	Working release joins releasing.
7021	Working release joins now.
7022	Working release friendship joins.
7023	Working release joins trust.
7024	Working release joins supported.
7025	Working release joins received.
7026	Working release joins joy.
7027	Working release joins ability.
7028	Working release joins building.
7029	Working release joins action.
7030	Working release trusting self.
7031	Working release trusting now.
7032	Working release trusting compromise.
7033	Working release trust blessing.
7034	Working release trusting supported.
7035	Working release trusting received.
7036	Working release trusting joy.
7037	Working release trusting ability.
7038	Working release trusting building.
7039	Working release trusting action.
7040	Working release supports releasing.
7041	Working release supports now.
7042	Working release supports compromise.
7043	Working release supports myn.
7044	Working release supports support.

Myn in Numbers

7045	Working release supports acceptance.
7046	Working release supports joy.
7047	Working release supports ability.
7048	Working release supports building.
7049	Working release supports action.
7050	Working release accept releasing.
7051	Working release accept now.
7052	Working release accept compromise.
7053	Working release accept trusting.
7054	Working release accept supported.
7055	Working release accept granted.
7056	Working release accept joy.
7057	Working release accept ability.
7058	Working release accept building.
7059	Working release accept action.
7060	Working release laugh releasing.
7061	Working release laugh now.
7062	Working release laugh joining.
7063	Working release laugh trusting.
7064	Working release laugh supporting.
7065	Working release laugh accepting.
7066	Working release laugh laugh.
7067	Working release laugh able.
7068	Working release joy builds.
7069	Working release joy action.
7070	Working release works release.
7071	Working release enables now.
7072	Working release enables compromise.
7073	Working release enables trust.
7074	Working release enables support.
7075	Working release enables received.
7076	Working release enables joy.
7077	Working release works ability.
7078	Working release enables building.

7079	Working release enables action.
7080	Working release builds soul.
7081	Working release builds now.
7082	Working release builds compromise.
7083	Working release builds trust.
7084	Working release builds support.
7085	Working release builds acceptance.
7086	Working release builds joy.
7087	Working release builds ability.
7088	Working release builds structure.
7089	Working release builds feelings.
7090	Working release tests releasing.
7091	Working release tests now.
7092	Working release tests compromise.
7093	Working release tests trust.
7094	Working release tests support.
7095	Working release tests acceptance.
7096	Working release tests joy.
7097	Working release tests ability.
7098	Working release tests building.
7099	Working release tests feelings.
7100	Working this self releasing.
7101	Working this my now.
7102	Working this my compromise.
7103	Working this my trust.
7104	Working this my support.
7105	Working this my acceptance.
7106	Working this my joy.
7107	Working this my ability.
7108	Working this my building.
7109	Working this my action.
7110	Working this now releases.
7111	Working this now done.
7112	Working this now compromise.

Myn in Numbers

7113	Working this now trusting.
7114	Working this now supported.
7115	Working this now accepted.
7116	Working this now joy.
7117	Working this now able.
7118	Working this now builds.
7119	Working this is action.
7120	Working this joins releasing.
7121	Working this joins now.
7122	Working this friendship joins.
7123	Working this joins myn.
7124	Working this joins supported.
7125	Working this joins received.
7126	Working this joins joy.
7127	Working this joins ability.
7128	Working this joins building.
7129	Working this joins action.
7130	Working this trust releasing.
7131	Working this trust now.
7132	Working this trust compromise.
7133	Working this trust myn.
7134	Working this trust supported.
7135	Working this trust received.
7136	Working this trust joy.
7137	Working this trust ability.
7138	Working this trust building.
7139	Working this trust action.
7140	Working this supports releasing.
7141	Working this supports now.
7142	Working this supports compromise.
7143	Working this supports myn.
7144	Working this means support.
7145	Working this supports acceptance.
7146	Working this supports joy.

7147	Working this supports ability.
7148	Working this supports building.
7149	Working this supports action.
7150	Working this receive releasing.
7151	Working this receive now.
7152	Working this receive compromise.
7153	Working this receive trust.
7154	Working this receive supported.
7155	Working this receive acceptance.
7156	Working this receive joy.
7157	Working this receive ability.
7158	Working this receive building.
7159	Working this receive action.
7160	Working this serves releasing.
7161	Working this serves now.
7162	Working this serves compromise.
7163	Working this serves myn.
7164	Working this serves supported.
7165	Working this serves received.
7166	Working this laugh content.
7167	Working this serves ability.
7168	Working this serves building.
7169	Working this serves action.
7170	Able now work releasing.
7171	Work is working now.
7172	Able now work compromise.
7173	Able now work trust.
7174	Able now work supported.
7175	Able now work acceptance.
7176	Able now work serving.
7177	Able now work ability.
7178	Able now work building.
7179	Able now work feelings.
7180	Working this builds releasing.

Myn in Numbers

7181	Working this builds now.
7182	Working this builds compromise.
7183	Working this builds myn.
7184	Working this builds supported.
7185	Working this builds received.
7186	Working this builds joy.
7187	Working this builds ability.
7188	Working this builds structure.
7189	Working this builds action.
7190	Working this tests releasing.
7191	Working this tests done.
7192	Working this tests compromise.
7193	Working this tests trust.
7194	Working this tests support.
7195	Working this tests acceptance.
7196	Working this tests joy.
7197	Working this tests ability.
7198	Working this tests building.
7199	Working this moves action.
7200	Work joins self releases.
7201	Work joins release now.
7202	Work joins my compromise.
7203	Work joins my trust.
7204	Work joins my support.
7205	Work joins my acceptance.
7206	Work joins my joy.
7207	Work joins my ability.
7208	Work joins my building.
7209	Work joins my action.
7210	Work joins now releasing.
7211	Work joins this now.
7212	Work joins this compromise.
7213	Work joins this trusted.
7214	Work joins now supported.

7215   Work joins now received.
7216   Work joins this joy.
7217   Work joins this ability.
7218   Work joins this building.
7219   Work joins this action.
7220   Work joins friend releases.
7221   Work joins friend now.
7222   Work joins friendship compromise.
7223   Work joins friend myn.
7224   Work joins friend supported.
7225   Work joins friend received.
7226   Work joins friend joy.
7227   Work joins friend ability.
7228   Work joins friend builds.
7229   Work joins friend action.
7230   Work joins trust releasing.
7231   Work joins trust now.
7232   Work joins trust compromise.
7233   Work joins trust prosperity.
7234   Work joins trust supported.
7235   Work joins trust received.
7236   Work joins trust joy.
7237   Work joins trust ability.
7238   Work joins trust builds.
7239   Work joins trust action.
7240   Work joins through releasing.
7241   Work joins through now.
7242   Work joins through compromise.
7243   Work joins through myn.
7244   Work joins through support.
7245   Work joins through acceptance.
7246   Work joins through joy.
7247   Work joins through ability.
7248   Work joins through building.

Myn in Numbers

7249 Work joins through action.
7250 Work joins accepting releasing.
7251 Work joins accept this.
7252 Work joins accepting compromise.
7253 Work joins accepting trust.
7254 Work joins accepting support.
7255 Work joins accepting received.
7256 Work joins accepting joy.
7257 Work joins accepting ability.
7258 Work joins accepting building.
7259 Work joins accepting action.
7260 Work joins joy release.
7261 Work joins joy now.
7262 Work joins joy compromise.
7263 Work joins joy trust.
7264 Work joins joy supported.
7265 Work joins joy acceptance.
7266 Work joins laugh content.
7267 Work joins joy ability.
7268 Work joins joy builds.
7269 Work joins joy action.
7270 Work joins capable release.
7271 Work joins capable now.
7272 Work joins capable compromise.
7273 Work joins capable trust.
7274 Work joins capable supported.
7275 Work joins capable acceptance.
7276 Work joins capable joy.
7277 Work joins working ability.
7278 Work joins capable building.
7279 Work joins capable action.
7280 Work joins building release.
7281 Work joins building now.
7282 Work joins building compromise.

7283	Work joins building trust.
7284	Work joins building support.
7285	Work joins building acceptance.
7286	Work joins building joy.
7287	Work joins building ability.
7288	Work joins building structure.
7289	Work joins building action.
7290	Work joins testing releasing.
7291	Work joins testing now.
7292	Work joins testing compromise.
7293	Work joins testing trust.
7294	Work joins testing supported.
7295	Work joins testing received.
7296	Work joins testing joy.
7297	Work joins testing ability.
7298	Work joins testing building.
7299	Work joins testing action.
7300	Work trusting my release.
7301	Work trusting my now.
7302	Work trusting my compromise.
7303	Work trusting my myn.
7304	Work trusting my supported.
7305	Work trusting my received.
7306	Work trusting my joy.
7307	Work trusting my ability.
7308	Work trusting my building.
7309	Work trusting my action.
7310	Work trusting this releasing.
7311	Work trusting this now.
7312	Work trusting this compromise.
7313	Work trusting this myn.
7314	Work trusting this supported.
7315	Work trusting this received.
7316	Work trusting this joy.

Myn in Numbers

7317	Work trusting this ability.
7318	Work trusting this building.
7319	Work trusting this action.
7320	Work trusting compromise releasing.
7321	Work trusting compromise now.
7322	Work trusting friendship compromise.
7323	Work trusting compromise myn.
7324	Work trusting compromise supported.
7325	Work trusting compromise received.
7326	Work trusting compromise joy.
7327	Work trusting compromise ability.
7328	Work trusting compromise building.
7329	Work trusting compromise action.
7330	Work trusting blessings releasing.
7331	Work trusting blessings now.
7332	Work trusting blessings compromise.
7333	Work trusting trust blessings.
7334	Work trusting blessings supported.
7335	Work trusting blessings received.
7336	Work trusting blessings joy.
7337	Work trusting blessings ability.
7338	Work trusting blessings building.
7339	Work trusting blessings action.
7340	Work trusting support releasing.
7341	Work trusting support now.
7342	Work trusting support compromise.
7343	Work trusting support trust.
7344	Work trusting through support.
7345	Work trusting support acceptance.
7346	Work trusting support joy.
7347	Work trusting support ability.
7348	Work trusting support building.
7349	Work trusting support action.
7350	Work trusting grant releasing.

7351   Work trusting grant now.
7352   Work trusting grant compromise.
7353   Work trusting grant trust.
7354   Work trusting grant support.
7355   Work trusting grant acceptance.
7356   Work trusting grant joy.
7357   Work trusting grant ability.
7358   Work trusting grant building.
7359   Work trusting grant move.
7360   Work trusting joy releasing.
7361   Work trusting joy now.
7362   Work trusting joy compromise.
7363   Work trusting joy blessing.
7364   Work trusting joy supported.
7365   Work trusting joy accepted.
7366   Work trusting content laugh.
7367   Work trusting joy ability.
7368   Work trusting joy builds.
7369   Work trusting joy action.
7370   Work trusting ability releasing.
7371   Work trusting ability now.
7372   Work trusting ability joins.
7373   Work trusting ability blesses.
7374   Work trusting ability supported.
7375   Work trusting ability accepted.
7376   Work trusting ability serves.
7377   Work trusting capable ability.
7378   Work trusting ability builds.
7379   Work trusting able action.
7380   Work trusting builds release.
7381   Work trusting build now.
7382   Work trusting builds compromise.
7383   Work trusting builds prosperity.
7384   Work trusting builds support.

Myn in Numbers

7385	Work trusting builds acceptance.
7386	Work trusting builds joy.
7387	Work trusting builds ability.
7388	Work trusting builds structure.
7389	Work trusting builds action.
7390	Work trusting action releases.
7391	Work trusting action now.
7392	Work trusting active compromise.
7393	Work trusting active blessing.
7394	Work trusting action support.
7395	Work trusting action accepted.
7396	Work trusting action joy.
7397	Work trusting action ability.
7398	Work trusting action builds.
7399	Work trusting feelings move.
7400	Work conveys my soul.
7401	Work conveys my now.
7402	Work conveys my compromise.
7403	Work conveys my trust.
7404	Work conveys my support.
7405	Work conveys my receiving.
7406	Work conveys my joy.
7407	Work conveys my ability.
7408	Work conveys my building.
7409	Work conveys my action.
7410	Work conveys this soul.
7411	Work conveys this now.
7412	Work conveys this compromise.
7413	Work conveys this blessing.
7414	Work conveys this conduit.
7415	Work conveys this received.
7416	Work conveys this joy.
7417	Work conveys this ability.
7418	Work conveys this building.

www.templeofgaia.com

7419 Work conveys this action.
7420 Work conveys compromise release.
7421 Work conveys compromise now.
7422 Work conveys friendship compromise.
7423 Work conveys compromise blessing.
7424 Work conveys compromise support.
7425 Work conveys compromise accepted.
7426 Work conveys compromise joy.
7427 Work conveys compromise ability.
7428 Work conveys compromise building.
7429 Work conveys compromise action.
7430 Work conveys prosperity releasing.
7431 Work conveys prosperity now.
7432 Work conveys prosperity compromise.
7433 Work conveys trusting blessing.
7434 Work conveys prosperity supported.
7435 Work conveys prosperity received.
7436 Work conveys prosperity joy.
7437 Work conveys prosperity ability.
7438 Work conveys prosperity building.
7439 Work conveys prosperity action.
7440 Work conveys through releasing.
7441 Work conveys through now.
7442 Work conveys through compromise.
7443 Work conveys through trust.
7444 Work conveys through support.
7445 Work conveys through acceptance.
7446 Work conveys through joy.
7447 Work conveys through ability.
7448 Work conveys through building.
7449 Work conveys through action.
7450 Work conveys granting releasing.
7451 Work conveys granting now.
7452 Work conveys granting compromise.

Myn in Numbers

7453	Work conveys granting myn.
7454	Work conveys granting supported.
7455	Work conveys granting received.
7456	Work conveys granting joy.
7457	Work conveys granting ability.
7458	Work conveys granting building.
7459	Work conveys granting action.
7460	Work conveys serving release.
7461	Work conveys serving now.
7462	Work conveys serving compromise.
7463	Work conveys serving trust.
7464	Work conveys serving supported.
7465	Work conveys serving acceptance.
7466	Work conveys content laugh.
7467	Work conveys serving ability.
7468	Work conveys serving structure.
7469	Work conveys serving action.
7470	Work conveys able releasing.
7471	Work conveys ability now.
7472	Work conveys able compromise.
7473	Work conveys able trust.
7474	Work conveys able support.
7475	Work conveys able acceptance.
7476	Work conveys able joy.
7477	Work conveys working ability.
7478	Work conveys able building.
7479	Work conveys able action.
7480	Work conveys building releasing.
7481	Work conveys building now.
7482	Work conveys building compromise.
7483	Work conveys building myn.
7484	Work conveys building supported.
7485	Work conveys building received.
7486	Work conveys building joy.

7487	Work conveys building ability.
7488	Work conveys building structure.
7489	Work conveys building action.
7490	Work conveys action releasing.
7491	Work conveys action now.
7492	Work conveys action compromise.
7493	Work conveys action myn.
7494	Work conveys action supported.
7495	Work conveys action received.
7496	Work conveys action joy.
7497	Work conveys action ability.
7498	Work conveys action building.
7499	Work conveys moving action.
7500	Work accepting my release.
7501	Work accepting my now.
7502	Work accepting my compromise.
7503	Work accepting my trust.
7504	Work accepting my support.
7505	Work accepting my presence.
7506	Work accepting my joy.
7507	Work accepting my ability.
7508	Work accepting my building.
7509	Work accepting my action.
7510	Work accepting this releasing.
7511	Work accepting this now.
7512	Work accepting this compromise.
7513	Work accepting this trust.
7514	Work accepting this support.
7515	Work accepting this granted.
7516	Work accepting this joy.
7517	Work accepting this ability.
7518	Work accepting this building.
7519	Work accepting this action.
7520	Work accepting joining release.

Myn in Numbers

7521	Work accepting joining now.
7522	Work accepting friendship joining.
7523	Work accepting joining myn.
7524	Work accepting joining supported.
7525	Work accepting joining received.
7526	Work accepting friend serves.
7527	Work accepting joining ability.
7528	Work accepting joining structure.
7529	Work accepting joining action.
7530	Work accepting trust releasing.
7531	Work accepting trust now.
7532	Work accepting trust compromise.
7533	Work accepting prosperity blessing.
7534	Work accepting trust supported.
7535	Work accepting trust received.
7536	Work accepting trust serves.
7537	Work accepting trust ability.
7538	Work accepting trust building.
7539	Work accepting trusted action.
7540	Work accepting through releasing.
7541	Work accepting through now.
7542	Work accepting through compromise.
7543	Work accepting through trust.
7544	Work accepting through support.
7545	Work accepting through acceptance.
7546	Work accepting through joy.
7547	Work accepting through ability.
7548	Work accepting through building.
7549	Work accepting through action.
7550	Work accepting present releasing.
7551	Work accepting present now.
7552	Work accepting present compromise.
7553	Work accepting present myn.
7554	Work accepting present supported.

7555	Work accepting present received.
7556	Work accepting present joy.
7557	Work accepting present ability.
7558	Work accepting present building.
7559	Work accepting present action.
7560	Work accepting joy releases.
7561	Work accepting joy now.
7562	Work accepting joy compromise.
7563	Work accepting joy blessing.
7564	Work accepting joy supported.
7565	Work accepting joy received.
7566	Work accepting laugh content.
7567	Work accepting joy ability.
7568	Work accepting joy building.
7569	Work accepting joy action.
7570	Work accepting ability releasing.
7571	Work accepting ability now.
7572	Work accepting ability compromise.
7573	Work accepting ability myn.
7574	Work accepting ability supported.
7575	Work accepting ability received.
7576	Work accepting ability joy.
7577	Work accepting capable ability.
7578	Work accepting ability building.
7579	Work accepting ability action.
7580	Work accepting builds releasing.
7581	Work accepting builds now.
7582	Work accepting builds compromise.
7583	Work accepting builds trust.
7584	Work accepting builds supported.
7585	Work accepting builds presence.
7586	Work accepting builds joy.
7587	Work accepting builds ability.
7588	Work accepting builds structure.

Myn in Numbers

7589	Work accepting builds action.
7590	Work accepting action releasing.
7591	Work accepting action now.
7592	Work accepting active compromise.
7593	Work accepting active trust.
7594	Work accepting action supported.
7595	Work accepting action received.
7596	Work accepting active joy.
7597	Work accepting active ability.
7598	Work accepting action building.
7599	Work accepting moving action.
7600	Working joy soul releases.
7601	Working joy my now.
7602	Working joy my compromise.
7603	Working joy my myn.
7604	Working joy my support.
7605	Working joy my acceptance.
7606	Working content my joy.
7607	Working joy my ability.
7608	Working joy my building.
7609	Working joy my action.
7610	Working joy now releasing.
7611	Working joy is now.
7612	Working joy now compromise.
7613	Working joy now trust.
7614	Working joy now supported.
7615	Working joy now received.
7616	Working joy this joy.
7617	Working joy now ability.
7618	Working joy now building.
7619	Working joy now action.
7620	Working joy compromise releases.
7621	Working joy compromise now.
7622	Working joy friendship compromise.

7623	Working joy compromise trust.
7624	Working joy compromise supported.
7625	Working joy compromise received.
7626	Working content compromise joy.
7627	Working joy compromise ability.
7628	Working joy compromise building.
7629	Working joy compromise action.
7630	Working joy trust releasing.
7631	Working joy trust now.
7632	Working joy trust compromise.
7633	Working joy trust myn.
7634	Working joy trust supported.
7635	Working joy trust received.
7636	Working joy trust joy.
7637	Working joy trust ability.
7638	Working joy trust building.
7639	Working joy trust action.
7640	Working joy through releasing.
7641	Working joy through this.
7642	Working joy through compromise.
7643	Working joy through trust.
7644	Working joy through support.
7645	Working joy through acceptance.
7646	Working joy through joy.
7647	Working joy through ability.
7648	Working joy through building.
7649	Working joy through action.
7650	Working joy receive releasing.
7651	Working joy receive now.
7652	Working joy receive compromise.
7653	Working joy receive trust.
7654	Working joy receive supported.
7655	Working joy receive acceptance.
7656	Working joy receive joy.

Myn in Numbers

7657 Working joy receive ability.
7658 Working joy receive building.
7659 Working joy receive action.
7660 Working joy joy releases.
7661 Working joy joy now.
7662 Working joy joy compromise.
7663 Working joy joy trusting.
7664 Working joy joy supported.
7665 Working joy joy received.
7666 Working joy laugh content.
7667 Working joy joy enables.
7668 Working joy joy builds.
7669 Working joy joy active.
7670 Working joy enables releasing.
7671 Working joy enables now.
7672 Working joy enables compromise.
7673 Working joy enables myn.
7674 Working joy enables supported.
7675 Working joy enables received.
7676 Working joy enables joy.
7677 Working joy working ability.
7678 Working joy enables building.
7679 Working joy enables action.
7680 Working joy builds releasing.
7681 Working joy builds now.
7682 Working joy builds compromise.
7683 Working joy builds trust.
7684 Working joy builds supported.
7685 Working joy builds received.
7686 Working joy builds joy.
7687 Working joy builds ability.
7688 Working joy builds structure.
7689 Working joy builds action.
7690 Working joy activates releasing.

Kevin J. Baird

7691   Working joy activates now.
7692   Working joy activates compromise.
7693   Working joy activates myn.
7694   Working joy activates supported.
7695   Working joy activates received.
7696   Working joy activates joy.
7697   Working joy activates ability.
7698   Working joy activates building.
7699   Working joy tests feelings.
7700   Working capable soul releases.
7701   Working capable self now.
7702   Working capable self compromise.
7703   Working capable self myn.
7704   Working capable self supported.
7705   Working capable self received.
7706   Working capable self joy.
7707   Working capable self ability.
7708   Working capable self building.
7709   Working capable self action.
7710   Working capable now releasing.
7711   Working capable is now.
7712   Working capable now compromise.
7713   Working capable now trust.
7714   Working capable now supported.
7715   Working capable now received.
7716   Working capable now joy.
7717   Working capable now ability.
7718   Working capable now building.
7719   Working capable now action.
7720   Working capable joins releasing.
7721   Working capable joins now.
7722   Working capable friendship joins.
7723   Working capable joins trust.
7724   Working capable joins supported.

Myn in Numbers

7725	Working capable joins received.
7726	Working capable joins joy.
7727	Working capable joins ability.
7728	Working capable joins building.
7729	Working capable joins active.
7730	Working capable prosperity releasing.
7731	Working capable prosperity now.
7732	Working capable prosperity compromise.
7733	Working capable trust prosperity.
7734	Working capable prosperity supported.
7735	Working capable prosperity received.
7736	Working capable prosperity joy.
7737	Working capable prosperity ability.
7738	Working capable prosperity building.
7739	Working capable prosperity action.
7740	Working capable through releasing.
7741	Working capable through this.
7742	Working capable through compromise.
7743	Working capable through trust.
7744	Working capable through support.
7745	Working capable through acceptance.
7746	Working capable through joy.
7747	Working capable through ability.
7748	Working capable through building.
7749	Working capable through action.
7750	Working capable receive releasing.
7751	Working capable receive now.
7752	Working capable receive compromise.
7753	Working capable receive myn.
7754	Working capable receive supported.
7755	Working capable receive received.
7756	Working capable receive joy.
7757	Working capable receive ability.
7758	Working capable receive building.

7759   Working capable receive action.
7760   Working capable joy releases.
7761   Working capable enjoy now.
7762   Working capable enjoy compromise.
7763   Working capable enjoy trust.
7764   Working capable joy supported.
7765   Working capable joy received.
7766   Working capable laugh content.
7767   Working capable enjoy ability.
7768   Working capable enjoy building.
7769   Working capable enjoy action.
7770   Working capable ability releases.
7771   Working capable ability now.
7772   Working capable ability joins.
7773   Working capable ability trusting.
7774   Working capable ability supported.
7775   Working capable ability accepted.
7776   Working capable ability joy.
7777   Working capable works ability.
7778   Working capable work builds.
7779   Working capable enables action.
7780   Working capable builds releasing.
7781   Working capable builds now.
7782   Working capable builds compromise.
7783   Working capable builds trust.
7784   Working capable builds supported.
7785   Working capable builds received.
7786   Working capable builds joy.
7787   Working capable builds ability.
7788   Working capable builds structure.
7789   Working capable builds action.
7790   Working capable activates releasing.
7791   Working capable activates now.
7792   Working capable activates compromise.

Myn in Numbers

7793 Working capable activates myn.
7794 Working capable activates supported.
7795 Working capable activates received.
7796 Working capable activates joy.
7797 Working capable activates ability.
7798 Working capable activates building.
7799 Working capable moves active.
7800 Work storing soul releases.
7801 Work storing self now.
7802 Work storing self compromise.
7803 Work storing self trust.
7804 Work storing self support.
7805 Work storing self acceptance.
7806 Work storing self joy.
7807 Work storing self ability.
7808 Work storing self building.
7809 Work storing self feelings.
7810 Work storing this releasing.
7811 Work storing this now.
7812 Work storing this compromise.
7813 Work storing this blessing.
7814 Work storing this supported.
7815 Work storing this acceptance.
7816 Work storing this joy.
7817 Work storing this ability.
7818 Work storing this building.
7819 Work storing this feeling.
7820 Work storing befriending self.
7821 Work storing friendship now.
7822 Work storing companion friendship.
7823 Work storing friendship blessing.
7824 Work storing friendship supported.
7825 Work storing friendship acceptance.
7826 Work storing friendship joy.

7827	Work storing friendship ability.
7828	Work storing friendship building.
7829	Work storing friendship feelings.
7830	Work storing blessing releasing.
7831	Work storing blessing now.
7832	Work storing blessing compromise.
7833	Work storing trust blessing.
7834	Work storing blessing supported.
7835	Work storing blessing received.
7836	Work storing blessing joy.
7837	Work storing blessing ability.
7838	Work storing blessing building.
7839	Work storing blessing feelings.
7840	Work storing through self.
7841	Work storing through this.
7842	Work storing through compromise.
7843	Work storing through trust.
7844	Work storing through support.
7845	Work storing through acceptance.
7846	Work storing through joy.
7847	Work storing through ability.
7848	Work storing through building.
7849	Work storing through action.
7850	Work storing present self.
7851	Work storing present now.
7852	Work storing present compromise.
7853	Work storing present myn.
7854	Work storing present supported.
7855	Work storing present received.
7856	Work storing present joy.
7857	Work storing present ability.
7858	Work storing present building.
7859	Work storing present action.
7860	Work storing joy releasing.

Myn in Numbers

7861	Work storing joy now.
7862	Work storing joy compromise.
7863	Work storing joy blessing.
7864	Work storing joy support.
7865	Work storing joy present.
7866	Work storing joy joy.
7867	Work storing joy ability.
7868	Work storing joy form.
7869	Work storing joy feelings
7870	Work stores ability release.
7871	Working stores ability now.
7872	Work storing ability compromise.
7873	Work stores able trust.
7874	Work storing ability supported.
7875	Work storing able acceptance.
7876	Work storing able joy.
7877	Work storing working ability.
7878	Work storing work storing.
7879	Work storing ability test.
7880	Work storing builds release.
7881	Work storing structure now.
7882	Work storing structured compromise.
7883	Work storing building trust.
7884	Work storing building supported.
7885	Work storing building received.
7886	Work storing building joy.
7887	Work storing building ability.
7888	Work storing builds structure.
7889	Work storing building action.
7890	Work storing active release.
7891	Work storing action now.
7892	Work storing active compromise.
7893	Work storing active trust.
7894	Work storing active support.

7895	Work storing active acceptance.
7896	Work storing active joy.
7897	Work storing active ability.
7898	Work storing active building.
7899	Work storing moving feelings.
7900	Working feelings soul releases.
7901	Working feelings my now.
7902	Working feelings my compromise.
7903	Working feelings my trust.
7904	Working feelings my support.
7905	Working feelings my acceptance.
7906	Working feelings my joy.
7907	Working feelings my ability.
7908	Working feelings my building.
7909	Working feelings my action.
7910	Working feelings now releasing.
7911	Working feelings is now.
7912	Working feelings now compromise.
7913	Working feelings now trusted.
7914	Working feelings is supported.
7915	Working feelings now received.
7916	Working feelings now joy.
7917	Working feelings now ability.
7918	Working feelings now building.
7919	Working feelings is action.
7920	Working feelings joins releasing.
7921	Working feelings joins now.
7922	Working feelings friendship compromise.
7923	Working feelings joins trust.
7924	Working feelings joins supported.
7925	Working feelings joins received.
7926	Working feelings joins joy.
7927	Working feelings joins ability.
7928	Working feelings joins building.

Myn in Numbers

7929	Working feelings joins action.
7930	Working feelings trust releases.
7931	Working feelings trust now.
7932	Working feelings trust compromise.
7933	Working feelings trust myn.
7934	Working feelings trust supported.
7935	Working feelings trust received.
7936	Working feelings trust joy.
7937	Working feelings trust ability.
7938	Working feelings trust building.
7939	Working feelings trust action.
7940	Working feelings through release.
7941	Working feelings through this.
7942	Working feelings through compromise.
7943	Working feelings through trust.
7944	Working feelings through support.
7945	Working feelings through acceptance.
7946	Working feelings through joy.
7947	Working feelings through ability.
7948	Working feelings through building.
7949	Working feelings through action.
7950	Working feelings receive releasing.
7951	Working feelings receive now.
7952	Working feelings receive compromise.
7953	Working feelings receive trust.
7954	Working feelings receive support.
7955	Working feelings receive acceptance.
7956	Working feelings receive joy.
7957	Working feelings receive ability.
7958	Working feelings receive building.
7959	Working feelings receive action.
7960	Working feelings joy releases.
7961	Working feelings enjoy now.
7962	Working feelings enjoy compromise.

7963	Working feelings enjoy myn.
7964	Working feelings enjoy support.
7965	Working feelings enjoy acceptance.
7966	Working feelings content laughing.
7967	Working feelings enjoy ability.
7968	Working feelings enjoy building.
7969	Working feelings enjoy action.
7970	Working feelings enables releasing.
7971	Working feelings enables now.
7972	Working feelings enables compromise.
7973	Working feelings enables myn.
7974	Working feelings enables supported.
7975	Working feelings enables received.
7976	Working feelings enables joy.
7977	Working feelings working ability.
7978	Working feelings enables building.
7979	Working feelings enables action.
7980	Working feelings builds releasing.
7981	Working feelings builds now.
7982	Working feelings builds compromise.
7983	Working feelings builds trust.
7984	Working feelings builds supported.
7985	Working feelings builds received.
7986	Working feelings builds joy.
7987	Working feelings builds ability.
7988	Working feelings builds structure.
7989	Working feelings builds feelings.
7990	Working feelings tests releasing.
7991	Working feelings tests now.
7992	Working feelings tests compromise.
7993	Working feelings tests trust.
7994	Working feelings tests supported.
7995	Working feelings tests received.
7996	Working feelings tests joy.

Myn in Numbers

7997 Working feelings tests ability.

7998 Working feelings tests building.

7999 Working feelings tests feelings.

Kevin J. Baird

Myn in Numbers

Build

8000-8999

When "8" leads the group your source is inviting you to "Build or store" as you conduct yourself in the group moment of the trailing numbers. Weigh the points and ponder the outcome.

***

8000	Building self releases self.
8001	Build self release now.
8002	Building self release joins.
8003	Building self self trust.
8004	Building self releases supported.
8005	Building self self accepted.
8006	Building self self serves.
8007	Building self my ability.
8008	Building self self building.
8009	Building self my action.
8010	Building self is releasing.
8011	Building self is now.
8012	Building self is compromise.
8013	Building self is trusting.

Kevin J. Baird

8014	Building self is supported.
8015	Building self is acceptance.
8016	Building self is joy.
8017	Building self is ability.
8018	Building self now building.
8019	Building self now tested.
8020	Building self joins releasing.
8021	Building self joins now.
8022	Building self joins friendship.
8023	Building self joins trusting.
8024	Building self joins supported.
8025	Building self joins acceptance.
8026	Building self joins serving.
8027	Building self joins ability.
8028	Building self joins building.
8029	Building self joins testing.
8030	Building self trusts releasing.
8031	Build self trusting now.
8032	Build self trusting friendship.
8033	Build self trusting blessings.
8034	Build self trusting support.
8035	Build self trusting acceptance.
8036	Build self trusting joy.
8037	Build self trusting ability.
8038	Build self trusting building.
8039	Build self trusting action.
8040	Build self supporting release.
8041	Build self support now.
8042	Build self supporting friendship.
8043	Build self supporting trust.
8044	Building self means support.
8045	Build self through acceptance.
8046	Build self through joy.
8047	Build self through ability.

Myn in Numbers

8048	Build self through building.
8049	Build self through action.
8050	Build self receiving releasing.
8051	Build self acceptance now.
8052	Build self receiving friendship.
8053	Build self receiving trust.
8054	Build self receiving support.
8055	Build self receiving acceptance.
8056	Build self receiving joy.
8057	Build self receiving ability.
8058	Build self receiving building.
8059	Build self receiving action.
8060	Build self serving releasing.
8061	Build self serves now.
8062	Build self serving friendship.
8063	Build self serving trust.
8064	Build self serving means.
8065	Build self serving acceptance.
8066	Build self serving joy.
8067	Build self serving ability.
8068	Build self serving structure.
8069	Build self serving action.
8070	Build self working releasing.
8071	Build self working now.
8072	Build self working friendship.
8073	Build self working trusted.
8074	Build self working support.
8075	Build self working acceptance.
8076	Building self working serves.
8077	Build self working ability.
8078	Build self working structure.
8079	Build self working feelings.
8080	Build self building release.
8081	Build self building now.

8082	Build self building friendship.
8083	Build self building trust.
8084	Build self building support.
8085	Build self building acceptance.
8086	Build self building joy.
8087	Build self building ability.
8088	Build self building structure.
8089	Build self building feelings.
8090	Build self testing self.
8091	Build self testing now.
8092	Build self testing friendship.
8093	Build self testing trust.
8094	Build self testing support.
8095	Build self testing acceptance.
8096	Build self testing joy.
8097	Build self testing ability.
8098	Build self testing structure.
8099	Build self testing feelings.
8100	Build now self release.
8101	Build now my now.
8102	Build now my compromise.
8103	Build now my trust.
8104	Build now my support.
8105	Build now my acceptance.
8106	Build now my joy.
8107	Build now my ability.
8108	Build now my structure.
8109	Build now my feelings.
8110	Build now done releasing.
8111	Build now is now.
8112	Build now is compromise.
8113	Build now this trust.
8114	Build now this support.
8115	Build now this acceptance.

Myn in Numbers

8116	Build now this joy.
8117	Build now this ability.
8118	Build now this building.
8119	Build now done feeling.
8120	Build now joining release.
8121	Build now joining this.
8122	Build now joining friendship.
8123	Build now joining trust.
8124	Build now joining supported.
8125	Build now joining acceptance.
8126	Build now joining joy.
8127	Build now joining ability.
8128	Build now joining building.
8129	Build now joining action.
8130	Build now trusting self.
8131	Build now trusting now.
8132	Build now trusting compromise.
8133	Build now trust blessing.
8134	Build now trusting means.
8135	Build now trusting acceptance.
8136	Build now trust joy.
8137	Build now trusting ability.
8138	Build now trusting building.
8139	Build now trusting feelings.
8140	Build now supporting self.
8141	Build now supporting done.
8142	Build now supporting friendship.
8143	Build now supporting trust.
8144	Build now supporting means.
8145	Build now supporting acceptance.
8146	Build now supporting joy.
8147	Build now supporting ability.
8148	Build now supporting building.
8149	Build now supporting feelings.

Kevin J. Baird

8150	Build now receiving releasing.
8151	Build now receiving now.
8152	Build now receiving compromise.
8153	Build now receiving trust.
8154	Build now receiving support.
8155	Build now receiving acceptance.
8156	Build now receiving joy.
8157	Build now receiving ability.
8158	Build now receiving building.
8159	Build now receiving feelings.
8160	Build now serving releases.
8161	Build now serving done.
8162	Build now serving compromise.
8163	Build now serving trust.
8164	Build now serving support.
8165	Build now serving acceptance.
8166	Build now serving joy.
8167	Build now serving ability.
8168	Build now serving building.
8169	Build now serving feelings.
8170	Build now work releasing.
8171	Build now work done.
8172	Build now work compromise.
8173	Build now work trusted.
8174	Build now work supported.
8175	Build now work acceptance.
8176	Build now work joy.
8177	Build now work ability.
8178	Build now work building.
8179	Build now work active.
8180	Build now building releasing.
8181	Build now building done.
8182	Build now building friendship.
8183	Build now building trust.

Myn in Numbers

8184	Build now building supported.
8185	Build now building acceptance.
8186	Build now building joy.
8187	Build now building ability.
8188	Build now building structure.
8189	Build now building feelings.
8190	Build now feeling release.
8191	Build now feeling done.
8192	Build now feeling compromise.
8193	Build now feeling trust.
8194	Build now feeling supported.
8195	Build now feeling accepted.
8196	Build now feeling joy.
8197	Build now feeling ability.
8198	Build now feeling building.
8199	Build now testing feelings.
8201	Building friendship releases done.
8202	Building friendship releases compromise.
8203	Building friendship releases blessing.
8204	Building friendship releases support.
8205	Building friendship releases acceptance.
8206	Building friendship releases joy.
8207	Building friendship releases ability.
8208	Building friendship releases stores.
8209	Building friendship releases feelings.
8210	Building friendship now releasing.
8211	Building friendship is now.
8212	Building friendship is compromise.
8213	Building friendship is trust.
8214	Building friendship is supported.
8215	Building friendship is acceptance.
8216	Building friendship is joy.
8217	Building friendship is ability.
8218	Building friendship is storing.

8219 Building friendship is feeling.
8220 Building friendship joins releasing.
8221 Building friendship joins now.
8222 Building friendship joins compromise.
8223 Building friendship joins trusting.
8224 Building friendship joins supported.
8225 Building friendship joins received.
8226 Building friendship joins joy.
8227 Building friendship joins ability.
8228 Building friendship joins building.
8229 Building friendship joins action.
8230 Build friendship trusting releasing.
8231 Build friendship trusting now.
8232 Build friendship trusting compromise.
8233 Building friendship trusting blessing.
8234 Build friendship trusting support.
8235 Build friendship trusting acceptance.
8236 Build friendship trusting joy.
8237 Build friendship trusting ability.
8238 Build friendship trusting structure.
8239 Build friendship trusting feelings.
8240 Building friendship means releasing.
8241 Building friendship means now.
8242 Building friendship means compromise.
8243 Building friendship means trusting.
8244 Building friendship means support.
8245 Building friendship means acceptance.
8246 Building friendship means joy.
8247 Building friendship means ability.
8248 Building friendship means building.
8249 Building friendship means feeling.
8250 Build friendship receiving release.
8251 Build friendship receiving now.
8252 Build friendship receiving compromise.

Myn in Numbers

8253	Build friendship receiving trust.
8254	Build friendship receiving support.
8255	Build friendship receiving acceptance.
8256	Build friendship receiving joy.
8257	Build friendship receiving ability.
8258	Build friendship receiving building.
8259	Build friendship receiving feelings.
8260	Build friendship serving release.
8261	Build friendship serving done.
8262	Build friendship serving compromise.
8263	Build friendship serving trust.
8264	Build friendship serving support.
8265	Build friendship serving acceptance.
8266	Build friendship serving joy.
8267	Build friendship serving ability.
8268	Build friendship serving building.
8269	Build friendship serving feelings.
8270	Build friendship working self.
8271	Build friendship working now.
8272	Build friendship working compromise.
8273	Build friendship working trusted.
8274	Build friendship working support.
8275	Build friendship working acceptance.
8276	Build friendship working joy.
8277	Building friendship working ability.
8278	Build friendship working structure.
8279	Build friendship working feelings.
8280	Building friendship forms release.
8281	Building friendship forms now.
8282	Building friendship forms compromise.
8283	Building friendship forms trust.
8284	Building friendship forms supported.
8285	Building friendship forms received.
8286	Building friendship forms joy.

8287 Building friendship forms ability.
8288 Building friendship forms structure.
8289 Building friendship forms action.
8290 Building friendship feels releasing.
8291 Building friendship feels done.
8292 Building friendship feels joining.
8293 Building friendship feels trusted.
8294 Building friendship feels supported.
8295 Building friendship feels accepted.
8296 Building friendship feels serving.
8297 Building friendship feels able.
8298 Building friendship feelings form.
8299 Building friendship feelings tested.
8300 Build trusting my release.
8301 Build trusting my now.
8302 Build trusting my compromise.
8303 Build trusting my blessing.
8304 Build trusting my support.
8305 Build trusting my acceptance.
8306 Build trusting my joy.
8307 Build trusting my ability.
8308 Build trusting my building.
8309 Build trusting my feelings.
8310 Build trusting now releasing.
8311 Build trusting this now.
8312 Build trusting this compromise.
8313 Build trusting this blessing.
8314 Build trusting this support.
8315 Build trusting this acceptance.
8316 Build trusting this joy.
8317 Build trusting this ability.
8318 Build trusting this building.
8319 Build trusting this feeling.
8320 Building trusts joining releasing.

Myn in Numbers

8321	Building trusts joining now.
8322	Building trusts friendship compromise.
8323	Building trusts joining prosperity.
8324	Building trusts joining support.
8325	Building trusts joining acceptance.
8326	Building trusts joining joy.
8327	Building trusts joining ability.
8328	Building trusts joining structure.
8329	Building trusts joining action.
8330	Build trust trusting self.
8331	Build trust trusting this.
8332	Build trust trusting compromise.
8333	Build trust trusting prosperity.
8334	Build trust trusting support.
8335	Build trust trusting acceptance.
8336	Build trust trusting joy.
8337	Build trust trusting ability.
8338	Build trust trusting structure.
8339	Build trust trusting feelings.
8340	Building trust means releasing.
8341	Building trust means now.
8342	Building trust means compromise.
8343	Building trust means trust.
8344	Building trust means support.
8345	Building trust means acceptance.
8346	Building trust means serving.
8347	Building trust means ability.
8348	Building trust supports building.
8349	Building trust supports feelings.
8350	Build trust presenting self.
8351	Build trust presenting now.
8352	Build trust presenting compromise.
8353	Build trust presenting trust.
8354	Build trust presenting support.

8355   Build trust presenting acceptance.
8356   Build trust presenting joy.
8357   Build trust presenting ability.
8358   Build trust presenting building.
8359   Build trust presenting feelings.
8360   Building trust serves release.
8361   Building trust serves now.
8362   Building trust serves compromise.
8363   Building trust serves myn.
8364   Building trust serves supported.
8365   Building trust serves received.
8366   Building trust serves joy.
8367   Building trust serves ability.
8368   Building trust serves building.
8369   Building trust serves feelings.
8370   Building trust enables releasing.
8371   Building trust enables now.
8372   Building trust enables compromise.
8373   Building trust enables trust.
8374   Building trust enables means.
8375   Building trust enables acceptance.
8376   Building trust enables joy.
8377   Building trust enables ability.
8378   Building trust enables building.
8379   Building trust enables feelings.
8380   Building trust building release.
8381   Building trust building now.
8382   Building trust building compromise.
8383   Building trust building trust.
8384   Building trust building supported.
8385   Building trust building received.
8386   Building trust building served.
8387   Building trust building ability.
8388   Building trust building structure.

Myn in Numbers

8389	Building trust building action.
8390	Build trusting feelings released.
8391	Build trusting feelings now.
8392	Build trusting feelings joined.
8393	Build trusting feelings trusted.
8394	Build trusting feelings supported.
8395	Build trusting feelings accepted.
8396	Build trusting feelings serve.
8397	Build trusting feelings working.
8398	Build trusting feelings building.
8399	Building trust moves feelings.
8400	Build supporting my release.
8401	Build supporting my now.
8402	Build supporting my compromise.
8403	Build supporting my trust.
8404	Build supporting my support.
8405	Build supporting my receiving.
8406	Build supporting my joy.
8407	Build supporting my ability.
8408	Build supporting my building.
8409	Build supporting my feelings.
8410	Build supporting this release.
8411	Build supporting this done.
8412	Build supporting is compromise.
8413	Build supporting is trust.
8414	Build supporting is means.
8415	Build supporting this received.
8416	Build supporting this joy.
8417	Build supporting this ability.
8418	Build supporting this building.
8419	Build supporting this feeling.
8420	Build supporting friendship release.
8421	Build supporting friendship now.
8422	Build supporting friendship compromise.

8423	Build supporting friendship trust.
8424	Build supporting friendship supported.
8425	Build supporting friendship received.
8426	Build supporting friendship serves.
8427	Build supporting friendship working.
8428	Build supporting friendship building.
8429	Build supporting friendship feelings.
8430	Build supporting myn releasing.
8431	Build supporting myn now.
8432	Build supporting myn compromise.
8433	Build supporting trust myn.
8434	Build supporting myn support.
8435	Build supporting trusting acceptance.
8436	Build supporting myn joy.
8437	Build supporting myn ability.
8438	Build supporting myn form.
8439	Build supporting trusting feelings.
8440	Build supporting supporting releasing.
8441	Build supporting supporting now.
8442	Build supporting supporting compromise.
8443	Build supporting supporting trust.
8444	Build supporting supporting support.
8445	Build supporting supporting received.
8446	Build supporting supporting joy.
8447	Build supporting supporting ability.
8448	Build supporting supporting building.
8449	Build supporting supporting action.
8450	Build supporting granted release.
8451	Build supporting granted now.
8452	Build supporting granted compromise.
8453	Build supporting granted prosperity.
8454	Build supporting granted support.
8455	Build supporting granted acceptance.
8456	Build supporting granted joy.

Myn in Numbers

8457	Build supporting granted ability.
8458	Build supporting accepted building.
8459	Build supporting granted action.
8460	Build supporting content self.
8461	Build supporting contentment now.
8462	Build supporting content compromise.
8463	Build supporting content trust.
8464	Build supporting content means.
8465	Build supporting content acceptance.
8466	Build supporting content joy.
8467	Build supporting content ability.
8468	Build supporting contentment building.
8469	Build supporting content action.
8470	Building supports working releasing.
8471	Building supports working now.
8472	Building supports working compromise.
8473	Building supports working myn.
8474	Building supports working supported.
8475	Building supports working received.
8476	Building supports working joy.
8477	Building supports working ability.
8478	Building supports working building.
8479	Building supports working feelings.
8480	Build supporting storing release.
8481	Build supporting storing now.
8482	Build supporting storing compromise.
8483	Build supporting storing trusted.
8484	Build supporting storing support.
8485	Build supporting storing acceptance.
8486	Build supporting storing joy.
8487	Build supporting storing ability.
8488	Build supporting storing structure.
8489	Build supporting storing feelings.
8490	Build supporting active release.

8491	Build supporting feelings now.
8492	Build supporting active compromise.
8493	Build supporting active trust.
8494	Build supporting active support.
8495	Build supporting active acceptance.
8496	Build supporting active joy.
8497	Build supporting active ability.
8498	Build supporting active building.
8499	Build supporting testing feelings.
8500	Building acceptance my releasing.
8501	Building acceptance my now.
8502	Building acceptance my compromise.
8503	Building acceptance my trust.
8504	Building acceptance my support.
8505	Building acceptance release granted.
8506	Building acceptance release serves.
8507	Building acceptance my ability.
8508	Building acceptance my building.
8509	Building acceptance my action.
8510	Building acceptance now releases.
8511	Building acceptance is now.
8512	Building acceptance is compromise.
8513	Building acceptance is myn.
8514	Building acceptance is supported.
8515	Building acceptance is received.
8516	Building acceptance is joy.
8517	Building acceptance is ability.
8518	Building acceptance is building.
8519	Building acceptance is action.
8520	Building acceptance joins release.
8521	Building acceptance joins now.
8522	Building acceptance friendship joins.
8523	Building acceptance joins trusting.
8524	Building acceptance joins supported.

Myn in Numbers

8525	Building acceptance joins received.
8526	Building acceptance joins joy.
8527	Building acceptance joins ability.
8528	Building acceptance joins building.
8529	Building acceptance joins action.
8530	Building acceptance myn releasing.
8531	Build acceptance trusting now.
8532	Build acceptance trusting compromise.
8533	Build acceptance trusting blessing.
8534	Build acceptance trusting support.
8535	Build acceptance trust received.
8536	Build acceptance trust joy.
8537	Build acceptance trusting ability.
8538	Build acceptance trusting building.
8539	Build acceptance trusting action.
8540	Building acceptance through releasing.
8541	Building acceptance through now.
8542	Building acceptance through compromise.
8543	Building acceptance through trust.
8544	Building acceptance through support.
8545	Building acceptance through acceptance.
8546	Building acceptance through joy.
8547	Building acceptance through ability.
8548	Building acceptance through building.
8549	Building acceptance through action.
8550	Building acceptance receive releasing.
8551	Building acceptance receive now.
8552	Building acceptance receive compromise.
8553	Building acceptance receive myn.
8554	Building acceptance receive supported.
8555	Building acceptance receive present.
8556	Building acceptance receive joy.
8557	Building acceptance receive ability.
8558	Building acceptance receive building.

www.templeofgaia.com

8559 Building acceptance receive action.
8560 Building acceptance serves releasing.
8561 Building acceptance serves now.
8562 Building acceptance serves compromise.
8563 Building acceptance serves myn.
8564 Building acceptance serves supported.
8565 Building acceptance serves received.
8566 Building acceptance content laugh.
8567 Building acceptance serves ability.
8568 Building acceptance serves building.
8569 Building acceptance serves feelings
8570 Building acceptance enables releasing.
8571 Building acceptance enables now.
8572 Building acceptance enables compromise.
8573 Building acceptance enables trust.
8574 Building acceptance enables supported.
8575 Building acceptance enables received.
8576 Building acceptance enables joy.
8577 Building acceptance enables ability.
8578 Building acceptance enables building.
8579 Building acceptance enables action.
8580 Building acceptance forms releasing.
8581 Building acceptance forms now.
8582 Building acceptance forms compromise.
8583 Building acceptance forms myn.
8584 Building acceptance forms supported.
8585 Building acceptance forms received.
8586 Building acceptance forms joy.
8587 Building acceptance forms ability.
8588 Building acceptance forms structure.
8589 Building acceptance forms action.
8590 Building acceptance activates releasing.
8591 Building acceptance activates now.
8592 Building acceptance activates compromise.

Myn in Numbers

8593   Building acceptance activates trust.
8594   Building acceptance activates supported.
8595   Building acceptance activates received.
8596   Building acceptance activates joy.
8597   Building acceptance activates ability.
8598   Building acceptance activates building.
8599   Building acceptance tests feelings.
8600   Building joy soul releases.
8601   Building joy my now.
8602   Building joy my compromise.
8603   Building joy releases trust.
8604   Building joy soul supported.
8605   Building joy soul receives.
8606   Building joy soul joy.
8607   Building joy soul ability.
8608   Building joy soul building.
8609   Building joy soul action.
8610   Building joy now releasing.
8611   Building joy is now.
8612   Building joy is compromise.
8613   Building joy is myn.
8614   Building joy is supported.
8615   Building joy is received.
8616   Building joy is joy.
8617   Building joy is ability.
8618   Building joy is building.
8619   Building joy is action.
8620   Building joy joins releasing.
8621   Building joy joins now.
8622   Building joy friendship compromise.
8623   Building joy joins trust.
8624   Building joy joins supported.
8625   Building joy joins received.
8626   Building joy joins joy.

8627	Building joy joins ability.
8628	Building joy joins building.
8629	Building joy joins action.
8630	Building joy blessing releasing.
8631	Building joy blessing now.
8632	Building joy blessing compromise.
8633	Building joy trust blessing.
8634	Building joy blessing supported.
8635	Building joy blessing received.
8636	Building joy blessing joy.
8637	Building joy blessing ability.
8638	Building joy blessing building.
8639	Building joy blessing action.
8640	Building joy through releasing.
8641	Building joy through this.
8642	Building joy through compromise.
8643	Building joy through blessing.
8644	Building joy through support.
8645	Building joy through acceptance.
8646	Building joy through joy.
8647	Building joy through ability.
8648	Building joy through form.
8649	Building joy through action.
8650	Building joy receive releasing.
8651	Building joy receive now.
8652	Building joy receive compromise.
8653	Building joy receive blessing.
8654	Building joy receive supported.
8655	Building joy receive acceptance.
8656	Building joy receive contentment.
8657	Building joy receive ability.
8658	Building joy receive building.
8659	Building joy receive action.
8660	Building content joy releases.

Myn in Numbers

8661	Building content joy now.
8662	Building content joy compromise.
8663	Building content joy trusting.
8664	Building content joy supported.
8665	Building content joy received.
8666	Building joy laughing content.
8667	Building content joy ability.
8668	Building content joy building.
8669	Building content joy action.
8670	Building joy ability releases.
8671	Building joy ability now.
8672	Building joy enables compromise.
8673	Building joy enables trust.
8674	Building joy ability supported.
8675	Building joy enables acceptance.
8676	Building joy enables joy.
8677	Building joy working enables.
8678	Building joy enables building.
8679	Building joy enables action.
8680	Building joy builds releasing.
8681	Building joy builds now.
8682	Building joy builds compromise.
8683	Building joy builds myn.
8684	Building joy builds supported.
8685	Building joy builds received.
8686	Building joy building joy.
8687	Building joy builds ability.
8688	Building joy builds structure.
8689	Building joy builds action.
8690	Building joy action releasing.
8691	Building joy active now.
8692	Building joy active compromise.
8693	Building joy active myn.
8694	Building joy action supported.

8695	Building joy active acceptance.
8696	Building joy active joy.
8697	Building joy active ability.
8698	Building joy active building.
8699	Building joy moving action.
8700	Building enables soul releases.
8701	Building enables my now.
8702	Building enables self joining.
8703	Building enables self.
8704	Building enables self support.
8705	Building enables self acceptance.
8706	Building enables self joy.
8707	Building enables self ability.
8708	Building enables self formation.
8709	Building enables released feelings.
8710	Building enables this releasing.
8711	Building enables this now.
8712	Building enables this compromise.
8713	Building enables this trust.
8714	Building enables this supported.
8715	Building enables this accepted.
8716	Building enables this joy.
8717	Building enables this ability.
8718	Building enables this stored.
8719	Building enables this action.
8720	Building enables joining release.
8721	Building enables compromise now.
8722	Building enables friendship compromise.
8723	Building enables joining trust.
8724	Building enables joining supported.
8725	Building enables joining received.
8726	Building enables joining content.
8727	Building enables joining ability.
8728	Building enables joining building.

Myn in Numbers

8729	Building enables joining action.
8730	Building enables trust releasing.
8731	Building enables trust now.
8732	Building enables trust compromise.
8733	Building enables trust myn.
8734	Building enables trust supported.
8735	Building enables trust received.
8736	Building enables trusting joy.
8737	Building enables trusting ability.
8738	Building enables trust building.
8739	Building enables trusting action.
8740	Building enables through releasing.
8741	Building enables through this.
8742	Building enables through compromise.
8743	Building enables through trusting.
8744	Building enables through support.
8745	Building enables through acceptance.
8746	Building enables through joy.
8747	Building enables through ability.
8748	Building enables through building.
8749	Building enables through action.
8750	Building enables receiving release.
8751	Building enables receiving now.
8752	Building enables receiving compromise.
8753	Building enables receiving trust.
8754	Building enables receiving supported.
8755	Building enables receiving acceptance.
8756	Building enables receiving joy.
8757	Building enables receiving ability.
8758	Building enables receiving structure.
8759	Building enables receiving action.
8760	Building enables enjoying release.
8761	Building enables enjoying now.
8762	Building enables enjoying compromise.

8763	Building enables enjoying trust.
8764	Building enables enjoying support.
8765	Building enables enjoying acceptance.
8766	Building enables content laugh.
8767	Building enables enjoying ability.
8768	Building enables enjoying building.
8769	Building enables enjoying action.
8770	Building enables working releasing.
8771	Building enables working now.
8772	Building enables working compromise.
8773	Building enables working trust.
8774	Building enables working supported.
8775	Building enables working acceptance.
8776	Building enables working service.
8777	Building enables working ability.
8778	Building enables working building.
8779	Building enables working feelings.
8780	Building enables forming release.
8781	Building enables forming now.
8782	Building enables forming compromise.
8783	Building enables forming myn.
8784	Building enables forming supported.
8785	Building enables forming received.
8786	Building enables forming joy.
8787	Building enables forming ability.
8788	Building enables forming structure.
8789	Building enables forming action.
8790	Building enables testing release.
8791	Building enables testing this.
8792	Building enables testing compromise.
8793	Building enables testing trust.
8794	Building enables testing support.
8795	Building enables testing acceptance.
8796	Building enables testing joy.

Myn in Numbers

8797	Building enables testing ability.
8798	Building enables testing building.
8799	Building enables tested feelings.
8800	Form storing my releases.
8801	Form storing release now.
8802	Form storing self compromise.
8803	Form storing self trust.
8804	Form storing self supported.
8805	Form storing self received.
8806	Form storing self joy.
8807	Form storing self ability.
8808	Form storing self building.
8809	Form storing self action.
8810	Form storing this release.
8811	Form storing this now.
8812	Form storing this compromise.
8813	Form storing this trusted.
8814	Form storing this supported.
8815	Form storing this received.
8816	Form storing this joy.
8817	Form storing this ability.
8818	Form storing this building.
8819	Form storing this action.
8820	Form storing partner release.
8821	Form storing compromise now.
8822	Form storing friendship compromise.
8823	Form storing joining trust.
8824	Form storing compromise support.
8825	Form storing compromise received.
8826	Form storing compromise serving.
8827	Form storing compromise ability.
8828	Form storing compromise building.
8829	Form storing compromise feelings.
8830	Form storing trust releasing.

8831   Form storing trust now.
8832   Form storing trust compromise.
8833   Form storing trust myn.
8834   Form storing trust supported.
8835   Form storing trust received.
8836   Form storing trust joy.
8837   Form storing trust ability.
8838   Form storing trust building.
8839   Form storing trusting feelings.
8840   Form storing means release.
8841   Form storing means now.
8842   Form storing means compromise.
8843   Form storing means myn.
8844   Form storing means support.
8845   Form storing means acceptance.
8846   Form storing means joy.
8847   Form storing means ability.
8848   Form storing means building.
8849   Form storing means action.
8850   Form storing present release.
8851   Form storing present done.
8852   Form storing present compromise.
8853   Form storing present trust.
8854   Form storing present support.
8855   Form storing present acceptance.
8856   Form storing present service.
8857   Form storing present ability.
8858   Form storing present building.
8859   Form storing present action.
8860   Form storing serving release.
8861   Form storing serving this.
8862   Form storing serving compromise.
8863   Form storing serving .
8864   Form storing serving supported.

Myn in Numbers

8865	Form storing serving received.
8866	Build build joy joy.
8867	Form storing serving ability.
8868	Form storing serving building.
8869	Form storing serving action.
8870	Form storing working release.
8871	Form storing ability now.
8872	Form storing ability compromise.
8873	Form storing ability trust.
8874	Form storing ability support.
8875	Form storing ability received.
8876	Form storing ability serving.
8877	Form storing working ability.
8878	Form storing ability building.
8879	Form storing ability action.
8880	Form storing building release.
8881	Form storing structure now.
8882	Form storing structured compromise.
8883	Form storing building trust.
8884	Form storing building support.
8885	Form storing building acceptance.
8886	Form storing building joy.
8887	Form storing building ability.
8888	Form storing building structure.
8889	Form storing building feelings.
8890	Form storing tested release.
8891	Form storing tested done.
8892	Form storing tested compromise.
8893	Form storing tested trust.
8894	Form storing tested support.
8895	Form storing tested acceptance.
8896	Form storing tested service.
8897	Form storing tested works.
8898	Form storing tested structure.

Kevin J. Baird

8899	Form storing moving feelings.
8900	Build feeling soul release.
8901	Build feeling releasing now.
8902	Build feeling release compromise.
8903	Build feeling release trusted.
8904	Build feeling release supported.
8905	Build feeling release received.
8906	Build feeling releasing joy.
8907	Build feeling releasing ability.
8908	Build feeling release build.
8909	Build feeling releasing action.
8910	Build feeling is releasing.
8911	Build feeling is now.
8912	Build feeling now joins.
8913	Build feeling this trusted.
8914	Build feeling now supported.
8915	Build feeling now received.
8916	Build feeling now serves.
8917	Build feeling this ability.
8918	Build feeling this build.
8919	Build feeling this action.
8920	Build feeling friendship release.
8921	Build feeling friendship now.
8922	Build feeling friendship compromise.
8923	Build feeling friendship trust.
8924	Build feeling friendship supported.
8925	Build feeling friendship received.
8926	Build feeling friendship joy.
8927	Build feeling friendship ability.
8928	Build feeling friendship building.
8929	Build feeling friendship action.
8930	Build feeling trusted release.
8931	Build feeling trusted now.
8932	Build feeling trusted compromise.

Myn in Numbers

8933	Build feeling trust trusted.
8934	Build feeling trust supported.
8935	Build feeling trust received.
8936	Build feeling trusted joy.
8937	Build feeling trusted ability.
8938	Build feeling trust building.
8939	Build feeling trusted action.
8940	Build feeling supported releasing.
8941	Build feeling supported now.
8942	Build feeling supported compromise.
8943	Build feeling supported trust.
8944	Build feeling supported means.
8945	Build feeling supportive acceptance.
8946	Build feeling supported service.
8947	Build feeling supported ability.
8948	Build feeling support forming.
8949	Build feeling supportive action.
8950	Build testing accepted release.
8951	Build testing accepted now.
8952	Build testing accepted compromise.
8953	Build testing accepted trust.
8954	Build testing accepted support.
8955	Build testing received acceptance.
8956	Build testing accepted joy.
8957	Build testing accepted ability.
8958	Build testing accepted structure.
8959	Build testing accepted feelings.
8960	Build feeling joy release.
8961	Build feeling joy now.
8962	Build feeling joy compromise.
8963	Build feeling joy trusted.
8964	Build feeling joy supported.
8965	Build feeling joy received.
8966	Build feeling content laugh.

8967	Build feeling joy ability.
8968	Build feeling joy storing.
8969	Build feeling joy active.
8970	Build feeling ability releasing.
8971	Build feeling ability now.
8972	Build feeling ability joins.
8973	Build feeling ability trusted.
8974	Build feeling ability supported.
8975	Build feeling ability accepted.
8976	Build feeling ability serves.
8977	Build feeling working ability.
8978	Build feeling ability building.
8979	Build feeling working action.
8980	Build feeling build releasing.
8981	Build feeling build now.
8982	Build feeling build compromise.
8983	Build feeling build trust.
8984	Build feeling build supported.
8985	Build feeling build accepted.
8986	Build feeling build joy.
8987	Build feeling build ability.
8988	Build feeling build structure.
8989	Build feeling build action.
8990	Build feeling active release.
8991	Build feeling active now.
8992	Build feeling active compromise.
8993	Build feeling action trusted.
8994	Build feeling action supported.
8995	Build feeling action accepted.
8996	Build feeling action serves.
8997	Build feeling action works.
8998	Build feeling action building.
8999	Build feeling feelings tested.

Myn in Numbers

Action

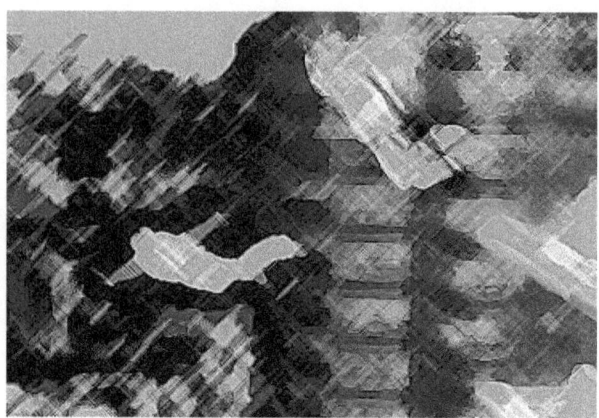

9000-9999

When "9" leads the group your source is inviting you to "Act" as you conduct yourself in the group moment of the trailing numbers. Weigh the points and ponder the outcome.

***

9000	Test releasing soul self.
9001	Test releasing self now.
9002	Test releasing self compromise.
9003	Test releasing self trust.
9004	Test releasing self supported.
9005	Test releasing self acceptance.
9006	Test releasing self joy.
9007	Test releasing self ability.
9008	Test releasing self building.
9009	Test releasing self action.
9010	Test releasing this self.
9011	Test releasing this now.
9012	Test releasing this compromise.
9013	Test releasing this myn.
9014	Test releasing this supported.

www.templeofgaia.com

9015	Test releasing this acceptance.
9016	Test releasing this joy.
9017	Test releasing this ability.
9018	Test releasing this building.
9019	Test releasing this action.
9020	Test release joining self.
9021	Test releasing compromise now.
9022	Test releasing friendship compromise.
9023	Test releasing compromise trust.
9024	Test releasing compromise supported.
9025	Test releasing compromise received.
9026	Test releasing compromise service.
9027	Test releasing compromise ability.
9028	Test releasing compromise building.
9029	Test releasing compromise action.
9030	Test releasing trusting releasing.
9031	Test releasing trusting now.
9032	Test releasing trusting compromise.
9033	Test releasing trust myn.
9034	Test releasing trusting support.
9035	Test releasing trusting acceptance.
9036	Test releasing trusting joy.
9037	Test releasing trusting ability.
9038	Test releasing trusting building.
9039	Test releasing trusting action.
9040	Test releasing through releasing.
9041	Test releasing through this.
9042	Test releasing through compromise.
9043	Test releasing through trust.
9044	Test releasing through support.
9045	Test releasing through acceptance.
9046	Test releasing through joy.
9047	Test releasing through ability.
9048	Test releasing through building.

Myn in Numbers

9049	Test releasing through action.
9050	Test releasing receiving releasing.
9051	Test releasing receiving now.
9052	Test releasing receiving compromise.
9053	Test releasing receiving trust.
9054	Test releasing receiving support.
9055	Test releasing receiving acceptance.
9056	Test releasing receiving joy.
9057	Test releasing receiving ability.
9058	Test releasing receiving building.
9059	Test releasing receiving action.
9060	Test releasing joy releasing.
9061	Test releasing joy now.
9062	Test releasing joy compromise.
9063	Test releasing joy myn.
9064	Test releasing joy supported.
9065	Test releasing joy received.
9066	Test releasing content laugh.
9067	Test releasing joy ability.
9068	Test releasing joy building.
9069	Test releasing joy action.
9070	Test releasing ability releasing.
9071	Test releasing ability now.
9072	Test releasing ability compromise.
9073	Test releasing ability trusted.
9074	Test releasing ability supported.
9075	Test releasing ability received.
9076	Test releasing ability serves.
9077	Test releasing working ability.
9078	Test releasing ability building.
9079	Test releasing ability action.
9080	Test releasing building releasing.
9081	Test releasing building now.
9082	Test releasing building compromise.

www.templeofgaia.com

9083	Test releasing building trust.
9084	Test releasing building supported.
9085	Test releasing building received.
9086	Test releasing building joy.
9087	Test releasing building ability.
9088	Test releasing building structure.
9089	Test releasing building action.
9090	Test releasing moves feelings.
9091	Test releasing action now.
9092	Test releasing action compromise.
9093	Test releasing moving trust.
9094	Test releasing active support.
9095	Test releasing action accepted.
9096	Test releasing active joy.
9097	Test releasing active ability.
9098	Test releasing active building.
9099	Test releasing moving action.
9100	Feel this my self.
9101	Feel this my now.
9102	Feel this my compromise.
9103	Feel this my myn.
9104	Feel this my supported.
9105	Feel this my received.
9106	Feel this my joy.
9107	Feel this my ability.
9108	Feel this my building.
9109	Feel this my action.
9110	Feel this now releasing.
9111	Action is now done.
9112	Feel this now compromise.
9113	Feel this now trusted.
9114	Feel this now supported.
9115	Feel this now received.
9116	Feel this now serves.

Myn in Numbers

9117	Feel this now ability.
9118	Feel this now building.
9119	Feel this now active.
9120	Feel this compromise releasing.
9121	Feel this compromise now.
9122	Feel this friendship compromise.
9123	Feel this compromise trusted.
9124	Feel this compromise supported.
9125	Feel this compromise accepted.
9126	Feel this compromise serves.
9127	Feel this compromise works.
9128	Feel this compromise builds.
9129	Feel this compromise active.
9130	Feel this trust releasing.
9131	Feel this trust now.
9132	Feel this trust compromise.
9133	Feel this trust myn.
9134	Feel this trust supported.
9135	Feel this trust received.
9136	Feel this trust joy.
9137	Feel this trust ability.
9138	Feel this trust building.
9139	Feel this trusting action.
9140	Feel this through releasing.
9141	Feel this through now.
9142	Feel this through compromise.
9143	Feel this through trust.
9144	Feel this through support.
9145	Feel this through acceptance.
9146	Feel this support serves.
9147	Feel this through ability.
9148	Feel this through building.
9149	Feel this through feelings.
9150	Feel this receiving release.

Kevin J. Baird

9151	Feel this receiving now.
9152	Feel this receiving compromise.
9153	Feel this receiving trust.
9154	Feel this receiving support.
9155	Feel this receiving acceptance.
9156	Feel this receiving joy.
9157	Feel this receiving ability.
9158	Feel this receiving building.
9159	Feel this receiving action.
9160	Feel this joy release.
9161	Feel this joy now.
9162	Feel this joy compromise.
9163	Feel this joy trusting.
9164	Feel this joy supported.
9165	Feel this joy accepting.
9166	Feel this laughing content.
9167	Feel this joy working.
9168	Feel this joy building.
9169	Feel this joy active
9170	Feel this working release.
9171	Feel this working now.
9172	Feel this working compromise.
9173	Feel this working trust.
9174	Feel this working supported.
9175	Feel this working accepted.
9176	Feel this working joy.
9177	Feel this working ability.
9178	Feel this working building.
9179	Feel this working action.
9180	Feel this building release.
9181	Feel this building now.
9182	Feel this building compromise.
9183	Feel this building trust.
9184	Feel this building supported.

Myn in Numbers

9185	Feel this building acceptance.
9186	Feel this building joy.
9187	Feel this building ability.
9188	Feel this building structure.
9189	Feel this building action.
9190	Feel this action releasing.
9191	Feel this action now.
9192	Feel this action joining.
9193	Feel this action trusted.
9194	Feel this action supported.
9195	Feel this action accepted.
9196	Feel this action serves.
9197	Feel this action working.
9198	Feel this action building.
9199	Feel this testing feelings.
9200	Active friendship soul self.
9201	Active friendship my now.
9202	Active friendship my compromise.
9203	Active friendship my myn.
9204	Active friendship my support.
9205	Active friendship my acceptance.
9206	Active friendship my joy.
9207	Active friendship my ability.
9208	Active friendship my building.
9209	Active friendship my action.
9210	Active friendship now releasing.
9211	Active friendship is now.
9212	Active friendship now compromise.
9213	Active friendship is myn.
9214	Active friendship now supported.
9215	Active friendship now received.
9216	Active friendship now joy.
9217	Active friendship now ability.
9218	Active friendship now building.

9219   Active friendship now action.
9220   Active friendship joins releasing.
9221   Active friendship joins now.
9222   Active friendship joins compromise.
9223   Active friendship joins trusting.
9224   Active friendship joins supported.
9225   Active friendship joins accepted.
9226   Active friendship joins serving.
9227   Active friendship joins able.
9228   Active friendship compromise builds.
9229   Active friendship joins action.
9230   Active friendship trusting soul.
9231   Active friendship trusting now.
9232   Active friendship trusting compromise.
9233   Active friendship prosperity blessing.
9234   Active friendship trusting supported.
9235   Active friendship trusting received.
9236   Active friendship trust serves.
9237   Active friendship trusting ability.
9238   Active friendship trust builds.
9239   Active friendship trusting feelings.
9240   Active friendship through releasing.
9241   Active friendship through this.
9242   Active friendship through compromise.
9243   Active friendship through trust.
9244   Active friendship through support.
9245   Active friendship through acceptance.
9246   Active friendship through joy.
9247   Active friendship through ability.
9248   Active friendship through building.
9249   Active friendship through action.
9250   Active friendship receive self.
9251   Active friendship receive now.
9252   Active friendship receive compromise.

Myn in Numbers

9253	Active friendship receive trust.
9254	Active friendship receive support.
9255	Active friendship receive acceptance.
9256	Active friendship receive joy.
9257	Active friendship receive ability.
9258	Active friendship receive building.
9259	Active friendship receive feelings.
9260	Active friendship joy releasing.
9261	Active friendship joy now.
9262	Active friendship joy compromise.
9263	Active friendship joy trusted.
9264	Active friendship joy supported.
9265	Active friendship joy accepted.
9266	Active friendship serves joy.
9267	Active friendship joy works.
9268	Active friendship joy builds.
9269	Active friendship serves feelings
9270	Active friendship works releasing.
9271	Active friendship works now.
9272	Active friendship works compromise.
9273	Active friendship works trust.
9274	Active friendship works supported.
9275	Active friendship works acceptance.
9276	Active friendship works joy.
9277	Active friendship working ability.
9278	Active friendship works building.
9279	Active friendship works action.
9280	Active friendship building release.
9281	Active friendship builds now.
9282	Active friendship builds compromise.
9283	Active friendship builds trust.
9284	Active friendship builds supported.
9285	Active friendship builds acceptance.
9286	Active friendship building joy.

www.templeofgaia.com

9287	Active friendship building ability.
9288	Active friendship builds form.
9289	Active friendship building feelings.
9290	Active friendship feelings release.
9291	Active friendship feelings done.
9292	Active friendship feelings compromise.
9293	Active friendship feelings trusted.
9294	Active friendship feelings supported.
9295	Active friendship feelings presented.
9296	Active friendship feelings serve.
9297	Active friendship feelings working.
9298	Active friendship feelings build.
9299	Active friendship testing feelings.
9300	Test trusting soul releases.
9301	Test trusting my now.
9302	Test trusting my compromise.
9303	Test trusting my blessing.
9304	Test trusting my support.
9305	Test trusting my acceptance.
9306	Test trusting my joy.
9307	Test trusting my ability.
9308	Test trusting my building.
9309	Test trusting my feelings.
9310	Test trusting this releasing.
9311	Test trusting this now.
9312	Test trusting this compromise.
9313	Test trusting this blessing.
9314	Test trusting this support.
9315	Test trusting this acceptance.
9316	Test trusting this joy.
9317	Test trusting this ability.
9318	Test trusting this building.
9319	Test trusting this feeling.
9320	Test trusting friend's releasing.

Myn in Numbers

9321	Test trusting friend's now.
9322	Test trusting joining friendship.
9323	Test trusting friend's trust.
9324	Test trusting friend's supported.
9325	Test trusting friend's received.
9326	Test trusting friend's joy.
9327	Test trusting friend's ability.
9328	Test trusting friend's form.
9329	Test trusting friend's feelings.
9330	Test trusting prosperity releasing.
9331	Test trusting prosperity now.
9332	Test trusting prosperity compromise.
9333	Test trusting prosperity blessing.
9334	Test trusting prosperity supported.
9335	Test trusting prosperity received.
9336	Test trusting prosperity serves.
9337	Test trusting prosperity works.
9338	Test trusting prosperity builds.
9339	Test trusting prosperity action.
9340	Test trusting through releasing.
9341	Test trusting through this.
9342	Test trusting through compromise.
9343	Test trusting through prosperity.
9344	Test trusting through support.
9345	Test trusting through acceptance.
9346	Test trusting through joy.
9347	Test trusting through ability.
9348	Test trusting through building.
9349	Test trusting through action.
9350	Test trusting receives self.
9351	Test trusting receiving this.
9352	Test trusting receiving compromise.
9353	Test trusting receiving prosperity.
9354	Test trusting receiving support.

9355 Test trusting receiving acceptance.
9356 Test trusting receiving service.
9357 Test trusting receiving ability.
9358 Test trusting receiving builds.
9359 Test trusting receiving feels.
9360 Test trusting joy release.
9361 Test trusting joy now.
9362 Test trusting joy compromise.
9363 Test trusting joy prosperity.
9364 Test trusting joy supported.
9365 Test trusting joy received.
9366 Test trusting content laugh.
9367 Test trusting joy ability.
9368 Test trusting joy building.
9369 Test trusting joy feelings
9370 Test trusting ability releasing.
9371 Test trusting ability now.
9372 Test trusting ability compromise.
9373 Test trusting ability blessing.
9374 Test trusting ability supported.
9375 Test trusting ability accepted.
9376 Test trusting ability serves.
9377 Test trusting working ability.
9378 Test trusting ability building.
9379 Test trusting ability feelings.
9380 Test trusting building release.
9381 Test trusting building this.
9382 Test trusting building compromise.
9383 Test trusting building blessing.
9384 Test trusting building support.
9385 Test trusting building acceptance.
9386 Test trusting building serves.
9387 Test trusting building ability.
9388 Test trusting building structure.

Myn in Numbers

9389	Test trusting building feelings.
9390	Test trusting feelings releasing.
9391	Test trusting feelings now.
9392	Test trusting feelings join.
9393	Test trusting feelings blessed.
9394	Test trusting feelings support.
9395	Test trusting feelings accepted.
9396	Test trusting feelings serve.
9397	Test trusting feelings worked.
9398	Test trusting feelings builds.
9399	Test trusting moving feelings.
9400	Feelings support my soul.
9401	Feelings support my now.
9402	Feelings support my compromise.
9403	Feelings support my trust.
9404	Feelings support my means.
9405	Feelings support my acceptance.
9406	Feelings support my joy.
9407	Feelings support my ability.
9408	Feelings support my building.
9409	Feelings support my action.
9410	Feelings support this soul.
9411	Feelings support this now.
9412	Feelings support this compromise.
9413	Feelings support this blessing.
9414	Feelings support this means.
9415	Feelings support this received.
9416	Feelings support this joy.
9417	Feelings support this ability.
9418	Feelings support this building.
9419	Feelings support this action.
9420	Feelings support compromise releasing.
9421	Feelings support compromise this.
9422	Feelings support friendship compromise.

9423 Feelings support compromise trust.
9424 Feelings support compromise means.
9425 Feelings support compromise acceptance.
9426 Feelings support compromise joy.
9427 Feelings support compromise ability.
9428 Feelings support compromise building.
9429 Feelings support compromise action.
9430 Feelings support trusting release.
9431 Feelings support trusting now.
9432 Feelings support trusting compromise.
9433 Feelings support trust blessing.
9434 Feelings support trusting supported.
9435 Feelings support trusting acceptance.
9436 Feelings support trusting joy.
9437 Feelings support trusting ability.
9438 Feelings support trusting building.
9439 Feelings support trusting action.
9440 Feelings supported through releasing.
9441 Feelings supported through this.
9442 Feelings supported through compromise.
9443 Feelings supported through trust.
9444 Feelings supported through means.
9445 Feelings supported through acceptance.
9446 Feelings supported through joy.
9447 Feelings supported through ability.
9448 Feelings supported through building.
9449 Feelings supported through action.
9450 Feelings supported receive releasing.
9451 Feelings supported receive now.
9452 Feelings supported receive compromise.
9453 Feelings supported receive trusted.
9454 Feelings supported receive means.
9455 Feelings supported receive acceptance.
9456 Feelings supported receive joy.

Myn in Numbers

9457	Feelings supported receive ability.
9458	Feelings supported receive building.
9459	Feelings supported receive action.
9460	Feelings support serving release.
9461	Feelings support serving now.
9462	Feelings support serving compromise.
9463	Feelings support serving trust.
9464	Feelings support serving means.
9465	Feelings support serving acceptance.
9466	Feelings support content laugh.
9467	Feelings support serving ability.
9468	Feelings support serving builds.
9469	Feelings support serving feelings
9470	Feelings support working release.
9471	Feelings support working now.
9472	Feelings support working compromise.
9473	Feelings support working trusted.
9474	Feelings support working supported.
9475	Feelings support working acceptance.
9476	Feelings support working joy.
9477	Feelings support working ability.
9478	Feelings support working form.
9479	Feelings support working action.
9480	Feelings support building release.
9481	Feelings support building now.
9482	Feelings support building compromise.
9483	Feelings support building trust.
9484	Feelings support building support.
9485	Feelings support building acceptance.
9486	Feelings support building joy.
9487	Feelings support building ability.
9488	Feelings support building structure.
9489	Feelings support building action.
9490	Feelings support moving released.

www.templeofgaia.com

9491	Feelings support moving now.
9492	Feelings support moving compromise.
9493	Feelings support move trusting.
9494	Feelings support moving supported.
9495	Feelings support move accepted.
9496	Feelings support moving serves.
9497	Feelings support moving works.
9498	Feelings support moving builds.
9499	Feelings support testing feelings.
9500	Active acceptance soul releases.
9501	Active acceptance my now.
9502	Active acceptance my compromise.
9503	Active acceptance my trusting.
9504	Active acceptance my support.
9505	Active acceptance my presence.
9506	Active acceptance release serves.
9507	Active acceptance my ability.
9508	Active acceptance my building.
9509	Active acceptance my feelings.
9510	Active acceptance now releasing.
9511	Active acceptance is now.
9512	Active acceptance now compromise.
9513	Active acceptance now trusted.
9514	Active acceptance now supported.
9515	Active acceptance now received.
9516	Active acceptance now joy.
9517	Active acceptance now ability.
9518	Active acceptance now building.
9519	Active acceptance is feelings.
9520	Active acceptance joins releasing.
9521	Active acceptance joins now.
9522	Active acceptance friendship joins.
9523	Active acceptance joins trusted.
9524	Active acceptance joins supported.

Myn in Numbers

9525 Active acceptance joins received.
9526 Active acceptance joins serving.
9527 Active acceptance joins ability.
9528 Active acceptance joins building.
9529 Active acceptance joins feelings.
9530 Active acceptance trusting release.
9531 Active acceptance trusting now.
9532 Active acceptance trusting compromise.
9533 Active acceptance trust trusting.
9534 Active acceptance trusting support.
9535 Active acceptance trusting presence.
9536 Active acceptance trusting joy.
9537 Active acceptance trusting ability.
9538 Active acceptance trusting building.
9539 Active acceptance trusting feelings.
9540 Active acceptance through releasing.
9541 Active acceptance through now.
9542 Active acceptance through compromise.
9543 Active acceptance through trust.
9544 Active acceptance through support.
9545 Active acceptance through receiving.
9546 Active acceptance through serving.
9547 Active acceptance through ability.
9548 Active acceptance through building.
9549 Active acceptance through action.
9550 Active acceptance receive release.
9551 Active acceptance receive now.
9552 Active acceptance receive compromise.
9553 Active acceptance receive trusting.
9554 Active acceptance receive supported.
9555 Active acceptance receiving acceptance.
9556 Active acceptance receive serving.
9557 Active acceptance receive ability.
9558 Active acceptance receive building.

9559 Active acceptance receive action.
9560 Active acceptance serves releasing.
9561 Active acceptance serves now.
9562 Active acceptance serves compromise.
9563 Active acceptance serves prosperity.
9564 Active acceptance serves supported.
9565 Active acceptance serves received.
9566 Active acceptance content laugh.
9567 Active acceptance serves ability.
9568 Active acceptance serves building.
9569 Active acceptance serves feelings.
9570 Active acceptance enables releasing.
9571 Active acceptance enables this.
9572 Active acceptance enables compromise.
9573 Active acceptance enables trust.
9574 Active acceptance enables support.
9575 Active acceptance enables receiving.
9576 Active acceptance enables serving.
9577 Active acceptance working ability.
9578 Active acceptance enables building.
9579 Active acceptance enables feelings.
9580 Active acceptance builds releasing.
9581 Active acceptance building this
9582 Active acceptance builds compromise.
9583 Active acceptance builds trust.
9584 Active acceptance builds supported.
9585 Active acceptance builds receiving.
9586 Active acceptance builds joy.
9587 Active acceptance builds ability.
9588 Active acceptance builds structure.
9589 Active acceptance builds feelings.
9590 Active acceptance tests release.
9591 Active acceptance tests now.
9592 Active acceptance testing compromise.

Myn in Numbers

9593 Active acceptance tests trust.
9594 Active acceptance tests supporting.
9595 Active acceptance testing received.
9596 Active acceptance testing joy.
9597 Active acceptance testing ability.
9598 Active acceptance testing building.
9599 Active acceptance moves active.
9600 Active laughing soul releases.
9601 Active laughing releases now.
9602 Active laughing releases compromise.
9603 Active laughing releases trusting.
9604 Active laughing releases supported.
9605 Active laughing releases received.
9606 Active laughing releases joy.
9607 Active laughing releases ability.
9608 Active laughing releases building.
9609 Active laughing releases action.
9610 Active laughing now releasing.
9611 Active laughing is now.
9612 Active laughing now compromise.
9613 Active laughing now trusted.
9614 Active laughing now supported.
9615 Active laughing now received.
9616 Active laughing now serves.
9617 Active laughing now working.
9618 Active laughing now building.
9619 Active laughing is feeling.
9620 Active laughing joins releasing.
9621 Active laughing joins now.
9622 Active laughing friendship joins.
9623 Active laughing joins trusted.
9624 Active laughing joins supported.
9625 Active laughing joins received.
9626 Active laughing joins serving.

Kevin J. Baird

9627	Active laughing joins ability.
9628	Active laughing joins building.
9629	Active laughing joins action.
9630	Active laughing trust releasing.
9631	Active laughing trust now.
9632	Active laughing trust compromise.
9633	Active laughing trust myn.
9634	Active laughing trust supported.
9635	Active laughing trust received.
9636	Active laughing trust joy.
9637	Active laughing trust ability.
9638	Active laughing trust building.
9639	Active laughing trust action.
9640	Active laughing through releasing.
9641	Active laughing through now.
9642	Active laughing through compromise.
9643	Active laughing through trust.
9644	Active laughing through support.
9645	Active laughing through acceptance.
9646	Active laughing through joy.
9647	Active laughing through ability.
9648	Active laughing through building.
9649	Active laughing through action.
9650	Active laughing receive releasing.
9651	Active laughing receive now.
9652	Active laughing receive compromise.
9653	Active laughing receive trust.
9654	Active laughing receive supported.
9655	Active laughing receive presented.
9656	Active laughing receive joy.
9657	Active laughing receive ability.
9658	Active laughing receive building.
9659	Active laughing receive action.
9660	Active laughing serves releasing.

Myn in Numbers

9661	Active laughing serves now.
9662	Active laughing serves compromise.
9663	Active laughing serves trust.
9664	Active laughing serves supported.
9665	Active laughing serves acceptance.
9666	Active laughing content laugh.
9667	Active laughing serves ability.
9668	Active laughing serves building.
9669	Active laughing serves feelings.
9670	Active laughing works releasing.
9671	Active laughing works now.
9672	Active laughing works compromise.
9673	Active laughing works trusting.
9674	Active laughing works supported.
9675	Active laughing works received.
9676	Active laughing enables joy.
9677	Active laughing working ability.
9678	Active laughing works building.
9679	Active laughing works action.
9680	Active laughing building releasing.
9681	Active laughing building now.
9682	Active laughing building compromise.
9683	Active laughing building trust.
9684	Active laughing building supported.
9685	Active laughing building acceptance.
9686	Active laughing building joy.
9687	Active laughing building ability.
9688	Active laughing building structure.
9689	Active laughing building feelings.
9690	Active laughing feelings releasing.
9691	Active laughing feelings now.
9692	Active laughing feelings joining.
9693	Active laughing feelings trusted.
9694	Active laughing feelings supported.

9695	Active laughing feelings accepted.
9696	Active laughing feelings serve.
9697	Active laughing feelings working.
9698	Active laughing feelings building.
9699	Active laughing moving feelings.
9700	Testing enables soul release.
9701	Testing enables my now.
9702	Testing enables my compromise.
9703	Testing enables my trust.
9704	Testing enables my support.
9705	Testing enables my acceptance.
9706	Testing enables my joy.
9707	Testing enables my ability.
9708	Testing enables my building.
9709	Testing enables my action.
9710	Testing enables this releasing.
9711	Testing enables this now.
9712	Testing enables this compromise.
9713	Testing enables this myn.
9714	Testing enables this supported.
9715	Testing enables this received.
9716	Testing enables this joy.
9717	Testing enables this ability.
9718	Testing enables this building.
9719	Testing enables this action.
9720	Testing enables friendship releasing.
9721	Testing enables friendship now.
9722	Testing enables friendship compromise.
9723	Testing enables friendship trust.
9724	Testing enables friendship support.
9725	Testing enables friendship acceptance.
9726	Testing enables friendship joy.
9727	Testing enables friendship ability.
9728	Testing enables friendship building.

Myn in Numbers

9729	Testing enables friendship action.
9730	Testing enables trust releasing.
9731	Testing enables trust now.
9732	Testing enables trust compromise.
9733	Testing enables trusting blessing.
9734	Testing enables trust supported.
9735	Testing enables trust received.
9736	Testing enables trust joy.
9737	Testing enables trust ability.
9738	Testing enables trust building.
9739	Testing enables trust action.
9740	Testing enables through releasing.
9741	Testing enables through now.
9742	Testing enables through compromise.
9743	Testing enables through myn.
9744	Testing enables through support.
9745	Testing enables through acceptance.
9746	Testing enables through joy.
9747	Testing enables through ability.
9748	Testing enables through building.
9749	Testing enables through action.
9750	Testing enables acceptable release.
9751	Testing enables acceptable now.
9752	Testing enables acceptable compromise.
9753	Testing enables acceptable trust.
9754	Testing enables acceptable support.
9755	Testing enables acceptable presence.
9756	Testing enables acceptable service.
9757	Testing enables acceptable ability.
9758	Testing enables acceptable ability.
9759	Testing enables acceptable action.
9760	Testing enables serving release.
9761	Testing enables serving this.
9762	Testing enables serving compromise.

www.templeofgaia.com

9763	Testing enables serving trusted.
9764	Testing enables serving supported.
9765	Testing enables serving received.
9766	Testing enables content laugh.
9767	Testing enables serving ability.
9768	Testing enables serving building.
9769	Testing enables serving feelings.
9770	Testing enables ability releasing.
9771	Testing enables ability now.
9772	Testing enables ability compromise.
9773	Testing enables able trust.
9774	Testing enables ability supported.
9775	Testing enables ability accepted.
9776	Testing enables working joy.
9777	Testing enables working ability.
9778	Testing enables ability building.
9779	Testing enables able action.
9780	Testing enables building release.
9781	Testing enables building now.
9782	Testing enables building compromise.
9783	Testing enables building trust.
9784	Testing enables building supported.
9785	Testing enables building acceptance.
9786	Testing enables building joy.
9787	Testing enables building ability.
9788	Testing enables building structure.
9789	Testing enables building action.
9790	Testing enables feelings releasing.
9791	Testing enables feelings now.
9792	Testing enables feelings compromise.
9793	Testing enables feelings trusted.
9794	Testing enables feelings supported.
9795	Testing enables feelings received.
9796	Testing enables feelings served.

Myn in Numbers

9797	Testing enables feelings able.
9798	Testing enables feelings building.
9799	Testing enables moving feelings.
9800	Active building soul releases.
9801	Active building my now.
9802	Active building my compromise.
9803	Active building my trust.
9804	Active building my support.
9805	Active building my acceptance.
9806	Active building release serves.
9807	Active building my ability.
9808	Active building my building.
9809	Active building my action.
9810	Active building now releasing.
9811	Active building is now.
9812	Active building now compromise.
9813	Active building now trust.
9814	Active building now supported.
9815	Active building now received.
9816	Active building now joy.
9817	Active building now ability.
9818	Active building now building.
9819	Active building now action.
9820	Active building compromise releasing.
9821	Active building compromise now.
9822	Active building friendship compromise.
9823	Active building compromise trust.
9824	Active building compromise supported.
9825	Active building compromise received.
9826	Active building compromise joy.
9827	Active building compromise ability.
9828	Active building compromise building.
9829	Active building compromise action.
9830	Active building trust releasing.

Kevin J. Baird

9831   Active building trust now.
9832   Active building trust compromise.
9833   Active building trust blessings.
9834   Active building trust supported.
9835   Active building trust received.
9836   Active building trust joy.
9837   Active building trust ability.
9838   Active building trust building.
9839   Active building trust action.
9840   Active building through releasing.
9841   Active building through this.
9842   Active building through compromise.
9843   Active building through trust.
9844   Active building through support.
9845   Active building through acceptance.
9846   Active building through joy.
9847   Active building through ability.
9848   Active building through building.
9849   Active building through action.
9850   Active building receive releasing.
9851   Active building receive now.
9852   Active building receive compromise.
9853   Active building receive trust.
9854   Active building receive supported.
9855   Active building receive acceptance.
9856   Active building receive joy.
9857   Active building receive ability.
9858   Active building receive building.
9859   Active building receive action.
9860   Active building serves releasing.
9861   Active building serves now.
9862   Active building serves compromise.
9863   Active building serves trusting.
9864   Active building serves supported.

Myn in Numbers

9865   Active building serves received.
9866   Active building content laugh.
9867   Active building serves ability.
9868   Active building serves building.
9869   Active building joy action.
9870   Active building enables releasing.
9871   Active building enables now.
9872   Active building enables compromise.
9873   Active building enables trust.
9874   Active building enables supported.
9875   Active building enables acceptance.
9876   Active building enables joy.
9877   Active building working ability.
9878   Active building enables building.
9879   Active building enables action.
9880   Active building builds releasing.
9881   Active building structure now.
9882   Active building structured compromise.
9883   Active building builds trusted.
9884   Active building builds supported.
9885   Active building builds accepted.
9886   Active building builds serving.
9887   Active building builds ability.
9888   Feeling forms building structure.
9889   Active building builds feelings.
9890   Active building moves releasing.
9891   Active building moves this.
9892   Active building moves compromise.
9893   Active building moves blessing.
9894   Active building moves supported.
9895   Active building moves acceptance.
9896   Active building moves joy.
9897   Active building moves ability.
9898   Active building moves building.

9899	Active building move feeling.
9900	Active feelings my release.
9901	Active feelings release now.
9902	Active feelings my compromise.
9903	Active feelings my blessing.
9904	Active feelings soul supported.
9905	Active feelings my acceptance.
9906	Active feelings my joy.
9907	Active feelings my ability.
9908	Active feelings my building.
9909	Active feelings my moving.
9910	Active feelings now releasing.
9911	Active feelings is now.
9912	Active feelings now join.
9913	Active feelings now blessed.
9914	Active feelings now supported.
9915	Active feelings now accepted.
9916	Active feelings now serves.
9917	Active feelings is working.
9918	Active feelings now building.
9919	Active feelings now tested.
9920	Active feelings compromises release.
9921	Active feelings compromise now.
9922	Active feelings join compromise.
9923	Active feelings compromise trust.
9924	Active feelings compromise support.
9925	Active feelings compromise acceptance.
9926	Active feelings compromise joy.
9927	Active feelings compromise ability.
9928	Active feelings compromise building.
9929	Active feelings join tested.
9930	Active feelings blessing self.
9931	Active feelings blessing now.
9932	Active feelings blessing compromise.

Myn in Numbers

9933	Active feelings trust blessing.
9934	Active feelings myn supported.
9935	Active feelings myn present.
9936	Active feelings myn serves.
9937	Active feelings myn enables.
9938	Active feelings myn builds.
9939	Active feelings myn moving.
9940	Active feelings through me.
9941	Active feelings supported now.
9942	Active feelings through compromise.
9943	Active feelings through blessing.
9944	Active feelings through support.
9945	Active feelings through acceptance.
9946	Active feelings through joy.
9947	Active feelings through ability.
9948	Active feelings through building.
9949	Active feelings through action.
9950	Active feelings receive releasing.
9951	Active feelings receive now.
9952	Active feelings receive compromise.
9953	Active feelings receive trusted.
9954	Active feelings receive supported.
9955	Active feelings receive accepted.
9956	Active feelings received serving.
9957	Active feelings receive enabled.
9958	Active feelings received builds.
9959	Active feelings receive action.
9960	Active feelings serve releasing.
9961	Active feelings serve now.
9962	Active feelings serve compromise.
9963	Active feelings serve myn.
9964	Active feelings serve supported.
9965	Active feelings serve received.
9966	Active feelings content laugh.

9967	Active feelings serve ability.
9968	Active feelings serve building.
9969	Active feelings serve action.
9970	Active feelings work releasing.
9971	Active feelings work now.
9972	Active feelings work compromise.
9973	Active feelings work trusted.
9974	Active feelings work supported.
9975	Active feelings work received.
9976	Active feelings work serves.
9977	Active feelings working ability.
9978	Active feelings work building.
9979	Active feelings work action.
9980	Active feelings building releasing.
9981	Active feelings building now.
9982	Active feelings building compromise.
9983	Active feelings building myn.
9984	Active feelings building supported.
9985	Active feelings building acceptance.
9986	Active feelings building joy.
9987	Active feelings building ability.
9988	Active feelings building structure.
9989	Active feelings building action.
9990	Active feelings tests releasing.
9991	Active feelings tests now.
9992	Active feelings tests compromise.
9993	Active feelings tests trust.
9994	Active feelings tests support.
9995	Active feelings tests acceptance.
9996	Active feelings tests joy.
9997	Active feelings tests ability.
9998	Active feelings tests building.
9999	Active feelings move action.

Myn in Numbers

DATE	NUMBER	DATE	NUMBER

Kevin J. Baird

DATE	NUMBER	DATE	NUMBER

Myn in Numbers

DATE	NUMBER	DATE	NUMBER

www.ingramcontent.com/pod-product-compliance
Lightning Source LLC
Chambersburg PA
CBHW022100150426
43195CB00008B/214